THE
EVERYTHING
CANCER-FIGHTING COOKBOOK

D0624621

Dear Reader,

As a nutritionist who specializes in helping those who have been diagnosed with cancer I have learned firsthand how important food is during these challenging times. With a goal of easing unpleasant treatment side effects and building resilience, I have found some foods provide more benefit than others. Some are just comforting because they are associated with better times and coincidentally give you extra calories when you need them. Others have easy-to-digest nutrients that help you withstand harsh therapies. Although food alone may not be sufficient to combat cancer, eating well is essential for treatment to be of optimal benefit.

It is with great pleasure that I share with you what I have learned from thousands of people who have taken this journey of handling a diagnosis of cancer and who have benefited from eating as well as they can.

I have laid this book out in an easy to follow way so loved ones and caregivers may also find it useful. I invite you to be creative and adjust seasonings if your taste buds change. For example, some people find that broths and foods rich in the savory flavor of *umami* is appealing, whereas others prefer much blander tastes. You are unique, your eating history is your own and I hope that these menus, recipes and suggestions will help to ease your therapy as well as rebuild your health so your diagnosis is not a restriction and eating remains one of life's great pleasures.

Eat well and Be well!

Warmly,

Carolyn Katzin, MS, CNS, MNT

Welcome to the EVERYTHING® Series!

These handy, accessible books give you all you need to tackle a difficult project, gain a new hobby, comprehend a fascinating topic, prepare for an exam, or even brush up on something you learned back in school but have since forgotten.

You can choose to read an Everything® book from cover to cover or just pick out the information you want from our four useful boxes: e-questions, e-facts, e-alerts, and e-ssentials.

We give you everything you need to know on the subject, but throw in a lot of fun stuff along the way, too.

We now have more than 400 Everything® books in print, spanning such wide-ranging categories as weddings, pregnancy, cooking, music instruction, foreign language, crafts, pets, New Age, and so much more. When you're done reading them all, you can finally say you know Everything®!

QUESTION

Answers to common questions

FACT

Important snippets of information

ALERT

Urgent warnings

ESSENTIAL

Quick handy tips

PUBLISHER Karen Cooper

DIRECTOR OF ACQUISITIONS AND INNOVATION Paula Munier

MANAGING EDITOR, EVERYTHING® SERIES Lisa Laing

COPY CHIEF Casey Ebert

ACQUISITIONS EDITOR Katrina Schroeder

SENIOR DEVELOPMENT EDITOR Brett Palana-Shanahan

EDITORIAL ASSISTANT Ross Weisman

EVERYTHING® SERIES COVER DESIGNER Erin Alexander

LAYOUT DESIGNERS Colleen Cunningham, Elisabeth Lariviere, Ashley Vierra, Denise Wallace

Visit the entire Everything® series at *www.everything.com*

THE
EVERYTHING®
CANCER-FIGHTING COOKBOOK

Carolyn F. Katzin, MS, CNS, MNT

Avon, Massachusetts

Dedicated to all the thousands of cancer
patients and their families I have worked with
who inspire and motivate me every day.

Copyright © 2011 by F+W Media, Inc. All rights reserved.
This book, or parts thereof, may not be reproduced
in any form without permission from the publisher; exceptions
are made for brief excerpts used in published reviews.

An Everything® Series Book.
Everything® and everything.com® are registered trademarks of F+W Media, Inc.

Published by Adams Media, a division of F+W Media, Inc.
57 Littlefield Street, Avon, MA 02322 U.S.A.
www.adamsmedia.com

ISBN 10: 1-4405-0746-5
ISBN 13: 978-1-4405-0746-5
eISBN 10: 1-4405-0747-3
eISBN 13: 978-1-4405-0747-2

Printed in the United States of America.

10 9 8 7 6 5 4 3 2 1

Library of Congress Cataloging-in-Publication Data
is available from the publisher.

This book is intended as general information only, and should not be used to diagnose or treat any health condition. In light of the complex, individual, and specific nature of health problems, this book is not intended to replace professional medical advice. The ideas, procedures, and suggestions in this book are intended to supplement, not replace, the advice of a trained medical professional. Consult your physician before adopting any of the suggestions in this book, as well as about any condition that may require diagnosis or medical attention. The author and publisher disclaim any liability arising directly or indirectly from the use of this book.

Many of the designations used by manufacturers and sellers to distinguish their products are claimed as trademarks. Where those designations appear in this book and Adams Media was aware of a trademark claim, the designations have been printed with initial capital letters.

This book is available at quantity discounts for bulk purchases.
For information, please call 1-800-289-0963.

Contents

Introduction

YOU PROBABLY PICKED THIS book up because you or someone you love has heard those dreaded words: "You have cancer." Remember, you may have been given a diagnosis of a condition called cancer, but it doesn't have you! This book is all about facing this challenge by mobilizing your body into fighting mode.

Cancer describes up to 250 different conditions with a similar origin. Each cell of your body has instructions that direct the lifespan and function of the cell and its environment. For example, a skin cell has a different function than a cell in your bone; however, they share the same DNA. If some damage should disrupt these instructions encoded in DNA (DeoxyriboNucleic Acid), and if this damage isn't stopped in its tracks, cancer may result. Every moment of your life, millions of cellular events are successfully prevented from progressing into a disease. As you age, some of these changes that don't cause cancer have become incorporated into your DNA and some may make your defenses less effective, which is why cancer is a disease more common in those over sixty years old. An exception to this is inheriting one or two copies of a defective gene like BRCA1 or 2 or p53. You have two copies of all of your genes, but if one copy is already compromised at birth there is a higher chance the other one will be altered by the random changes that occur throughout life than someone who has two copies that are both fully operational. These genes code for proteins important in protecting your cells from cancer. If one of these genes malfunctions, you have a higher risk of developing cancer.

Another aspect of risk involves lifestyle. If you are exposed to carcinogens or chemicals likely to cause mutations or deleterious changes in DNA, you are more likely to develop cancer as you age. Smoking is an example of this, as tobacco products contain many carcinogens. No amount of healthy eating will defend your body from the harm tobacco can cause—don't smoke!

There are some general guidelines for healthy eating that apply once you begin the fight against cancer, and there are some that are specific to you based on where your cancer has been discovered and how you are to receive your treatment. In this book, you will find recipes and eating suggestions to help you personalize your approach.

Many people are concerned about weight loss during treatment; however, weight gain may sometimes occur, especially with longer-term adjuvant therapies such as hormone-modulating medications like tamoxifen. Balancing your food intake with your calorie output isn't always easy when your energy is low yet you crave comfort foods. To help with this, there are some delicious options to help you modify your favorite recipes.

Fighting cancer with your fork will empower you. Let's get started!

CHAPTER 1

Eating to Fight Cancer

Good food serves three important functions: it provides essential fuel, essential nutrients, and pleasure. No single food has to provide all three things at once, but you should aim to have more nourishing foods than usual when you are fighting cancer. Let's begin by figuring out what you can and cannot eat during treatment, then we'll plan out some menus. Next, we can modify these menus as needed. Remember, you don't need to completely change everything you normally do just because you have received a diagnosis of cancer. If you are already eating well but feel a lack of confidence because you received this diagnosis, that is a normal reaction, but don't stop your healthy practices now. They are empowering and do make a difference not only in how you feel about yourself but also in how you build up your resilience during treatment and after treatment has ended.

What Can I Eat During Treatment?

Treatments for cancer often have side effects that affect your typical healthy eating patterns. Fighting back means taking care of yourself by getting as much rest as you can, taking regular gentle exercise, and eating small, easy-to-digest meals. Here are some typical symptoms you may experience with some specific eating suggestions to combat them.

Fatigue

Most treatments for cancer, as well as the emotions surrounding the whole cancer process, can leave you feeling exhausted. When you feel more tired than usual you don't have the energy to chew on whole grains, vegetables, and bulky, fiber-rich foods. One solution to fatigue is to temporarily eat more energy-dense foods (those with more calories coming from healthy oils like almond butter). You can purée vegetables into a comforting root vegetable or bean soup. Another solution to fatigue is to incorporate some healthy stimulants such as dark chocolate or green tea. Dehydration is a common cause of fatigue and one that is often overlooked. Make sure you have some fluids in the form of water, juices, and other beverages as well as soups every few hours throughout active treatment for cancer. If you press your thumb and first finger together and the indentation doesn't immediately bounce back, you may be dehydrated.

Taste and Smell Changes

Another common side effect of cancer treatment is change of taste and smell sensations. Some people complain of food tasting metallic or unpalatable, while others simply don't smell or taste much at all, making food bland and unappealing. Such changes in taste, also called dysgeusia, are usually temporary, but they can have devastating effects on your weight and strength. Ginger is a traditional remedy for nausea, and many people find the flavor appealing. Try crystallized ginger or ginger tea before you try to eat other foods. Several flavors that mask other less appealing ones include cherry and strawberry. Remember that texture and aroma are also important in taste appreciation.

Getting Enough to Eat

How often you eat is almost as important as what you eat. Many people are so fatigued in the evenings that they go to bed early, so it may be as long as twelve hours before they have any calories again. Because the early hours of the morning are when your body is in its heightened repair mode, this is the time when your body's demand for energy and essential nutrients is at its greatest. For this reason, you should have a nourishing beverage before you go to sleep, such as a warm malted milk (soy or almond milk are good alternatives to dairy), and have a couple of sips of a tropical-fruit beverage like papaya or mango nectar whenever you awake during the night. These simple modifications can make the difference between weight loss and weight maintenance during treatment without disturbing your rest. If weight gain is your challenge, you can have a small glass of skim milk or half a banana to help you sleep well without the added calories.

QUESTION

What Is a Liquid or Soft Diet?
This is diet that is very gentle and easy to tolerate right after surgery or radiation. Some choices that will comply with a diet that doesn't need to be clear but still has to be liquid or soft in consistency include cream of rice or wheat and puréed or mashed vegetables and cream soups. A high-speed blender will combine chicken, turkey, and meats so the consistency is soft and easy to swallow. Cottage cheese, yogurt, and pasta with cheese sauce are good choices. Try ice creams and fruit mousses for something sweet.

Difficulties Swallowing

Texture is an important part of swallowing. Sometimes, damage to the nerve endings in the mouth can make it difficult to sense the thickness or thinness of a food or beverage. Try single-texture foods such as mashed potatoes or puréed vegetables instead of mixed-texture dishes like stews or soups with chunks of meat or veggies that may get stuck in your throat. Very slippery foods like macaroni or gelatin might go down too fast and cause you to choke, so try relaxing and going slowly, taking one swallow at a time. If it is helpful, you can try tilting your head forward a little, as this may make swallowing easier. Other tricks for improving swallowing include using a straw or cup for liquids and soups or trying carbonated beverages.

Changes in Digestion

Because our digestive system is lined with rapidly dividing cells, treatments that target cancer cells also affect the delicate cells that line our digestive system. Damage to these cells affects how we process our foods and absorb nutrients. Starting in the mouth, lack of saliva can make chewing and swallowing difficult. Foods that encourage saliva production include baked crackers like Melba toast; the vegetable okra, which can be made into a gumbo; and gelatin, which can be incorporated into desserts and soup. Saliva is also released when we think of salty or tart foods, so it isn't just what we put in our mouth that affects chewing and swallowing, but also how we are thinking at the time. You may find it helpful to eat in a relaxed environment and focus on pleasant memories.

ESSENTIAL

Small meals or snacks may be more appealing than full meals. Flavored milks, milk shakes, and protein smoothies are perfect, along with a couple of macaroons or ginger snap cookies. Tiny peanut butter and jelly or almond butter sandwiches cut into bite-sized pieces are another idea for a mini meal. Try deviled eggs or little croutons topped with a savory dip. Don't forget a colorful garnish, such as a sprig of parsley or lemon wedge.

Avoid acid indigestion by having small, frequent meals of easily digested foods such as pasta, rice, or slow-cooked casserole dishes. Protein smoothies are a good standby for boosting your protein intake by half, which is what most oncologists recommend during treatment. In the following chapters you'll find recipes for homemade smoothies as well as how to tailor commercial ones to your own tastes. Some people find that certain foods and beverages are best avoided during this time, including tomatoes, citrus fruits, and drinks with caffeine, as these may all cause burning sensations. There is no one-size-fits-all in selecting which foods to eat during treatment, but a good approach is to think of this as a temporary time to eat an expedient diet that keeps your intake of essential nutrients as high as possible. Eating small, frequent, easy-to-digest snack-sized meals is usually the best approach. Once the treatment is completed you will be able to compensate with an extra-good diet.

Changes in Bowel Habits

Medications used to treat cancer, as well as pain therapies, may result in constipation or diarrhea. Both conditions are improved by making sure you get enough fluids on a regular basis. Water, including high water-content foods, and beverages including smoothies, soups, and juices are all good ways to keep your fluid intake high. If you feel dehydrated, you can make a homemade remedy by adding a pinch of salt and a teaspoon of sugar to a cup of water. There are many commercial rehydration beverages available as well.

FACT

Sometimes you want to stay away from dietary fiber and have foods that don't form too much bulk or require you to go to the bathroom more often. Eggs, fish, pasta, white bread, pancakes, plain cakes, saltine or oyster-type crackers, gelatin desserts, and sorbet are all good choices. Flavored milks, yogurt, and low-fat cottage cheese are also suitable, although some people find staying away from dairy products helps their digestive system get back to normal faster.

Fruits that are gentle laxatives include the pitted fruits plums, apricots, peaches, cherries, and their dried versions, as well as rhubarb and figs. Prune juice and syrup of figs are traditional treatments for constipation.

Foods that help with diarrhea management include bananas, rice, apple sauce, and toast or fortified breakfast cereals. Chicken noodle soup is a traditional remedy. The inside of a baked potato served plain is also bland, easy to prepare, and easy to tolerate.

Skin and Peripheral Nerve Sensitivity

Many of the newer molecularly targeted therapies for cancer have the side effect of making your skin more sensitive, resulting in a rash. There are a few vegetables that may make this worse, as some chemicals in them, called psoralens, may interact with ultraviolet light. Avoid parsley, celery, carrot, fennel, anise, caraway, chervil, and cilantro if you have a rash and see if this helps reduce it.

Nerve sensitivity, particularly in the hands and feet, may also occur as a result of several treatments, including radiation. Foods rich in vitamin E may prevent this, so include foods rich in vitamin oils such as sunflower seeds (tahini is made from these and would be gentle on your digestive system), almond, and almond butter. You may also wish to take a mixed tocopherol type of vitamin E supplement during treatment, as there have been a couple of studies that suggest this protects the digestive system.

Menu Planning

Use this chart or make up your own eating plan to suit your and your family's eating patterns. The idea is to set up a basic daily template that you can modify if needed. Below is an example of a daily menu plan for someone who has a good appetite and can eat without any restrictions. Try to plan ahead for at least three days at a time. If you are going to be undergoing treatment, you may wish to set up a seven- or fourteen-day plan.

MEAL	WHAT TO EAT
Upon Awakening:	Beverage choice (if you take medications, for example)
Breakfast:	Protein source (scrambled eggs) with toast and butter *or* high-fiber cereal (oatmeal) with cinnamon or raisins *or* fruit or fruit juice
Snack:	Piece of fresh fruit
Lunch:	Protein source (broiled chicken with papaya and mango salsa) with green vegetables and brown rice
Snack:	Whole-grain crackers with nut butter
Dinner:	Protein source (salmon broiled with a little lemon juice and olive oil) with red and orange vegetables and garlic mashed potatoes

MEAL	WHAT TO EAT
Snack:	Fresh berries and Greek-style yogurt
Before bedtime beverage (if taking medications):	Warm drink (malted milk)
Extras:	Dark chocolate, ginger cookies, or macaroons

Once you have set up your menu plan for the week you can also set up shopping lists. These will be useful if you need to ask someone else to shop for you.

▼ SHOPPING LIST FOR PREVIOUS MENU PLAN

Perishables	Chicken, salmon, papaya, mango, carrots, green leafy vegetables, red and green peppers, milk, yogurt
Basics	Whole-grain crackers, high-fiber cereal, oatmeal, cinnamon, raisins, hazelnut and almond butters, olive oil, butter, garlic, brown rice, potatoes, lemons
Seasonal	Fresh berries
Extras	Dark chocolate, ginger cookies, macaroons

These are just some suggestions to get you started. The idea is to have sufficient staple items on hand, such as crackers, rice, pasta, prepared pasta sauce, soups, and long-life milk (the type that comes in cartons and doesn't require refrigeration).

ALERT

Sodas were originally conceived as digestive aids and they are still a good standby. Ginger flavors, such as crystallized ginger or ginger ale, are also easy to tolerate. Frozen yogurt may taste good, or a frozen banana. Try some hot sweet tea or chai with a graham or other plain type of cookie. Perhaps a hot cereal like cream of wheat or oatmeal is soothing and bland enough in flavor. Remember, cold temperatures reduce flavors, whereas hot temperatures bring them out, and choose according to whether your taste buds are overaroused or numbed.

Super Foods That Help Fight Cancer

Cancer is a condition that arises because of crucial changes in the DNA or blueprint of a cell that isn't corrected and results in a progressively chaotic situation. Although this error of DNA may occur in one place, it may spread or metastasize to other locations in the body. Super foods are foods that provide nutrients that protect the DNA from damage in the first place; these nutrient chemicals are called antioxidants. Anticarcinogens are nutrient chemicals that protect DNA damage even more by alerting the immune system to changes in DNA and then doing damage control. Another consideration in protecting DNA from damage is inflammation. When cells divide more often than usual, they may make mistakes more often. This is one reason why anti-inflammatory foods are also helpful in fighting cancer. Cancer cells divide faster than normal cells and anti-inflammatory foods may be helpful in slowing this process down. The good news is that many delicious foods are rich in all three types of health-promoting chemicals—antioxidants, anticarcinogens, and anti-inflammatories.

Examples of cancer-fighting super foods include berries, pomegranates, lemons, and other citrus fruit, as sources of antioxidants; curry powder (contains turmeric, cumin, and other spices that have anticancer activity), salmon, flax, and chia seeds as sources of omega-3 oils, which are anti-inflammatory. In addition, there are some foods that have natural aspirin-like activity or anti-inflammatory properties, such as apricots and broccoli. Marinades and rubs made of cancer-fighting herbs and spices are useful ways to prevent possible harmful amine production when food is heated. Recipes in this book use as many cancer-fighting super foods as possible.

Cancer-Fighting Vegetables

All vegetables have cancer-fighting benefits; however, some are particularly beneficial.

- **Cruciferous vegetables:** Vegetables from the cabbage and garlic family are especially helpful in fighting cancer. The cruciferous or brassica family of vegetables includes cabbage, broccoli, Brussels sprouts, cauliflower, collard greens, mustard, kale, Swiss chard, and watercress.

These vegetables are rich in sulfurophanes and are effective at fighting cancer by triggering enzymes that remove possibly harmful environmental toxins, including those found in smog and smoke.

- **Allium vegetables:** The allium family includes garlic, onions, chives, scallions, shallots, and leeks. These vegetables also contain sulfur-rich compounds, including allicin, and help stimulate detoxification processes that protect against carcinogens. Choose a serving from each of these vegetable groups often, as these are known cancer fighters.

Cancer-Fighting Fruits

All fruits provide vitamin C and other helpful cancer-fighting phytonutrients, but some are particularly helpful.

- **Apples:** The phrase "An apple a day keeps the doctor away" has some truth in it. Apples are delicious cancer-fighting fruits rich in flavonoids such as quercetin and catechins. Researchers have shown that apple flavonoids protect epithelial cells that line the bladder and lungs from mutagens, or cancer-causing agents.
- **Berries:** Blueberries are a wonderful source of antioxidants and are tasty, low in calories, and high in fiber. They are rich in colored pigments called anthocyanins, which are a type of flavonoid that is excellent at quenching or trapping possibly harmful free radicals. Choose blueberries if you are exposed to high-energy radiation such as x-rays, flying long distances (especially if this includes going over one of the Poles), or if you have had any infections, as these increase free radical formation.

    Black raspberries are another type of berry that thrives in cool and rainy regions such as Oregon. Researchers at Ohio State University have shown that black raspberries are particularly effective at fighting cancers of the upper airways and esophagus. Strawberries are a delicious source of vitamin C and ellagic acid, both cancer-fighting phytonutrients. Choose them often for low-sugar, tasty cancer-fighting desserts and cereal toppings or as a snack.
- **Tropical Fruit:** Mango, although not as high in antioxidants, has been shown to have anticancer activity against breast and other common

cancer cell types. Gallotannins are thought to be the active anticancer ingredients. These anticarcinogens are also found in black and green teas.

- **Pomegranates:** These fruits are especially rich in vitamin C and other antioxidants, including punicalagins and ellagic acid (see *walnuts* later in this chapter). A small glass of pomegranate juice is a great way to start the day.

Cancer-Fighting Herbs and Spices

Herbs and spices have been been used in cooking as well as medicinal purposes by every culture. Herbs rich in antioxidants and other cancer-fighting phytonutrients include rosemary, oregano, mint, marjoram, sage, thyme, and lavender. Spices include those from the ginger family, including Chinese ginger and turmeric. Other spices include those used in curry powder, including cumin and coriander.

ALERT

Glucose and fructose are sugars found in sugar and starches. When you eat a meal that has sugar or white rice or white flour, your blood sugar rises quickly. But if you add some dietary fiber, such as beans or vegetables, the rise in blood sugar is slowed down and the glycemic load is improved. Glycemic is from *gly-* for sugar and *-emic* for blood. Although an individual food may have a glycemic index (usually rated against white sugar), combinations of foods eaten at the same time have a glycemic load.

Other Cancer-Fighting Super Foods

- **Avocados:** These delicious fruits are a wonderful cancer-fighting food. They are easy to digest and provide many antioxidants and glutathione. Glutathione is an important part of detoxification processes and protects against mutagens or cancer-causing agents. Among the antioxidants, avocados contain vitamins A, C, and E as well as an exceptionally rich amount of lutein. Cancer-fighting carotenoids need to be present in a balanced amount for appropriate protection, and avocados provide all of these perfectly. Studies have shown that avocado extract inhibits prostate cancer cell growth, but only when all of the carotenoids, including lutein, are present together.

- **Cocoa and dark chocolate:** Cocoa and chocolate that is made from this bean contain many cancer-fighting flavonoids, including epicatechin and procyanidins. Cocoa flavonoids have been shown to provide antioxidants and protect against prostate cancer in animals. Dark chocolate may be particularly helpful during treatment to prevent nerve damage associated with many chemotherapies.

- **Mushrooms:** These are the fruiting bodies of a fungus. We are most familiar with white button mushrooms, but there are hundreds of other edible mushrooms including Shiitake, Maitake, Portabella, and Enoki. White button mushrooms and some other edible mushrooms need to be cooked thoroughly, as they contain hydrazines, which are known carcinogens. However, mushrooms are also rich in beta glucans, which increase natural killer cell (a type of white blood cell) immune activity. Overall, mushrooms have been shown to have significant cancer-fighting capacity and would be a good addition to your diet as long as you cook them well.

- **Tomatoes:** Lycopene, the bright-red pigment found in tomatoes, is also found in apricots, guavas, persimmons, pink grapefruit, and watermelon. People who eat diets rich in tomatoes, especially if they have a particular genetic variation, appear to be protected from various cancers including lung, stomach, and prostate. Tomato sauce made from cooked tomatoes and tomato paste, along with oregano and other culinary herbs and olive oil, is an ideal way to eat these cancer-fighting foods. Eat them cooked and raw because they are colorful, rich in vitamin C and other antioxidants, and are delicious, too!

- **Walnuts:** Walnuts are particularly rich in alpha linolenic acid (ALA), an omega-3 fatty acid. This is an important anti-inflammatory nutrient protecting cells from mistakes in DNA that may cause cancer. Walnuts are rich in ellagic acid, also found in berries and pomegranates. This is a plant chemical or phytochemical that inhibits carcinogens such as nitrosamines and polycyclic aromatic hydrocarbons (PAH). They are also a rich source of vitamin B complex and vitamin E and contain about 15 percent protein.

Foods to Be Cautious about or Completely Avoid During Treatment

As your digestive system may be more sensitive than usual, avoid harsh, rough-edged sources of dietary fiber during this time. Examples include wheat bran or coarse-cut chopped nuts. A better solution would be to include whole-wheat pasta or nut butters.

Lactose (milk sugar) is poorly digested by as many as 75 percent of the world's population; most people of European descent have evolved a genetic variation that allows milk, soft cheese, or ice cream. During treatment, you may find that you are no longer able to tolerate dairy products unless they have had the enzyme added. Yogurt and hard cheeses are usually well tolerated. Greek-style yogurt has a creamy texture and has the beneficial gut flora, or probiotics, added back. This is a good choice for many people during treatment.

FACT

Meats form chemicals called amines when exposed to high temperatures. These amines have been associated with cancer and are found in many processed meats, such as sausage (including pepperoni), bacon, and other cured meats. Amines also form on the surface of meats that are broiled or barbecued. Try to avoid these meats or prepare by cooking slowly at a lower temperature.

Honey is very sweet but may contain spores of *botulinum* toxin. Just as children under one year old are told to avoid honey, it makes sense to avoid it during cancer treatment. The likelihood of exposure is very low, but your immune system is often compromised by treatment, so you may be more vulnerable to poisoning by this powerful toxin.

Some people suggest avoiding sugar altogether after a diagnosis of cancer. However, the science behind this is not conclusive. If a little sugar adds to the palatability of food, then add it. If you find you are drinking sweetened beverages and more than 10 percent of your calories are coming from sugar, you may want to consider including more berries or other low-sugar fruits in its place, as they add more nutrients with fewer calories but are still sweet.

What about Alcohol?

Some medications or chemotherapy treatments may be affected by alcohol. It would be wise to check with your pharmacist before drinking alcohol during treatment. Alcohol is found in some mouthwashes and may be irritating to the delicate lining of the mouth and oral cavity. You may wish to look for a version without alcohol for this reason. On the positive side, a glass of red wine with dinner may stimulate appetite be relaxing you and also help with digestion.

What about Soy?

Some women who have been diagnosed with estrogen receptor positive breast cancer have been told to avoid soy and other foods containing phytoestrogens (plant substances with estrogen-like activity). Some soy products like soy sauce and soy oil have such tiny quantities of the phytoestrogens (isoflavones including genistein, daidzein or equols) that they can be safely eaten by everyone. However, edamame should be limited for women with this particular diagnosis. According to the American Cancer Society, current research suggests that the amount of soy found in typical Asian diets is probably safe to consume, as the soy is in a fermented form and has not been shown to affect breast cancer survivors either positively or negatively. Check labels of protein drinks and other supplements designed with women in mind, as many of these have concentrated soy isoflavones, which may counteract estrogen-blocking therapies such as tamoxifen.

Should You Cut Out all Sugar?

As noted above, it is not necessary to cut out all sugar for your diet to be an effective cancer fighter. Added sugars in sodas and other sweetened beverages often marketed as healthful like green tea or pomegranate juices only offer empty calories and should be avoided. If you have a larger waist size than ideal (larger than half your height), you would want to be especially careful to cut out added sugars, including natural types like agave or honey. Your first goal will be to reduce your waist measurement, and the easiest way to do this is to cut back on candy, desserts, and sweets. White rice and white flour are digested almost as fast as sugar in some people, so when consuming these you may also want to include beans or other high-fiber foods at the same time to reduce the glycemic load. This will help you feel less hungry soon after eating.

Weight Management

Many cancers appear to be fueled by messenger chemicals produced by certain fat cells. This means that if you have a round shape, indicating too much belly fat, you may be producing more of these chemicals, so it makes sense to fight back by shaping back your waist. This may be a challenge, as many people seek comfort foods during stressful times. The recipes in this book are set up so that you don't need to feel deprived, yet the overall effect doesn't trigger these chemicals. Remember that weight gain is usually associated with eating more than we need and moving less. When you are dealing with fatigue and looking to comfort foods to give you a lift, you may also find that you gain unwanted weight. Without going on a rigid restriction program, you may want to be aware of this tendency and monitor your waist size to make sure you keep it in the healthy range (half your height or less).

ESSENTIAL

If your doctor recommends a clear liquid diet, perhaps because of some imaging that needs to be completed, try miso or consommé (clear bouillon made from bone broth and clarified with egg white), which are both good ways to get some protein. For sweeter liquids, try clear fruit juices such as cranberry, cherry, or grape juice. These can also be made into popsicles or jelly. You can also strain orange, lemon, or lime juice or drink tea sweetened with a little sugar.

If you are underweight, you can modify the recipes in this book by including those with higher calorie counts and following some of the tips below. To add calories:

1. Include avocado often, as it is a good source of other important nutrients, including glutathione and essential fatty acids. Use as a dip, on top of crackers or in sandwiches.
2. Add Greek-style yogurt, sour cream, or buttermilk to soups.

3. Include high-quality ice cream in your milk shakes or protein smoothies.
4. Include nut butters by adding to crackers or just eating straight up.
5. Include a little more olive or nut oils in your cooking preparations; oils are about 110 calories for each tablespoon.
6. Include puddings, mousses, custards, and other smooth-textured dishes that are easy to eat.
7. Place a little dish of extra-virgin olive oil on the dinner table for dunking whole-wheat bread. Just like in some restaurants, this is a delicious and healthy way to boost calories. Rosemary-flavored breads are especially good.

Staying Active

Part of any cancer-fighting recipe book has to include activity. Walking, stretch types of yoga, swimming, and resistance weight training are good for your circulation and can help with your appetite and mood. Stay as active as possible without overstraining yourself throughout your treatment and beyond.

Fresh-ground flax, pumpkin, sunflower, or hemp seeds are a great way to increase fiber and improve your healthy oil intake at the same time. You can grind seeds yourself or buy some ready ground and eat right away, as they go rancid quickly. Sprinkling wheat germ is another good boost to cereals or sprinkled on top of salads. Include snacks of dried fruit or add on top of your breakfast cereal or include them in muffins or desserts.

Hygiene in the Kitchen During Cancer Treatment

The word "hygiene" derives from the Greek for healthy; in other words, free of contamination. Contamination can arise from bacteria, viruses, or parasites that thrive on food and dirt. Contaminated food often smells and tastes fine, which is one reason there are some 9,000 deaths due to food-borne illness in the United States every year. You need to make sure the cleanliness of your kitchen and the way you prepare food does not lead to contaminated food or food-preparation surfaces.

Keep the kitchen clean by using proprietary cleansers. Run any sponges and brushes through each dishwasher cycle and throw them away after two weeks. A spotless-looking kitchen may be contaminated if the sponge you clean with is spreading germs from place to place. Regular wiping down of food-preparation surfaces with dilute bleach solution (one part bleach to ten parts water) is a wise precaution. Here are some tips to prevent food-borne illness. This is especially important if your white blood cell count is lower than usual because of treatment for cancer.

1. Always thaw frozen meat in the refrigerator, never at room temperature. You may use a microwave or rapid defroster, but remember, once defrosted it is vulnerable to contamination and should be either cooked or consumed quickly.
2. Never leave poultry or meats at room temperature for more than twenty minutes.
3. Cook fish and poultry thoroughly. Use a meat thermometer to be sure.
4. Avoid eating raw or undercooked eggs, as these may contain harmful salmonella bacteria.
5. Never keep foods warm (temperatures below 140°F) for more than one hour.
6. If you have a cut or open place on your skin, you *must* cover it well, preferably with a latex glove.
7. Use shallow dishes to distribute heat evenly and cool rapidly.
8. When in doubt, chuck it out!
9. Put perishable goods (fresh fish, meats, frozen and refrigerated goods) away as quickly as possible after purchase. Select frozen foods last when shopping, go straight home afterward, and avoid leaving food in a hot car. Never refreeze frozen meat unless it has been cooked in between.
10. Always keep kitchen utensils and preparation surfaces scrupulously clean. Scrub wooden chopping boards after use with salt and a little cool water. Use a germicide on other surfaces.
11. Never mix cooked and raw foods together. A common cause of food poisoning is barbecuing meat or chicken and then returning the cooked

pieces to the dish they were marinated in. Keep all cooked and raw foods separate in the refrigerator, also.

12. Never use the same knife, spoon, or other utensil to mix cooked and raw foods.

Now you have all the tools you need to fight cancer. All you need now is good food itself and lots of love! Be well!

CHAPTER 2

Appetizers

Artichokes with Aioli

Whole cooked artichokes are usually eaten leaf by delicious leaf, dipped in melted butter while still warm or chilled like this recipe and dipped in aioli. Health benefits are in the heart, but don't forget to remove the fuzzy "choke" first.

INGREDIENTS | SERVES 4

4 whole artichokes
1 lemon, cut in half
1½ cups water
½ cup dry white wine
1 clove garlic, minced
1 tablespoon olive oil
1 teaspoon fresh lemon juice
¾ cup mayonnaise

1. Prepare the artichokes by cutting the stems off the bottoms first. Rub the cut lemon on all the places of the artichokes you will cut to prevent browning. Next cut the top 1" off each artichoke with a serrated knife and discard. Rub the lemon on the cut. Snip the thorny tips off the remaining leaves with kitchen scissors and rub the cut surface with the lemon.

2. Pull out the center leaves to expose the fuzzy choke in the center, and then scoop out the choke with a melon baller. Squeeze lemon juice into the center of each artichoke.

3. Pour the water and white wine into the bottom of a large pot. Place a steamer rack in the bottom of the pot and put the artichokes upside-down on the rack. Cover the pot with a tight-fitting lid; simmer 50 minutes, or until a leaf can be pulled easily from artichoke. Remove the artichokes and let them drain and cool upside-down. Turn them over and chill them in the refrigerator.

4. Combine garlic, olive oil, lemon juice, and mayonnaise in food processor to create aioli while artichokes chill. Chill until ready to serve.

5. Put each chilled artichoke on an appetizer plate, spoon aioli into middle of each artichoke, and serve.

PER SERVING Calories: 412 | Fat: 36g | Sodium: 343mg | Carbohydrates: 16g | Fiber: 7g | Protein: 5g

Marinated Baby Artichokes

Artichokes are a member of the thistle family. They have no fat or cholesterol and lots of fiber. They are nutrient dense and contain an ingredient, cynarin, that may protect your liver.

INGREDIENTS | SERVES 4

1 lemon, cut in half
8 cups water
6 baby artichokes
1 teaspoon ground coriander
3 tablespoons olive oil
1 tablespoon Dijon mustard
1 shallot, peeled and minced
⅛ teaspoon black pepper

Baby Artichokes

Baby artichokes are not young artichokes, but small buds that grow on the sides of the plant's main stem. They are more tender and mild than regular artichokes. They usually don't have a choke, or collection of prickly leaves, in the center. When you cut the cooked baby artichokes, check if there is a choke; if there is, remove carefully with a spoon.

1. Cut lemon in half and squeeze juice. Place half of the juice in large bowl filled with cold water.

2. Pull off outer leaves of artichokes until you reach yellow leaves. Cut off stem. Cut off top ⅓ of artichoke and discard. As you work, drop trimmed artichokes into bowl of lemon water.

3. In large pot, combine cold water, ground coriander, and squeezed lemon halves. Bring to a boil. Add the artichokes and bring back to a boil. Cover, reduce heat, and simmer for 10–15 minutes, or until artichokes are tender.

4. In small bowl, combine remaining half of lemon juice, olive oil, mustard, shallot, and pepper, and whisk to blend.

5. When artichokes are tender, drain and rinse with cold water. Cut artichokes in quarters lengthwise. If necessary, carefully remove prickly choke from center with a spoon. Arrange artichokes on serving plate and drizzle with olive oil mixture.

PER SERVING Calories: 150 | Fat: 11g | Sodium: 140mg | Carbohydrates: 13g | Fiber: 5g | Protein: 3g

Artichokes Stuffed with Couscous

Garlic mayonnaise is good for dipping the leaves and seasoning the artichoke bottoms after the couscous is eaten.

INGREDIENTS | SERVES 2

1 cup water

½ cup pomegranate juice

1 teaspoon olive oil

1 cup uncooked couscous

¾ cup toasted pine nuts

10 dried apricots, coarsely chopped

½ cup cilantro leaves

Pinch salt

2 very large globe artichokes, trimmed and cooked

Sea Salt

Commercial salt is highly refined—99.5 percent is made up of sodium chloride, with additives of anticaking chemicals, potassium iodide, and sugar (dextrose) to stabilize the iodine. Instead, look for a high-quality sea salt, which is loaded with minerals and, in moderation, can actually give you energy and minimize dehydration, a common side effect of cancer treatments.

1. Combine water and the pomegranate juice in a saucepan and heat to boiling, then stir in the olive oil and couscous. Remove from the heat and cover; set aside for 5 minutes.

2. In a mixing bowl, combine the pine nuts, apricots, cilantro leaves, and salt, stirring well. Fold in the couscous.

3. Part the artichoke leaves to expose the center. Using a spoon, scoop out the choke and discard. Spoon the couscous mixture into the artichokes, mounding it up to fill them completely. Serve hot or at room temperature.

PER SERVING Calories: 970 | Fat: 38g | Sodium: 240mg | Carbohydrates: 146g | Fiber: 16g | Protein: 24g

Black Bean Guacamole

Sneaking some extra fiber and protein into a traditional Mexican guacamole makes this dip a more nutritious appetizer.

INGREDIENTS | **YIELDS 2 CUPS; SERVING SIZE: ¼ CUP**

1 (15-ounce) can black beans
3 avocados
1 tablespoon fresh lime juice
3 scallions, chopped
1 large tomato, diced
2 cloves garlic, minced
½ teaspoon chili powder
¼ teaspoon salt
1 tablespoon chopped fresh cilantro

1. Using a fork or a potato masher, mash the beans in a medium-sized bowl just until they are halfway mashed, leaving some texture.

2. Combine all the remaining ingredients, and mash together until mixed.

3. Adjust seasonings to taste. Allow to sit for at least 10 minutes before serving to allow the flavors to set. Gently mix again just before serving.

PER SERVING Calories: 160 | Fat: 12g | Sodium: 350mg | Carbohydrates: 17g | Fiber: 0g | Protein: 1g

Black Bean Dip

This hearty dip can be served on its own or used as the basis for layered dips. Use bell pepper strips and crackers for dippers.

INGREDIENTS | **YIELDS 2 CUPS; SERVING SIZE: ¼ CUP**

2 (15-ounce) cans black beans, rinsed and drained
2 jalapeño peppers, minced
2 cloves garlic, minced
1 large tomato, chopped
1 red bell pepper, chopped
2 tablespoons minced fresh cilantro
¼ teaspoon black pepper

1. In a food processor, combine beans, jalapeños, and garlic; process until smooth.

2. Transfer to a medium bowl and stir in remaining ingredients.

3. Cover and chill for 2 to 3 hours before serving.

PER SERVING Calories: 70 | Fat: 1g | Sodium: 530mg | Carbohydrates: 19g | Fiber: 7g | Protein: 5g

Chickpeas in Lettuce Wraps

*This fabulous creamy and flavorful spread can also be spread
on toasted bread or used as an appetizer dip.*

INGREDIENTS | SERVES 6–8

1 (15-ounce) can chickpeas
3 tablespoons olive oil
3 tablespoons fresh lemon juice
3 cloves garlic, minced
1 tablespoon chopped fresh mint
½ cup diced red onion
8 lettuce leaves
1 cup chopped tomatoes
1 cup chopped yellow bell pepper

1. Drain the chickpeas; rinse, and drain again. Place half in a blender or food processor. Add olive oil, lemon juice, garlic, and mint. Blend or process until smooth.

2. Place in medium-size bowl and stir in remaining chickpeas and red onion; stir until combined.

3. To wrap, place lettuce leaves on work surface. Divide chickpea mixture among leaves; top with tomatoes and bell pepper. Roll up, folding in sides, to enclose filling. Serve immediately.

PER SERVING Calories: 130 | Fat: 6g | Sodium: 160mg | Carbohydrates: 16g | Fiber: 3g | Protein: 3g

Fava Bean Hummus with Kalamata Olives and Pistachios

*If you need extra liquid to help purée the fava beans, you may add olive oil or a splash of vegetable
or chicken stock, but don't overdo it; the hummus should be thick, not runny. Serve this
with toasted pita pieces or bagel chips or with fresh vegetables for dunking.*

INGREDIENTS | SERVES 6

1 (15-ounce) can fava beans, drained and rinsed
3 cloves garlic, or to taste
Juice from 1 lemon, or more to taste
1 tablespoon flax oil
2 tablespoons olive oil, or more as needed to process
1–2 tablespoons tahini paste
Salt and black pepper, to taste
½ cup minced fresh parsley
¾ cup toasted pistachios

1. Put the beans, garlic, lemon juice, flax oil, olive oil, tahini, salt, and pepper into a food processor or blender and purée.

2. Spoon the mixture into a bowl and stir in the parsley and pistachios. Chill until serving time.

PER SERVING Calories: 230 | Fat: 16g | Sodium: 140mg | Carbohydrates: 17g | Fiber: 5g | Protein: 7g

Eggplant Crostini

Eggplant is a most versatile and delicious vegetable. You don't have to salt or soak the Japanese eggplants to get the bitterness out as you do with their larger relatives.

INGREDIENTS | **SERVES 4; SERVING SIZE 4 SLICES**

1 baguette loaf of bread
½ cup olive oil, divided
6 cloves garlic, peeled
2 Japanese eggplants
1 teaspoon salt
½ cup grated pecorino Romano cheese
¼ cup diced roasted red bell pepper

1. Preheat the oven to 350°F. Slice the baguette into ¼"-thick rounds and lay them out on a cookie sheet. Brush both sides with olive oil, then toast them in the oven for about 5 minutes. Turn them over and toast the other side.

2. Remove from oven, rub one side of each toast with garlic clove, and set aside.

3. Slice the eggplants into ¼"-thick slices, brush them with olive oil, and sprinkle them with salt.

4. Grill the eggplant rounds on both sides for about 10 minutes total.

5. Top each toast with a grilled eggplant round, sprinkle the cheese over the eggplant, and garnish each with the roasted red pepper.

PER SERVING Calories: 700 | Fat: 33g | Sodium: 1460mg | Carbohydrates: 84g | Fiber: 13g | Protein: 16g

Endive Petals

Belgian endive is a slightly bitter lettuce grown in a mound of earth to control photosynthesis so that its color is a pale shade of red or green. Remember to store the endive out of the light or the leaves will become green and taste too bitter.

INGREDIENTS | SERVES 6

4 heads Belgian endive lettuce

1 cup minced cooked chicken

¼ cup minced whole green onions

¼ cup hoisin sauce

½ cup chopped roasted peanuts

¼ cup diced red bell pepper, seeds removed

1 teaspoon sesame oil

2 tablespoons minced fresh cilantro

Petal Possibilities

You can alternately fill your endive petals with bay shrimp and basil mayonnaise; chunky ham salad; or blue cheese, currants, and walnuts. If your endive leaves are ragged around the edges, give them a trim with scissors before filling them. Dress up a salad with a julienne of the smaller inner leaves.

1. Separate the individual leaves of the endive by cutting off the bottoms of the stalks.

2. Mix together the chicken, green onions, hoisin sauce, ¼ cup of the peanuts, bell pepper, sesame oil, and cilantro.

3. Put a teaspoon of chicken filling onto the bottom end of each endive leaf. Sprinkle a pinch of the remaining peanuts onto the filling.

4. Serve chilled or at room temperature. You want the endive to remain crisp and not get limp.

PER SERVING Calories: 200 | Fat: 9g | Sodium: 260mg | Carbohydrates: 19g | Fiber: 12g | Protein: 14g

Stuffed Mushrooms

Classic stuffed mushrooms can be jazzed up with a variety of ingredients. Try adding crabmeat, bacon, cream cheese, pesto, or blue cheese to the filling in this recipe. Or wrap the (unbroiled) stuffed mushrooms in puff pastry or phyllo dough and bake 15 minutes for a more substantial appetizer.

INGREDIENTS | SERVES 6

16 ounces fresh mushrooms

3 tablespoons olive oil

½ cup finely chopped onion

1 tablespoon chopped fresh thyme

¼ cup cream

¾ cup dry bread crumbs

2 tablespoons ground flax seeds

¼ cup grated Parmesan cheese

½ teaspoon salt

¼ teaspoon black pepper

Duxelles

Duxelles is a mushroom stuffing traditionally used in the classic dish Beef Wellington. Chopped mushrooms are twisted in a tea towel to squeeze out excess moisture. Then they are sautéed in butter with shallots, seasoned with parsley, salt, and pepper, and cooled. This simple, delicious concoction can be added to rice pilaf, stirred in sauces, or spread on toast.

1. Wipe the mushrooms clean with a tea towel. Remove the stems and set the caps aside. Chop the stems in a fine dice.

2. Heat olive oil in a sauté pan, add the onions and sauté for 1 minute. Add the mushroom stems and thyme and cook for about 4 minutes. Add cream, stir to combine.

3. Transfer mixture to bowl. Add bread crumbs, ground flax seeds, half of the Parmesan cheese, salt, and pepper to the bowl and mix well with mushroom mixture. Set aside.

4. Put the mushroom caps on a baking sheet, gill sides up. Stuff each cap with a teaspoon of the mushroom stem mixture. Sprinkle with remaining Parmesan.

5. Broil mushrooms in the oven for about 5 minutes, until stuffing is nicely browned. Serve warm.

PER SERVING Calories: 200 | Fat: 13g | Sodium: 360mg | Carbohydrates: 15g | Fiber: 3g | Protein: 6g

Salmon Cakes with Mango Salsa

If you cannot find almond or pecan meal, you can make your own by grinding a cup of raw almonds or pecans in a food processor until a flour consistency is achieved. Be careful not to run it so long it becomes an oily paste.

INGREDIENTS | SERVES 4

1 (14-ounce) can salmon
¼ cup minced chives
1 large egg, beaten
1 cup almond or pecan flour
Sea salt, to taste
1 mango
½ red pepper, minced
½ sweet onion, minced
3" piece ginger root
Juice of 1 lemon

Grilled Salmon and Salsa

A beautiful fillet of grilled salmon would benefit from a few tablespoons of mango or tomato salsa. The juices will enrich the dry meat, and the sweet-sour taste will only complement the smoky flavor of the fish. Serve alongside some steamed broccoli tossed with garlic sautéed in olive oil and a salad of cooked kale and walnuts.

1. Preheat oven to 350°F.

2. In a medium bowl, combine salmon, chives, beaten egg, nut flour, and sea salt. Mix well; form into 4 patties.

3. Place on a well-oiled baking sheet; bake 15–20 minutes, or cook in an oiled skillet, browning on both sides.

4. To make the salsa, peel and chop mango into small pieces; place in a medium-size bowl. Add red pepper and onion.

5. Peel and grate ginger, extracting juice by pressing the fiber against the side of a shallow dish; pour juice into bowl with mango mixture.

6. Juice lemon and add to mango mixture; mix well.

7. Cover and refrigerate until ready to serve. For a hotter, spicier version, add a fresh, minced jalapeño pepper.

PER SERVING Calories: 330 | Fat: 17g | Sodium: 410mg | Carbohydrates: 18g | Fiber: 5g | Protein: 32g

Roasted Garlic

Believe it or not, roasted garlic is a fabulous treat eaten all by itself. You can also spread it on bread, mash it into some low-fat cream cheese for a sandwich spread, or add to sauces.

INGREDIENTS | **SERVES 6**

1 head garlic
2 teaspoons olive oil
Pinch salt
1 teaspoon fresh lemon juice

Freezing Roasted Garlic

Make several heads of roasted garlic. When the garlic is cool, squeeze the cloves out of the papery covering; discard the covering. Place the garlic in a small bowl and work into a paste. Freeze in ice cube trays until solid, then place in heavy-duty freezer bags, label, and freeze up to 3 months. To use, just cut off the amount you want and thaw in the fridge.

1. Preheat oven to 400°F. Peel off some of the outer skins from the garlic head, leaving the head whole. Cut off the top ½" of the garlic head; discard top.

2. Place on a square of heavy-duty aluminum foil, cut side up. Drizzle with the olive oil, making sure the oil runs into the cloves. Sprinkle with salt and lemon juice.

3. Wrap garlic in the foil, covering completely. Place on a baking sheet and roast for 40–50 minutes or until garlic is very soft and golden brown.

4. Let cool for 15 minutes, then serve or use in recipes.

PER SERVING | Calories: 32 | Fat: 1g | Sodium: 28mg | Carbohydrates: 4g | Fiber: 0g | Protein: 1g

Roasted Walnut Tapenade

This is a versatile sauce that can be served over grilled chicken, meat, or fish dishes. It will also serve well as a dip with vegetable crudités or thin slices of toasted bread.

INGREDIENTS | YIELDS 2 CUPS; SERVING SIZE: 1 TABLESPOON

1 cup walnut halves
4 black or green olives
2 cloves garlic
½ cup olive oil
½ cup water
2 teaspoons balsamic vinegar
½ teaspoon sea salt

Roasting Walnuts

To roast walnuts, preheat oven to 350°F. Spread walnuts out on baking sheet and place them in oven about 8–10 minutes. Make sure to set an oven timer to remind you when they are done. To toast, place in a skillet with a little bit of oil and cook over medium-low heat, stirring often.

1. Preheat oven to 350°F. Roast walnuts until lightly browned, about 8 minutes. Remove from oven and allow to cool.

2. Chop walnuts in a food processor using the pulsing action.

3. Add olives and garlic; continue to pulse for a chunky texture.

4. With the chute open, add olive oil in a slow stream while you pulse ingredients.

5. Add water, vinegar, and sea salt; continue to pulse until you have a smooth, paste-like consistency.

PER SERVING Calories: 50 | Fat: 6g | Sodium: 50mg | Carbohydrates: 1g | Fiber: 0g | Protein: 0g

Zesty Almond Spread

Serve this spread with crackers or chopped veggies.

INGREDIENTS | YIELDS ABOUT ¼ CUP; SERVING SIZE: 1 TABLESPOON

30 unsalted almonds
2 teaspoons honey
1 teaspoon chili powder
¼ teaspoon garlic powder
Pinch of salt (optional)

1. Place all ingredients in food processor or blender.

2. Process to desired consistency.

PER SERVING, WITHOUT SALT Calories: 50 | Fat: 4g | Sodium: 1mg | Carbohydrates: 4g | Fiber: 1g | Protein: 2g

White Bean Dip

This dip is similar to hummus, but is made with white beans instead of garbanzo beans and may be more digestible. Many Italian antipasti platters include this dip with toasted chunks of multigrain bread. You can vary the seasonings by adding fresh basil or oregano.

INGREDIENTS | SERVES 4; SERVING SIZE: ½ CUP

2 cloves garlic, peeled
½ teaspoon salt
1½ cups cooked white beans
⅓ cup tahini
2 tablespoons fresh lemon juice
2 tablespoons olive oil
1 teaspoon thyme

1. Purée the garlic and salt in a food processor. Drain and add the white beans and purée to a paste.

2. Add the remaining ingredients and process until smooth, scraping down the sides of the bowl.

3. Transfer the finished purée to a bowl and serve with crackers or pita bread and carrot sticks.

PER SERVING Calories: 300 | Fat: 17g | Sodium: 310mg | Carbohydrates: 28g | Fiber: 7g | Protein: 11g

Crispy Rice Balls

Fry these little balls right before serving. They're crisp and savory, with a tender center. For variety, try molding the rice around a tiny square of cheese before frying. These make delicious bite-sized snacks.

INGREDIENTS | **SERVES 8**

1 cup medium-grain rice

2 cups water

1 tablespoon olive oil

½ cup minced onion

3 cloves garlic, minced

1 egg

½ teaspoon salt

⅛ teaspoon cayenne pepper

2 tablespoons prepared horseradish

½ teaspoon dried thyme leaves

1 cup crushed puffed-rice cereal

1 cup sesame oil

Cooking Rice

There are three main types of rice: long grain, medium grain, and short grain. They differ in the amount and kind of starch they contain. Long-grain rice cooks up fluffier because it has less amylopectin, which is a kind of starch that makes rice sticky. Medium-grain rice has more amylopectin, so it is perfect for rice balls and risotto.

1. In medium saucepan, combine rice and water. Bring to a boil over high heat, then reduce heat to low; simmer 18–23 minutes, or until rice is tender and water is absorbed.

2. Meanwhile, heat olive oil over medium heat. Add onion; cook and stir until onion begins to brown, about 8–9 minutes.

3. Stir in garlic for 1 minute, then stir into hot cooked rice. Let cool for 30 minutes.

4. Add egg, salt, pepper, horseradish, and thyme. Form mixture into 1" balls; roll in crushed cereal to coat.

5. Heat oil in heavy skillet over medium heat. Fry rice balls, turning carefully, until golden brown and crisp, about 4–5 minutes. Drain on paper towels.

PER SERVING Calories: 166 | Fat: 6g | Sodium: 167mg | Carbohydrates: 25g | Fiber: <1g | Protein: 3g

Corn Quesadillas

Corn tortillas are a great choice for appetizers, for making your own chips, and for using as the bread for sandwich wraps.

INGREDIENTS | SERVES 6

1 tablespoon olive oil
3 cloves garlic, minced
2 jalapeño peppers, minced
1½ cups frozen corn
1 (15-ounce) can black beans, drained and rinsed
½ cup Zesty Black Bean Salsa (Chapter 12) or Super Spicy Salsa (Chapter 12)
12 (6") corn tortillas
½ cup Cheddar cheese
1 cup shredded pepper Jack cheese

1. In a small saucepan, heat olive oil over medium heat. Add the garlic and jalapeños and cook, stirring every 2–3 minutes, until softened.

2. Add corn; cook and stir for 4–5 minutes longer, until hot. Remove from heat and stir in the black beans and salsa.

3. Arrange half of the tortillas on work surface. Spread each with some of the cheese. Divide corn mixture among tortillas, then top with the pepper Jack cheese. Top with remaining tortillas.

4. Heat a large skillet or griddle over medium heat. Grill quesadillas, turning once, until cheese melts and tortillas are toasted. Cut into wedges and serve with salsa.

PER SERVING Calories: 300 | Fat: 11g | Sodium: 500mg | Carbohydrates: 46g | Fiber: 9g | Protein: 12g

Crisp Polenta Squares

Polenta is made from cornmeal that has been cooked until soft. When chilled, sliced, and fried, it becomes a crisp and delectable snack.

INGREDIENTS | **SERVES 4–6**

3 cups water

1 cup tomato juice

4 cloves garlic, minced

1 teaspoon salt

⅛ teaspoon black pepper

1 cup cornmeal

½ cup olive oil

1. In large saucepan, combine water, tomato juice, garlic, salt, and pepper and bring to a boil.

2. Stir in cornmeal; cook and stir over low heat until very thick, about 12–17 minutes.

3. Pour mixture into oiled baking dish; spread about ½" thick. Cover and chill until very firm.

4. When ready to eat, cut into 2" squares. Heat olive oil over medium-high heat until about 375°F. Fry polenta squares, a few at a time, until very crisp. Drain on paper towels. Serve with any spicy salsa or dip.

PER SERVING Calories: 260 | Fat: 19g | Sodium: 500mg | Carbohydrates: 20g | Fiber: 2g | Protein: 2g

CHAPTER 3

Soups

Chicken Stock

Chicken stock is easy to make and really wholesome. Once you learn how to make it, this recipe will become almost second nature. Collagen from the bones is especially nourishing and forms the gelatin that helps add protein and consistency as it cools.

INGREDIENTS | **YIELDS 8 CUPS; SERVING SIZE: 1 CUP**

Olive oil

2 pounds chicken, cut up and left on the bone

8 cups water

1 tablespoon chopped fresh ginger root

1 onion, sliced

3 stalks celery, chopped

3 carrots, chopped

1 bay leaf

2 whole cloves

1 teaspoon salt

⅛ teaspoon white pepper

1. In large pot, heat olive oil and add chicken. Cook 10–12 minutes, or until chicken begins to brown.

2. Add water, ginger, onion, celery, carrots, bay leaf, and cloves; bring to a boil, then reduce heat, cover, and simmer for 55 minutes.

3. Cool; remove chicken from bone; discard bone and store chicken for another use.

4. Strain liquid into another large pot; season to taste with salt and pepper. Place in refrigerator overnight. Remove fat that accumulates on surface.

5. Store stock in refrigerator 3 days or freeze for longer storage.

PER SERVING Calories: 110 | Fat: 7g | Sodium: 340mg | Carbohydrates: 4g | Fiber: 1g | Protein: 8g

Beef Stock

*Your own beef stock is not only nourishing to eat, it's also delicious.
Make a batch or two and freeze in 1 cup amounts.*

INGREDIENTS | YIELDS 8 CUPS;
SERVING SIZE: 1 CUP

4 pounds meaty beef bones

½ cup water

1 onion, chopped

2 carrots, chopped

1 potato, peeled and cubed

1 (14-ounce) can diced tomatoes, undrained

1 bay leaf

1½ teaspoons salt

¼ teaspoon black pepper

1 teaspoon dried marjoram

½ teaspoon dried thyme

10 cups water

Freezing Stocks

All stocks and broths freeze very well. Cool the liquid completely, then skim off any fat that accumulates on the surface. Divide into 2-cup hard-sided freezer containers, leaving about 1" of headspace for expansion during freezing. Label the containers, seal, and freeze for up to 3 months. To use, let stand in refrigerator overnight to thaw.

1. In large soup pot, brown the bones, a couple of batches at a time, over medium-high heat, about 10–12 minutes per batch. Remove bones and set aside.

2. Add ½ cup water to pot and bring to a boil; scrape up drippings and bits stuck to pot.

3. Return beef to pot along with all remaining ingredients. Bring to a boil over high heat. Then skim off the surface, reduce heat to low, cover, and simmer 4–5 hours.

4. Strain stock, pressing on solids to get all of the liquid possible. Cool stock in refrigerator overnight and remove excess fat.

5. Store in refrigerator up to 2 days or freeze up to 3 months. This stock is a great base for soups or stews.

PER SERVING Calories: 80 | Fat: 4g | Sodium: 480mg | Carbohydrates: 9g | Fiber: 2g | Protein: 5g

Artichoke Lentil Soup

There is enough sodium in the canned artichoke hearts to flavor the entire soup. Drain and rinse them well before using.

INGREDIENTS | SERVES 6

3 tablespoons olive oil

2 onions, chopped

4 cloves garlic, minced

1 cup green lentils, rinsed

3 cups Chicken Stock (Chapter 3) or Beef Stock (Chapter 3)

3 cups water

2 tablespoons fresh lemon juice

2 tablespoons arrowroot

1 cup half-and-half

1 (14-ounce) can artichoke hearts, drained

⅛ teaspoon white pepper

½ cup chopped flat-leaf parsley

3 tablespoons grated Parmesan cheese

1 teaspoon grated lemon zest

Lentils

Green lentils, also known as French green lentils or Puy lentils, are considered the most delicate and flavorful of the lentil family. They remain firm after cooking, holding their shape better than brown lentils. Pick over them carefully and rinse thoroughly before using. Most lentils cook in just about an hour; taste to make sure they're tender.

1. In a large stockpot, heat olive oil over medium heat. Add the onions and garlic; cook and stir until crisp-tender, about 4 minutes.

2. Add lentils, stock, and water and bring to a simmer. Cover and simmer for 1 hour.

3. In small bowl, combine lemon juice with arrowroot and half-and-half. Stir into soup with wire whisk.

4. Finely chop artichoke hearts and add to soup along with pepper. Heat until soup steams.

5. In small bowl, combine parsley, Parmesan, and lemon zest, and mix well.

6. Ladle soup into heated bowls, sprinkle with parsley mixture, and serve.

PER SERVING Calories: 330 | Fat: 14g | Sodium: 340mg | Carbohydrates: 36g | Fiber: 6g | Protein: 15g

Spring Asparagus Soup

In February, the first asparagus comes in with a taste of spring. This puréed soup can also be made with other vegetables, like sugar-snap peas or baby peas.

INGREDIENTS | SERVES 4

1 tablespoon olive oil
3 scallions, chopped
½ cup finely chopped sweet onion
1 clove garlic, minced
2 new potatoes, peeled and chopped
1 pound asparagus
4 cups Chicken Stock (Chapter 3)
1 tablespoon fresh lemon juice
1 teaspoon lemon zest
1 tablespoon fresh thyme leaves
⅛ teaspoon white pepper
1 cup half-and-half

1. In large soup pot, heat olive oil over medium heat. Add scallions, sweet onion, and garlic; cook and stir for 3 minutes. Then add potatoes; cook and stir for 5 minutes longer.

2. Snap the asparagus spears and discard ends. Chop asparagus into 1" pieces and add to pot along with stock. Bring to a boil, reduce heat, cover, and simmer for 10 minutes.

3. Using an immersion blender, purée soup until smooth. If you do not have an immersion blender, purée soup in 4 batches in blender or food processor, then return to pot and continue with recipe.

4. Add lemon juice, lemon zest, thyme, pepper, and half-and-half; heat until steaming and serve. You can also serve it chilled.

PER SERVING Calories: 270 | Fat: 13g | Sodium: 370mg | Carbohydrates: 25g | Fiber: 4g | Protein: 12g

Minestrone Vegetable Soup

This Italian soup is full of high-fiber vegetables and legumes such as cabbage, celery, zucchini, navy beans, and garbanzos. If you need to reduce foods that cause abdominal gas, cut back on the garbanzo beans and cabbage and add more carrots instead.

INGREDIENTS | SERVES 6

½ cup chopped onion

½ cup chopped carrots

¼ cup chopped celery

2 tablespoons olive oil

2 cloves garlic, minced

1 cup chopped cabbage

4 cups Chicken Stock (Chapter 3)

1 cup chopped, peeled tomatoes

2 cups chopped zucchini

½ cup cooked navy beans

½ cup cooked garbanzo beans

½ cup broken whole-wheat spaghetti

Salt and black pepper, to taste

¼ cup basil pesto

½ cup grated Parmesan cheese

1. Sauté the onions, carrots, and celery in the olive oil for 15 minutes.

2. Add garlic and cabbage and cook until cabbage is wilted.

3. Add chicken stock, tomatoes, zucchini, navy beans, and garbanzo beans and bring to a boil. Simmer 15 minutes.

4. Add spaghetti and simmer 15 minutes longer. Season with salt and pepper.

5. Serve hot with pesto and Parmesan cheese.

PER SERVING Calories: 260 | Fat: 13g | Sodium: 400mg | Carbohydrates: 23g | Fiber: 5g | Protein: 11g

Soaking Beans

To help keep the gas factor down, dried beans need a soak. Fill a saucepan with 1½ quarts water and add 1 cup beans. Bring the water and beans to a boil and simmer for 2 minutes. Turn the heat off and let the beans sit in the water overnight, or at least 8 hours. Most of the gas-causing elements will dissolve into the water. Discard the soaking water and add fresh water to cook the beans.

Pumpkin Soup

This soup is packed with a triple play of fiber in the pumpkin, dried cranberries, and pumpkin seeds. Pumpkin is also one of the highest sources of vitamin A on the list.

INGREDIENTS | SERVES 4

2 tablespoons olive oil
½ cup chopped shallots
2 tablespoons chopped fresh sage
4 cups Chicken Stock (Chapter 3) or vegetable stock
2 cups canned pumpkin
½ cup plain yogurt
Salt, to taste
White pepper, to taste
½ cup dried cranberries
½ cup roasted pumpkin seeds

1. Heat olive oil in a soup pot over medium heat. Sauté shallots and sage for 5 minutes.

2. Add chicken or vegetable broth and pumpkin; bring to a boil. Simmer until pumpkin is cooked, about 45 minutes.

3. Purée soup in a blender until smooth.

4. Stir in yogurt and season with salt and white pepper.

5. Serve garnished with dried cranberries and roasted pumpkin seeds sprinkled on top.

PER SERVING Calories: 310 | Fat: 13g | Sodium: 370mg | Carbohydrates: 39g | Fiber: 6g | Protein: 11g

Creamy Chilled Avocado Soup

This is a perfect summer starter or a light lunch with a nice pink shrimp or chunk of crabmeat floated on top.

INGREDIENTS | SERVES 4

2 ripe avocados
2 tablespoons fresh lime juice
1 cup frozen lima beans, thawed
½ cup chopped sweet onion
1 clove garlic, minced
¼ teaspoon Tabasco sauce
⅛ teaspoon white pepper
2½ cups Chicken Stock (Chapter 3) or vegetable stock
1 cup plain yogurt

1. Peel avocados and chop coarsely; place in blender or food processor. Sprinkle with lime juice.

2. Add all remaining ingredients, cover, and blend or process until soup is smooth.

3. Place in medium-size bowl and place plastic wrap directly on the surface of the soup. Cover and chill for 2 hours before serving.

PER SERVING Calories: 320 | Fat: 19g | Sodium: 270mg | Carbohydrates: 30g | Fiber: 10g | Protein: 11g

Southwest Tortilla Soup

From corn to avocados, this soup is packed with fiber and flavor.

INGREDIENTS | **SERVES 6**

1 small onion, diced

1 celery stalk, diced

2 tablespoons olive oil

2 garlic cloves, minced

1 cup corn kernels

4 cups Chicken Stock (Chapter 3)

½ cup diced roasted red bell pepper

1 cup diced, peeled tomatoes

½ cup tomato purée

3 blue corn tortillas, cut in ¼" strips

1 teaspoon ground cumin

1 tablespoon chili powder

2 teaspoons puréed chipotle peppers in adobo sauce

Salt and black pepper, to taste

¼ cup chopped fresh cilantro

2 avocados, diced

1 cup crushed Baked Tortilla Chips (Chapter 9)

1 cup shredded Monterey jack cheese

1. Sauté onion and celery in olive oil until translucent.

2. Add garlic, corn, chicken stock, bell pepper, tomatoes, and tomato purée. Bring to a boil.

3. Add tortilla strips, cumin, chili powder, and chipotle purée; simmer 30 minutes.

4. Remove from heat. Season the soup with salt, pepper, and cilantro.

5. Serve soup hot, garnished with diced avocado, baked tortilla chips, and cheese.

PER SERVING Calories: 410 | Fat: 25g | Sodium: 480mg | Carbohydrates: 38g | Fiber: 8g | Protein: 14g

Creamy Tortilla Soup

This recipe is for a broth version of tortilla soup. To transform this recipe into a creamy tortilla soup, simply purée the corn kernels before adding them. The starch in the puréed corn will thicken the soup into a creamy yellow version studded with a colorful confetti of vegetables.

Tomato Vegetable Soup

This recipe calls for canned tomatoes, but if your garden is overflowing with ripe tomatoes, consider using fresh peeled tomatoes instead.

INGREDIENTS | SERVES 6

1 tablespoon olive oil

2 teaspoons minced garlic

⅔ teaspoon ground cumin

2 carrots, chopped

2 stalks celery, diced

1 medium onion, chopped

⅔ cup tomato paste

½ teaspoon red pepper flakes

2 cups canned peeled tomatoes, with juice

⅔ teaspoon chopped fresh oregano

3 cups Chicken Stock (Chapter 3)

3 cups Beef Stock (Chapter 3)

2 cups diced potatoes

2 cups shredded cabbage

½ cup green beans

½ cup fresh or frozen corn kernels

½ teaspoon black pepper

¼ cup fresh lime juice or balsamic vinegar

1. Heat olive oil in a large stockpot; sauté garlic, cumin, carrot, and celery for 1 minute. Add onion; cook until transparent.

2. Stir in tomato paste; sauté until it begins to brown.

3. Add remaining ingredients except for lime juice or vinegar. Bring to a boil; reduce heat and simmer for 20–30 minutes, adding additional stock or water if needed.

4. Just before serving, add lime juice or balsamic vinegar.

PER SERVING Calories: 220 | Fat: 5g | Sodium: 430mg | Carbohydrates: 35g | Fiber: 6g | Protein: 10g

Easy Measures

Consider freezing stock in an ice cube tray. Most ice cube tray sections hold ⅛ cup (2 tablespoons) of liquid. Once stock is frozen, you can transfer cubes to freezer bag or container. This makes it easy to measure out the amount you need for recipes.

Nutty Greek Snapper Soup

You can make this soup using leftover fish or substitute halibut, cod, or sea bass for the snapper.

INGREDIENTS | SERVES 4

1 pound (16 ounces) red snapper fillet

2 large cucumbers

4 green onions, chopped

4 cups plain yogurt

1 cup packed fresh parsley, basil, cilantro, arugula, and chives, mixed

3 tablespoons fresh lime juice

Salt and black pepper, to taste (optional)

¼ cup chopped walnuts

Fresh herb sprigs for garnish (optional)

1. Rinse red snapper fillet and pat dry with paper towels. Broil fillet until opaque through the thickest part, about 4 minutes on each side depending on the thickness of fillet. Let cool. (Alternatives would be to steam or poach the fillets.)

2. Peel and halve cucumbers and scoop out and discard seeds. Cut into 1" pieces.

3. Put half of cucumbers with green onions in bowl of food processor; pulse to coarsely chop. Transfer to a large bowl.

4. Add remaining cucumbers, yogurt, and herb leaves to food processor; process until smooth and frothy. (Alternatively, you can grate cucumbers, finely mince green onion and herbs, and stir together with yogurt in large bowl.)

5. Stir in lime juice and season with salt and pepper to taste, if using. Cover and refrigerate for at least 1 hour, or up to 8 hours; the longer the soup cools, the more the flavors will mellow.

6. While soup cools, break cooled red snapper fillets into large chunks, discarding skin and any bones.

7. Ladle chilled soup into shallow bowls and add red snapper. Sprinkle chopped walnuts over soup, garnish with herb sprigs, and serve.

PER SERVING Calories: 340 | Fat: 15g | Sodium: 200mg | Carbohydrates: 19g | Fiber: 3g | Protein: 35g

Winter Squash and Red Pepper Soup

You don't have to wait until winter to warm up with this delicious soup!

INGREDIENTS | SERVES 6

3½ cups winter squash, cooked

1 tablespoon olive oil

1 cup onion, chopped

1 tablespoon garlic, chopped

4 ounces roasted red pepper

3 cups Chicken Stock (Chapter 3)

½ cup dry white wine

2 teaspoons agave syrup

1 teaspoon cinnamon

½ teaspoon dried ginger

1 tablespoon sour cream (optional)

1. Wash and cut squash in half; core out seeds. Place face-down on oiled 9" × 13" glass baking dish; bake at 400°F for 50–60 minutes, or until squash is cooked tender. When cool enough to handle, scoop squash out of shells and set aside.

2. In large nonstick skillet, heat olive oil. Add onions and garlic; sauté until tender and continue to cook until the onions are soft and have turned brown (caramelized).

3. Add roasted pepper and chicken stock; simmer for another 16 minutes.

4. Add cooked winter squash, white wine, agave syrup, cinnamon, and ginger; simmer for another 5 minutes.

5. Transfer to food processor or blender; purée until smooth. Depending on size of processor or blender, you may need to purée a partial portion at a time.

6. If desired, stir in reduced-fat sour cream and serve.

PER SERVING Calories: 150 | Fat: 4.5g | Sodium: 180mg | Carbohydrates: 21g | Fiber: 4g | Protein: 5g

Salmon Chowder

Customize this dish with your favorite vegetables.

INGREDIENTS | SERVES 4

1 (7½-ounce) can salmon

2 teaspoons olive oil

1 medium onion, chopped

2 stalks celery, chopped

1 sweet green pepper, seeded and chopped

1 clove garlic, minced

4 carrots, peeled and diced

4 small potatoes, peeled and diced

1 cup Chicken Stock (Chapter 3)

1 cup water

½ teaspoon black pepper

½ teaspoon dill seed

1 cup diced zucchini

1 cup half-and-half

1 (8¾-ounce) can cream-style corn

Black pepper, to taste

½ cup chopped fresh parsley (optional)

1. Drain and flake salmon; discard liquid.

2. In a large nonstick saucepan, add olive oil over medium heat; sauté onion, celery, green pepper, garlic, and carrots, stirring often, until tender, about 5 minutes.

3. Add potatoes, stock, water, pepper, and dill seed; bring to boil. Reduce heat, cover, and simmer for 20 minutes, or until potatoes are tender.

4. Add zucchini; simmer, covered, for another 5 minutes.

5. Add salmon, half-and-half, corn, and pepper; cook over low heat just until heated through.

6. Just before serving, add parsley, if desired.

PER SERVING Calories: 410 | Fat: 14g | Sodium: 650mg | Carbohydrates: 58g | Fiber: 8g | Protein: 21g

Black Bean and Corn Soup

To add flavor and spice to any of your dishes, add chili powder, jalapeño peppers, chipotle peppers, cayenne pepper, red pepper, or serrano peppers.

INGREDIENTS | **SERVES 6**

4 cups black beans
1 teaspoon olive oil
1 clove garlic, minced
½ teaspoon all-purpose seasoning
2 cups frozen corn
2 cups tomatoes, diced
2 cups crushed tomatoes
½ cup green onions, sliced
2 tablespoons chili powder
1 teaspoon ground cumin
½ cup bell peppers, diced
1 cup Chicken Stock (Chapter 3)
1 cup water

1. Combine all ingredients in a large saucepan.

2. Cook on medium heat for 15 minutes.

3. Simmer for another 10 minutes, then serve.

PER SERVING Calories: 267 | Fat: 3g | Sodium: 292mg | Carbohydrates: 50g | Fiber: 15g | Protein: 15g

Black Beans

Black beans help lower cholesterol and are high in fiber, which helps slow rising blood sugar levels. Black beans are rich in antioxidants and other cancer-fighting nutrients including folate. They are also a particularly wise choice for people with diabetes or hypoglycemia. They are a virtually fat-free protein as well.

Extra Red Soup

*If you'd like to serve this soup cold, swirl 1 cup of plain yogurt or sour cream
into it just before serving for a creamy and delicious flavor.*

INGREDIENTS | SERVES 4

8 medium red bell peppers, seeded
and sliced

1 cup yellow onions, sliced

1½ cups pumpkin, cubed

2 garlic cloves, crushed

1 green chili, chopped

1½ cups tomatoes, diced

2 cups Chicken Stock (Chapter 3), Beef
Stock (Chapter 3), or vegetable stock

2 tablespoons fresh basil, chopped

Salt and black pepper, to taste

1. Add bell peppers, onions, pumpkin, garlic, chili, tomatoes, and stock to a large saucepan and bring to a boil.

2. Simmer for 25 minutes, or until bell peppers and pumpkin are soft. Drain, keeping vegetables and liquid in separate bowls.

3. Blend vegetables in a food processor and place back in saucepan with liquid. Add basil, salt, and pepper to soup and heat thoroughly.

PER SERVING Calories: 189 | Fat: 3g | Sodium: 826mg | Carbohydrates: 39g | Fiber: 8g | Protein: 7g

Lentil Vegetable Soup

This soup makes a great fall treat. Consider serving with some crusty bread, warmed in the oven.

INGREDIENTS | SERVES 4

5 cups water, Chicken Stock (Chapter 3),
or Beef Stock (Chapter 3)

1 medium-size sweet potato, peeled
and chopped

1 cup uncooked lentils

2 medium onions, chopped

¼ cup barley

2 tablespoons dried parsley flakes

2 carrots, sliced

1 celery stalk, chopped

2 teaspoons ground cumin

1. Combine all ingredients in soup pot.

2. Simmer until lentils are soft, about 1 hour.

PER SERVING Calories: 273 | Fat: 1g | Sodium: 34mg | Carbohydrates: 53g | Fiber: 19g | Protein: 16g

Tuscan Bean Soup

Tuscan cuisine combines a mixture of vegetables with the flavor of Mediterranean aromatic herbs.

INGREDIENTS | SERVES 6

1 clove garlic, minced

2 cups zucchini, sliced

1 teaspoon oregano

½ cup bell peppers, diced

2 cups tomatoes, diced

1 teaspoon all-purpose seasoning

1 teaspoon ground cumin

½ cup carrots, sliced

1 cup red wine

3 cups white beans, cooked

4 cups Chicken Stock (Chapter 3)

½ teaspoon black pepper

1 tablespoon tomato paste

½ cup celery, sliced

1. Combine all ingredients in a large saucepan.

2. Cook on medium-high heat for 15 minutes.

3. Simmer for another 10 minutes, then serve.

PER SERVING Calories: 242 | Fat: 4g | Sodium: 595mg | Carbohydrates: 33g | Fiber: 9g | Protein: 14g

Doubling Recipes

You can double most cooking recipes—that is, soups, broiled and grilled meats, and casseroles. Don't try to double baking recipes because they usually won't work. If you do double, or even triple a recipe, be careful with seasonings. Use less than double and then add more if you think the recipe needs it.

Corn Polenta Chowder

Turkey bacon helps reduce the fat in this excellent thick chowder,
but it is high in salt, so no additional salt is needed.

INGREDIENTS | SERVES 6

2 strips turkey bacon

1 tablespoon olive oil

1 red onion, chopped

3 cloves garlic, minced

1 red bell pepper, chopped

2 jalapeño peppers, minced

2 Yukon Gold potatoes, chopped

5 cups Chicken Stock (Chapter 3), divided

⅓ cup cornmeal

2 tablespoons adobo sauce

2 (10-ounce) packages frozen corn, thawed

1 cup half-and-half

¼ cup chopped fresh cilantro

⅛ teaspoon cayenne pepper

1. In large soup pot, cook bacon until crisp. Remove from heat, crumble, and set aside.

2. To drippings remaining in pot, add olive oil, then onion and garlic; cook and stir until tender, about 5 minutes.

3. Stir in bell peppers, jalapeños, potatoes, and 3 cups of the stock. Bring to a boil, then reduce heat, cover, and simmer for 20 minutes until potatoes are tender.

4. Meanwhile, in small microwave-safe bowl, combine cornmeal and 1 cup chicken stock. Microwave on high for 2 minutes, remove and stir, then microwave for 2–4 minutes longer or until mixture thickens.

5. Stir in adobo sauce and remaining 1 cup chicken broth. Add to soup along with corn. Simmer for another 10 minutes.

6. Add the half-and-half, cilantro, and pepper and stir well. Heat until steam rises, then sprinkle with reserved bacon and serve immediately.

PER SERVING Calories: 350 | Fat: 13g | Sodium: 1400mg | Carbohydrates: 51g | Fiber: 5g | Protein: 13g

Cream of Broccoli Soup

Silken tofu makes an excellent substitute for dairy cream or milk in this simple, tasty soup. Top with toasted pine nuts for that extra crunchy flavor.

INGREDIENTS | SERVES 8

2 heads of broccoli

½ onion, chopped

2 cloves garlic, minced

1 tablespoon olive oil

½ cup fresh parsley, minced

6 cups Chicken Stock (Chapter 3) or vegetable stock

3 tablespoons white or yellow miso

1 (12-ounce) package silken tofu

Salt, to taste

White pepper, to taste

Toasted pine nuts (optional)

Two Kinds of Tofu

Basic tofu is made by crushing dried soybeans with water, and extracting the liquid to produce soy milk. This soy milk is then boiled, and a coagulant such as a natural food acid or a salt is added to produce curds. The resultant solid mass is then cut and packaged for sale.

1. Cut the florets off the broccoli stems; peel and chop.

2. In a large heavy saucepan, sauté the onion and garlic in oil until just tender; add half the parsley, setting the rest aside to use as garnish.

3. Add the stock and broccoli; bring to a boil; reduce heat and simmer until broccoli is tender, about 15 minutes.

4. Remove a small amount of broth to a bowl; dissolve the miso. Return to the soup pot; remove pot from heat.

5. Crumble silken tofu into broth; use a hand wand mixer to purée until smooth. An alternative is to ladle the soup into a blender in batches and purée until smooth.

6. Add salt and pepper to taste; serve either warm or chilled, topped with toasted pine nuts and minced parsley.

PER SERVING Calories: 170 | Fat: 5g | Sodium: 540mg | Carbohydrates: 21g | Fiber: 5g | Protein: 13g

Roasted Cauliflower Soup

Roasting vegetables gives them a whole new flavor by bringing out the natural sugars as they caramelize.

INGREDIENTS | SERVES 4

1 head cauliflower
1 chopped onion
3 large carrots
4 cloves garlic, minced
3 tablespoons olive oil
½ teaspoon salt
3 cups Chicken Stock (Chapter 3)
1 tablespoon fresh thyme leaves
1 cup milk
⅛ teaspoon white pepper

Cauliflower

Cauliflower is a member of the broccoli family and is full of antioxidants and fiber. Purchase cauliflower florets at your supermarket, wash them, and keep in small plastic containers in the refrigerator for instant snacking. This vegetable is fresh, delicious, crunchy, and so good for you.

1. Preheat oven to 400°F.

2. Remove leaves from cauliflower, wash, trim, and cut into florets. Peel carrots and cut into 2" pieces.

3. Toss cauliflower, onion, carrots, and garlic with olive oil in large roasting pan. Sprinkle with salt.

4. Roast for 45–55 minutes, until cauliflower is lightly golden, stirring twice during roasting time.

5. Scrape all of the vegetables into large soup pot. Rinse roasting pan with ½ cup chicken stock, scraping to remove browned bits. Add to soup pot along with remaining chicken stock and thyme. Bring to a simmer over medium heat; simmer for 10 minutes.

6. Remove from heat and, using an immersion blender, purée. Add milk and pepper and stir well with wire whisk. Heat until soup steams, and serve.

PER SERVING Calories: 290 | Fat: 15g | Sodium: 670mg | Carbohydrates: 31g | Fiber: 8g | Protein: 12g

Vegetable Beef Barley Stew

This amount of meat adds rich flavor without significantly increasing the cholesterol or saturated-fat content of the stew.

INGREDIENTS | SERVES 8

¾ pound beef round steak

2 tablespoons arrowroot

1 teaspoon paprika

2 tablespoons olive oil

2 onions, chopped

4 cups Beef Stock (Chapter 3), divided

4 carrots, thickly sliced

3 potatoes, cubed

1 (8-ounce) package sliced mushrooms

3 cups water

1 teaspoon dried marjoram leaves

1 bay leaf

¼ teaspoon salt

¼ teaspoon black pepper

¾ cup hulled barley

Barley

Barley contains a substance called beta-glucan that has been shown to be effective in reducing cholesterol levels in clinical studies. You can buy barley in several forms. Hulled barley is the most nutritious, while pearl barley is more polished and cooks more quickly. Barley flakes and grits are also available for quick-cooking recipes.

1. Trim beef and cut into 1" pieces. Sprinkle with arrowroot and paprika and toss to coat.

2. In large skillet, heat olive oil over medium heat. Add beef; brown, stirring occasionally, for about 5–6 minutes. Remove to a 4- to 5-quart slow cooker.

3. Add onions to skillet along with ½ cup beef stock. Bring to a boil, then simmer, scraping the bottom of the skillet, for 3–4 minutes. Add to slow cooker along with all remaining ingredients.

4. Cover and cook on low for 8–9 hours, or until barley and vegetables are tender. Stir, remove bay leaf, and serve immediately.

PER SERVING Calories: 270 | Fat: 8g | Sodium: 160mg | Carbohydrates: 36g | Fiber: 6g | Protein: 17g

Curried Chicken Mushroom Soup

Chopped turkey breast can be substituted for the chicken if you'd prefer. Top this easy soup with some chopped fresh parsley for more color.

INGREDIENTS | SERVES 4

1 ounce mixed dried mushrooms

2 cups boiling water

1 tablespoon olive oil

2 boneless, skinless chicken breasts, chopped

1½ cups chopped leek

2 cups chopped cremini mushrooms

1 tablespoon curry powder

2 tablespoons arrowroot

⅛ teaspoon white pepper

½ teaspoon dried chervil leaves

1 cup milk

1 cup Chicken Stock (Chapter 3)

1. In a small bowl, combine the dried mushrooms with the boiling water; set aside for 20 minutes to rehydrate.

2. In a large saucepan, heat olive oil over medium heat. Add chicken breasts; cook and stir until almost cooked, about 4 to 5 minutes. Remove chicken from saucepan and set aside.

3. Add leeks and cremini mushrooms to saucepan; cook and stir for 4 to 5 minutes or until crisp-tender.

4. Add curry powder, arrowroot, pepper, and chervil to saucepan; cook and stir until bubbly.

5. Add milk and chicken stock; stir well and bring to a simmer.

6. Meanwhile, drain rehydrated mushrooms, reserving liquid. Squeeze out excess liquid and coarsely chop mushrooms. Strain liquid through a coffee filter.

7. Add to soup along with the mushrooms and chicken. Bring to a simmer; simmer for 10 to 15 minutes to blend flavors. Serve immediately.

PER SERVING Calories: 240 | Fat: 8g | Sodium: 150mg | Carbohydrates: 19g | Fiber: 3g | Protein: 21g

Sweet Potato Coconut Soup

Despite the sweet ingredients, this is a hearty and delicious soup. Increase the coconut milk to a full can if you want a richer coconut flavor. You can toast the cinnamon, Garam masala, and cumin in a dry skillet over medium-high heat. Once they release their aroma, remove from heat and add to soup mixture.

INGREDIENTS | **SERVES 6–8**

3 large sweet potatoes

1 cup red lentils

1 cup Chicken Stock (Chapter 3) or vegetable stock

4 cups water

½ teaspoon cinnamon

2 teaspoons Garam masala (Indian spice mix)

1 teaspoon ground cumin

½ (14-ounce) can coconut milk

Salt, to taste

Toasted pine nuts (optional)

Plain yogurt (optional)

Garam Masala

This combination of Indian spices is a traditional mix of cinnamon, roasted cumin, green or black cardamom, nutmeg, cloves, and mace. Garam masala helps warm the body and adds depth to a recipe. Make your own by buying the ingredients separately and grinding them in an electric coffee grinder or with a mortar and pestle.

1. Peel and chop potatoes; rinse and drain lentils.

2. Combine all ingredients except coconut milk and salt in a large saucepan; bring to a boil.

3. Reduce heat; simmer until potatoes are tender.

4. Skim off any foam that forms on the surface while cooking.

5. When done, add coconut milk and salt.

6. Using a hand wand or a blender, purée until smooth.

7. Serve topped with toasted pine nuts and a dollop of plain yogurt.

PER SERVING Calories: 180 | Fat: 6g | Sodium: 70mg | Carbohydrates: 28g | Fiber: 5g | Protein: 8g

Apple Squash Soup

This sweet soup is packed full of vitamin A and fiber. It's smooth and silky without any cream.

INGREDIENTS | SERVES 8

2 tablespoons olive oil

2 onions, chopped

3 cloves garlic, minced

6 cups water

3 pounds butternut squash, peeled and cubed

3 Granny Smith apples, peeled and cubed

⅓ cup old-fashioned rolled oats, ground

2 tablespoons minced fresh ginger root

2 tablespoons curry powder

½ teaspoon salt

⅛ teaspoon white pepper

Apples and Squash

Apples and squash come into season around the same time, so they are natural partners. They are both sweet, but using an apple that is also tart will result in the most balanced flavor.

1. Heat oil in large soup pot over medium heat. Add onion and garlic; cook and stir until tender, about 6–7 minutes.

2. Add water and squash and bring to a simmer. Simmer for 15–20 minutes, or until squash is almost tender.

3. Stir in apples and remaining ingredients. Bring back to a simmer and cook for 10–15 minutes, or until apples and squash are tender.

4. Using an immersion blender, blend the soup until it's smooth and creamy. Serve immediately.

PER SERVING Calories: 160 | Fat: 4g | Sodium: 160mg | Carbohydrates: 32g | Fiber: 8g | Protein: 3g

CHAPTER 4

Beans, Pasta, and Rice

Baked Beans

These slow-cooked beans are a delicious side dish or light evening meal with whole-grain toast. This is a staple supper in England, and is easy fast food.

INGREDIENTS	SERVES 6; SERVING SIZE: 1 CUP

4 cups cooked white beans

1 cup sliced onion

4 slices turkey bacon, chopped

1 teaspoon dry mustard

½ cup brown sugar

½ cup maple syrup

2 tablespoons ketchup

½ teaspoon salt

1 teaspoon black pepper

1½ cups water

1. Preheat oven to 350°F.

2. Drain the beans and layer them with the onions and bacon in a casserole dish.

3. Combine the dry mustard, brown sugar, maple syrup, ketchup, salt, pepper, and water, and pour the mixture over the beans.

4. Cover and bake for 2 hours.

5. Uncover and bake for 15 minutes more.

PER SERVING Calories: 340 | Fat: 2g | Sodium: 360mg | Carbohydrates: 70g | Fiber: 8g | Protein: 13g

Beans for Your Budget

The variety of dried beans numbers in the hundreds. They are packed with flavor, protein, and both soluble and insoluble fiber. Very little, if any, meat is necessary when beans are combined with onions, garlic, carrots, and tomatoes. They also marry happily with parsley, cilantro, rosemary, basil, and tarragon. They should be the basis of every high-fiber diet. Canned beans are an easy alternative, but home baked are lower in sodium.

Black Beans and Polenta

Polenta is cooked cornmeal. It's easy to make, and provides complete protein when eaten with black beans.

INGREDIENTS | SERVES 6

1 tablespoon olive oil
1 onion, chopped
3 cloves garlic, minced
1 (8-ounce) package button mushrooms
1 (15-ounce) can black beans, drained
1 cup Spaghetti Sauce (Chapter 12)
4 cups Chicken Stock (Chapter 3)
1 cup yellow cornmeal
½ teaspoon salt
⅛ teaspoon black pepper

1. Preheat oven to 350°F.

2. In a large skillet, heat the olive oil over medium heat. Add the onion and garlic; cook and stir until crisp-tender, about 6 minutes.

3. Add the mushrooms; cook and stir 5 minutes longer.

4. Add the beans and Spaghetti Sauce and bring to a simmer. Reduce heat and simmer while preparing polenta.

5. In large pot, bring stock to a boil over high heat. Stir in cornmeal, salt, and pepper. Reduce heat to medium and cook, stirring constantly, until mixture is thick.

6. Pour into prepared dish and smooth into an even layer. Top with black bean mixture.

7. Bake 20–30 minutes, or until food is hot. Cut into squares to serve.

PER SERVING Calories: 250 | Fat: 6g | Sodium: 830mg | Carbohydrates: 42g | Fiber: 7g | Protein: 11g

Hearty Bean Stew

This quick stew is scrumptiously filling and easy to make. Add any vegetable you like to the mixture to make it your own.

INGREDIENTS | SERVES 8

1 pound lean ground beef

3 stalks celery, chopped

1 onion, diced

2 tablespoons arrowroot

1 cup milk

1 cup Beef Stock (Chapter 3)

2 (15-ounce) cans Great Northern beans, drained

2 cups frozen corn, thawed

1 (14-ounce) can diced tomatoes, drained

⅛ teaspoon black pepper

Dash Tabasco sauce

½ cup grated Cotija cheese

1. In a large saucepan, cook ground beef over medium heat, stirring to break up meat. Drain off the additional fat and liquid.

2. Add celery and onion; cook and stir until crisp-tender, about 5 minutes.

3. Add arrowroot; cook and stir until bubbly.

4. Add milk and broth; cook and stir until thickened.

5. Add remaining ingredients except the cheese and heat through.

6. Sprinkle with cheese and serve immediately.

PER SERVING Calories: 320 | Fat: 7g | Sodium: 210mg | Carbohydrates: 41g | Fiber: 8g | Protein: 25g

Canned Beans

Canned beans are an excellent addition to a low-fat diet. They are full of fiber and protein, but they can be high in sodium. Look for lower-sodium varieties, especially in health food stores and co-ops. To reduce sodium content, you can thoroughly drain and rinse the beans, then drain again before using in the recipe. You can use canned beans if you are short on time.

Fried Chickpeas with Yogurt

A flavorful Indian favorite spiked with chutney, this entrée comes together in minutes and is a perfect accompaniment to cooked basmati rice and hot, fresh naan, the popular Indian bread.

INGREDIENTS | SERVES 2

2 tablespoons olive oil

1 onion, diced

1 tomato, diced

2 tablespoons minced ginger

1 tablespoon minced garlic

1 teaspoon ground turmeric

1 (15¼-ounce) can chickpeas, drained and rinsed

1 teaspoon curry powder, or more to taste

1 teaspoon ground cumin

½ bunch fresh cilantro, coarsely chopped

Salt, to taste

½ cup plain yogurt

½ cup Mango Chutney (Chapter 12), or to taste

1. Heat the oil in a large skillet over medium heat and sauté the onion and tomato until the vegetables soften.

2. Add the ginger, garlic, and turmeric and cook 2–3 minutes more, or until the flavors are combined.

3. Add the chickpeas, curry powder, and cumin and cook, stirring often, for about 5 minutes.

4. Add the cilantro and salt, stirring well.

5. Stir in the yogurt and cook 2 minutes more.

6. Serve with a dollop of chutney on each portion.

PER SERVING Calories: 700 | Fat: 20g | Sodium: 840mg | Carbohydrates: 121g | Fiber: 17g | Protein: 17g

Connie's Delicious Refried Beans

Although canned refried beans are convenient, starting from scratch yields a spectacular flavor absent in the canned version. This Americanized take on refried beans packs a wonderful punch, and is a dish you'll want to make often, especially if you like burritos, tacos, and quesadillas.

INGREDIENTS | SERVES 6

1 (1-pound) bag dried pinto beans, rinsed and picked clean

1 cup chopped onion, or more if desired

1 package dried hot chili seasoning

1 package dried mild chili seasoning

1 tablespoon roasted whole cumin seeds, pounded with a mortar and pestle

1 jalapeño chili, seeded and diced

Super Spicy Salsa (Chapter 12), to taste

Salt, to taste

2 tablespoons canola oil, or more as needed

Cooking Beans

To cook beans, first pick over them to remove extraneous material, then rinse and drain. Cover with cold water and let stand overnight. The next day, drain beans and rinse again. Cover with cold water and bring to a simmer. Cover pan and simmer for 1½–2 hours, until tender. Drain and store in refrigerator up to 3 days.

1. Rinse beans and soak overnight covered by 2" in cold water. Drain them well and rinse the beans again.

2. Put the beans and the onion in a large saucepan with about 8 cups water, or to cover by 2". Bring the water to a boil and reduce the heat to medium-low and skim off any scum.

3. Stir in the chili seasonings, the cumin seeds, and the jalapeño. Cook, checking on the water level and stirring occasionally, for 3–4 hours, or until the beans are tender and the water is almost absorbed.

4. Add the salsa and salt.

5. Heat the oil in a large skillet and put beans in skillet by spoonfuls. Using a potato masher or the back of a large spoon, mash and fry them until the beans are relatively smooth, repeating until all the beans are mashed and fried.

PER SERVING Calories: 320 | Fat: 6g | Sodium: 95mg | Carbohydrates: 51g | Fiber: 15g | Protein: 18g

Chicken Asparagus Pasta

Chicken and asparagus taste like spring, especially when flavored with lemon juice. This is a good recipe for a last-minute meal.

INGREDIENTS | SERVES 6

3 boneless, skinless chicken breasts
½ teaspoon salt
⅛ teaspoon cayenne pepper
2 tablespoons arrowroot
2 tablespoons olive oil
⅓ cup sliced green onion
1 cup sliced mushrooms
1 pound fresh asparagus, cut into 1" pieces
1 (12-ounce) package whole-wheat spaghetti
1 tablespoon fresh lemon juice
⅓ cup grated Parmesan cheese

1. Bring a large pot of water to a boil.

2. Meanwhile, cut chicken into 1" cubes. Toss with salt, pepper, and arrowroot.

3. In large skillet, heat olive oil over medium heat. Add chicken; cook and stir until browned but not cooked through, about 4–5 minutes. Remove chicken from skillet and set aside.

4. Add onions, mushrooms, and asparagus to skillet. Cook and stir until crisp-tender, about 4–6 minutes.

5. Meanwhile, cook pasta according to package directions.

6. Return chicken to skillet along with a ladle of pasta cooking water and lemon juice. Bring to a simmer, then simmer 3–6 minutes, until chicken is thoroughly cooked and vegetables are tender.

7. Drain pasta and add to skillet. Cook and stir 1–2 minutes to blend flavors.

8. Sprinkle with cheese and serve immediately.

PER SERVING Calories: 360 | Fat: 8g | Sodium: 310mg | Carbohydrates: 49g | Fiber: 9g | Protein: 26g

Penne Primavera

Spring vegetables are full of fiber and their crunchy texture goes well with the chewy pasta. You can also spike your primavera with a garnish of chopped Italian flat-leaf parsley, a few tiny grape or currant tomatoes, a bit of hot red pepper flakes, and toasted walnuts.

INGREDIENTS | SERVES 4; SERVING SIZE: 2 CUPS

½ cup diced onion
½ cup diced carrot
¼ cup diced red bell pepper
2 tablespoons olive oil
½ cup Chicken Stock (Chapter 3)
1 cup asparagus tips
1 cup broccoli florets
½ cup cream
½ cup peas
½ cup grated Parmesan cheese
Salt and black pepper, to taste
4 cups cooked penne pasta

1. Sauté onions, carrots, and red bell pepper in oil until tender.

2. Add chicken stock, asparagus and broccoli and simmer for 5 minutes.

3. Add cream and peas and simmer for 5 minutes.

4. Stir in Parmesan cheese and remove from heat.

5. Season with salt and pepper and serve over pasta.

PER SERVING Calories: 670 | Fat: 23g | Sodium: 250mg | Carbohydrates: 96g | Fiber: 6g | Protein: 23g

Primavera

In Italian, primavera means spring. Thus, it's appropriate to use young baby vegetables in this dish. You can use frozen baby peas, but sugar snaps are excellent and a fine source of fresh great-tasting fiber, too. Some primavera recipes also call for bits of chicken or chopped shrimp—all delicious.

Vermicelli with Tuna and Anchovies

Vermicelli is thinner than spaghetti and is a good pasta choice for light sauces that won't weigh it down.

INGREDIENTS | SERVES 4

1 tablespoon olive oil

1 onion, chopped

3 cloves garlic, minced

1 (14-ounce) can diced tomatoes, undrained

½ teaspoon dried oregano leaves

1 (12-ounce) package vermicelli pasta

1 anchovy fillet, finely chopped

2 tablespoons capers, rinsed

1 (6-ounce) can white chunk tuna, drained

¼ cup grated Parmesan cheese

2 tablespoons chopped fresh flat-leaf parsley

Cooking Pasta

Pasta should be cooked in a large quantity of rapidly boiling, salted water. When you add the pasta to the water, stir gently so the pasta doesn't stick together. Do not add oil to the pasta water; control the boiling and foaming by stirring and slightly reducing the heat. Drain pasta when al dente, or still slightly firm in the center, and use immediately.

1. Bring a large pot of water to a boil.

2. In a large skillet, heat oil over medium heat. Add onion and garlic; cook and stir until tender, about 6 minutes.

3. Add tomatoes carefully along with oregano and stir; simmer for 5 minutes.

4. Cook pasta in boiling water until al dente, according to package directions. Drain, reserving ½ cup pasta cooking water.

5. Add pasta to tomato mixture along with anchovies, capers, and tuna; cook and stir over medium heat for 2–3 minutes, adding reserved cooking water as necessary, until sauce thickens slightly.

6. Sprinkle with cheese and parsley and serve immediately.

PER SERVING Calories: 462 | Fat: 7g | Sodium: 410mg | Carbohydrates: 73g | Fiber: 5g | Protein: 25g

Greens in Garlic with Pasta

Use any pasta or noodle that you have on hand in this dish. Also feel free to substitute gluten-free pasta made out of brown rice or quinoa, found in the natural food aisle of your grocery store.

INGREDIENTS | SERVES 4

4 teaspoons olive oil, divided

4 cloves garlic, crushed

6 cups tightly packed loose-leaf greens (baby mustard, turnip, chard)

2 cups cooked pasta

¼ cup freshly grated Parmesan cheese

Salt and black pepper, to taste (optional)

Sweet or Salty?

In most cases, when you add a pinch (less than ⅛ teaspoon) of sugar to a recipe, you can reduce the amount of salt without noticing a difference. Sugar acts as a flavor enhancer and magnifies the effect of the salt, and vice versa.

1. Place a sauté pan over medium heat. When hot, add 2 teaspoons of olive oil and garlic. Cook, stirring frequently, until golden brown, 3–5 minutes, being careful not to burn garlic, as that makes it bitter.

2. Add the greens; sauté until coated in garlic oil. Remove from heat.

3. In a large serving bowl, add the pasta, cooked greens, 2 teaspoons of olive oil, and Parmesan cheese; toss to mix.

4. Season as desired and serve immediately.

PER SERVING Calories: 170 | Fat: 7g | Sodium: 100mg | Carbohydrates: 22g | Fiber: 4g | Protein: 7g

Fusion Lo Mein

No need to get takeout when you can recreate delicious Chinese classics at home!

INGREDIENTS | SERVES 6

2 tablespoons rice vinegar

2 tablespoons thawed pineapple-orange juice

2 teaspoons minced shallots

2 teaspoons fresh lemon juice

1 teaspoon arrowroot

1 teaspoon Worcestershire sauce

1 teaspoon agave syrup

2 cloves garlic, minced

1 teaspoon olive oil

¾ cup chopped green onions

1 cup diagonally sliced (¼" thick) carrots

1 cup julienned yellow bell pepper

1 cup julienned red bell pepper

3 cups small broccoli florets

1 cup fresh bean sprouts

1½ cups cooked pasta

1. In a food processor or blender, combine vinegar, juice concentrate, shallots, lemon juice, arrowroot, Worcestershire, agave syrup, and garlic; process until smooth.

2. Heat a wok or large nonstick skillet coated with cooking spray over medium-high heat until hot; add the olive oil. Add the onions and stir-fry for 1 minute.

3. Add the carrots, bell peppers, and broccoli; stir-fry another minute. Cover pan and cook for 2 more minutes.

4. Add vinegar mixture and sprouts. Bring mixture to a boil; cook, uncovered for 30 seconds, stirring constantly.

5. Add cooked pasta and toss to mix.

PER SERVING Calories: 140 | Fat: 2g | Sodium: 45mg | Carbohydrates: 27g | Fiber: 3g | Protein: 6g

Whole-Grain Noodles with Caraway Cabbage

Whole-grain noodles are gaining popularity and can now be found in almost any variety and shape.

INGREDIENTS | **SERVES 6**

2 tablespoons olive oil
½ cup onion, chopped
2 cups cabbage, coarsely chopped
1½ cups Brussels sprouts, trimmed and halved
2 teaspoons caraway seed
1½ cups Chicken Stock (Chapter 3)
¼ teaspoon black pepper
¼ teaspoon salt
6 ounces whole-grain noodles

1. Heat olive oil in large saucepan; sauté onions for about 5 minutes until translucent.

2. Add cabbage and Brussels sprouts; cook over medium heat for 3 minutes.

3. Stir in caraway seed, stock, pepper, and salt; cover and simmer for 5–8 minutes, until vegetables are crisp-tender.

4. Cook noodles in boiling water until tender; drain. Mix noodles and vegetables in large bowl and serve.

PER SERVING Calories: 190 | Fat: 6g | Sodium: 200mg | Carbohydrates: 29g | Fiber: 6g | Protein: 7g

Tuscan Pasta Fagioli

The Mediterranean diet is known for simple yet deliciously flavored dishes, such as this easy pasta recipe.

INGREDIENTS | **SERVES 6**

2 tablespoons olive oil
⅓ cup onion, chopped
3 cloves garlic, minced
½ pound tomatoes, peeled and chopped
5 cups Chicken Stock (Chapter 3) or vegetable stock
¼ teaspoon black pepper
3 cups cannellini beans, rinsed and drained
2½ cups whole-grain pasta shells
2 tablespoons Parmesan cheese

1. Heat olive oil in a large pot; gently cook the onions and garlic until soft but not browned. Add tomatoes, stock, and pepper.

2. Purée 1½ cups of cannellini beans in a food processor or blender; add to stock. Cover and simmer 20–30 minutes. While stock is simmering, cook pasta until al dente; drain.

3. Add remaining beans and pasta to stock; heat through. Serve with Parmesan cheese.

PER SERVING Calories: 400 | Fat: 9g | Sodium: 590mg | Carbohydrates: 62g | Fiber: 7g | Protein: 17g

Fresh Tomato and Clam Sauce with Whole-Grain Linguini

This recipe works well with canned clams if you are unable to get fresh. Canned clams are quite high in sodium, which may need to be taken into consideration. If using canned clams, you will need 1 (8-ounce) can of minced clams and 1 (10-ounce) can of whole clams. Reserve the clam juice and add to the sauce.

INGREDIENTS | **SERVES 4**

3 dozen (36) littleneck clams
Cold Water
Cornmeal, handful
2 tablespoons olive oil
5 cloves garlic, chopped
½ cup red bell pepper, chopped
4 cups fresh tomatoes, peeled and chopped
3 tablespoons fresh parsley, chopped
1 tablespoon fresh basil, chopped
¼ teaspoon salt
¼ teaspoon red pepper flakes
½ teaspoon oregano
½ cup dry white wine
8 ounces whole-grain linguini

1. Before preparing this dish (preferably several hours or more), place clams in bowl of cold water with handful of cornmeal added; keep refrigerated. This will help purge clams of any sand or other debris. When ready to cook, rinse and scrub clams.

2. Heat olive oil, garlic, and red pepper in a deep skillet. Add chopped tomatoes, parsley, basil, salt, red pepper flakes, and oregano, bring to quick boil, then reduce heat and simmer 15–20 minutes.

3. Stir in white wine.

4. Add clams on top of tomato sauce. Cover and steam until clams open.

5. Meanwhile, boil water and cook pasta to al dente.

6. Serve tomato sauce and clams over pasta.

PER SERVING | Calories: 350 | Fat: 9g | Sodium: 180mg | Carbohydrates: 54g | Fiber: 10g | Protein: 15g

Broccoli Penne

This green pasta sauce looks like pesto, but it's full of broccoli, vitamins, and minerals.

INGREDIENTS | SERVES 4

4 tablespoons olive oil, divided
1 onion, chopped
4 cloves garlic, minced
1 tablespoon grated ginger root
2 cups broccoli florets
¼ cup water
2 tablespoons fresh lemon juice
½ teaspoon salt
⅛ teaspoon cayenne pepper
¼ cup fresh basil leaves
1 (12-ounce) package whole-wheat penne pasta
⅓ cup grated Parmesan cheese

Al Dente

Al dente is an Italian term which means "to the tooth." It describes how pasta should feel when it's properly cooked. Never cook pasta until it's very soft or it will lose its character. When you taste cooked pasta, there should be a little bit of resistance at the center. When you look at the bitten end, you should see a small opaque line.

1. Bring a large pot of water to a boil.

2. In large saucepan, heat 1 tablespoon olive oil over medium heat. Add onion, garlic, and ginger; cook and stir until crisp-tender, about 5 minutes.

3. Add broccoli; cook and stir 4 minutes longer.

4. Add water; bring to a simmer, cover pan, and cook 3–5 minutes, until broccoli is tender. Drain and place in food processor.

5. Add lemon juice, salt, pepper, basil, and remaining 3 tablespoons olive oil; process until smooth. Return to saucepan over low heat.

6. Cook pasta according to package directions; drain.

7. Add pasta to saucepan with sauce. Toss to coat over low heat, then sprinkle with cheese. Serve immediately.

PER SERVING Calories: 480 | Fat: 17g | Sodium: 410mg | Carbohydrates: 72g | Fiber: 9g | Protein: 17g

Whole-Wheat Spaghetti and Meatballs

This simple recipe is full of vitamins C and A. Serve it with toasted Hearty-Grain French Bread (Chapter 13) and some red wine.

INGREDIENTS | SERVES 6–8

1 recipe Sirloin Meatballs in Sauce (Chapter 7)

1 (8-ounce) can tomato sauce

½ cup grated carrots

1 (16-ounce) package whole-wheat spaghetti

½ cup grated Parmesan cheese, divided

Whole-Wheat Spaghetti

Whole-wheat spaghetti has a much stronger taste than regular pasta. It should be served with strongly flavored sauces until your family is used to the taste. You can also gradually switch to whole-wheat pastas by starting out using just a third whole-wheat pasta (and the other two thirds plain) and increasing the proportion of whole wheat each time you serve it.

1. Bring a large pot of water to a boil.

2. Prepare the Sirloin Meatballs in Sauce, adding tomato sauce and grated carrots to the sauce. Simmer until meatballs are cooked.

3. Cook spaghetti in water according to package directions or until almost al dente. Drain spaghetti, reserving ¼ cup cooking water.

4. Add spaghetti to meatballs in sauce along with ¼ cup cheese. Simmer, stirring gently, for 5–6 minutes, or until pasta is al dente, adding reserved cooking water if necessary for desired consistency.

5. Sprinkle with remaining Parmesan and serve immediately.

PER SERVING Calories: 620 | Fat: 16g | Sodium: 840mg | Carbohydrates: 88g | Fiber: 16g | Protein: 37g

Fruited Fall Quinoa

Cranberries and apricots make a sweet combo. Add some sage and thyme to give it more warm flavors, and it would make an excellent Thanksgiving entrée.

INGREDIENTS | SERVES 4

1 cup quinoa
2 cups apple juice
1 cup water
½ onion, diced
2 ribs celery, diced
2 tablespoons canola oil
½ teaspoon nutmeg
½ teaspoon cinnamon
¼ teaspoon cloves
½ cup dried cranberries
½ cup dried apricots, chopped
1 teaspoon fresh minced parsley
¼ teaspoon salt

1. In a large pot, combine quinoa, apple juice, and water. Cover and simmer for 15 minutes or until done.

2. In a large skillet, heat onion and celery in oil, stirring frequently, until soft.

3. Over low heat, combine onions and celery with quinoa.

4. Add remaining ingredients, tossing gently to combine. Heat for 3–4 more minutes.

PER SERVING Calories: 380 | Fat: 10g | Sodium: 200mg | Carbohydrates: 71g | Fiber: 6g | Protein: 7g

Quinoa and Whole Grains

Quinoa is a good source of those important antioxidants that help reduce inflammation, including one with the tongue-twister name of superoxide dismutase. It's also a good source of folate and magnesium.

Curried Rice and Lentils

With no added fat, this is a very simple one-pot side-dish recipe. Personalize it with some chopped greens, browned chicken breast, or a veggie mix.

INGREDIENTS | **SERVES 4**

1½ cups white or brown rice, uncooked

1 cup lentils

2 tomatoes, diced

3½ cups water, Chicken Stock (Chapter 3), or vegetable stock

1 bay leaf (optional)

1 tablespoon curry powder

½ teaspoon ground cumin

½ teaspoon turmeric

½ teaspoon garlic powder

Salt and black pepper, to taste

1. Combine all ingredients except salt and pepper in a large soup or stock pot. Bring to a slow simmer, then cover and cook for 20 minutes, stirring occasionally, until rice is done and liquid is absorbed.

2. Season with salt and pepper to taste. Remove bay leaf before serving.

PER SERVING Calories: 460 | Fat: 2.5g | Sodium: 5mg | Carbohydrates: 91g | Fiber: 10g | Protein: 21g

Stuff It!

Rice makes excellent stuffing for poblano or green bell peppers. Carefully remove the top of the bell peppers or, for poblanos, slice down the middle. Fill with cooked curried rice and lentils, Fruited Fall Quinoa (Chapter 4), or leftover Risotto Curry (Chapter 4) and bake at 375°F for 25 minutes, or 15 minutes for poblano peppers.

Asian Stir-Fried Rice

When cooking tofu, you need to press out the excess water, otherwise it splatters in hot oil and doesn't brown well. To do this, slice a block of tofu in half and wrap the cut pieces in layers of paper towels, changing the towels for new sheets when these get soaked.

INGREDIENTS | SERVES 4

3 tablespoons sesame oil

8 ounces firm tofu, cubed

3 cloves garlic, crushed and minced

1 onion, diced

1 tablespoon minced fresh ginger, or to taste

1 cup cubed winter squash, such as butternut or kabocha

1 cup shelled edamame

1 (8-ounce) can sliced bamboo shoots, drained

2 long green chilis, thinly sliced

2 cups cooked short-grain brown rice, chilled

3 tablespoons soy sauce, or to taste

½ cup Chicken Stock (Chapter 3), vegetable stock, or water, as needed

1. Heat the oil in a large wok or skillet over medium-high heat. Add tofu; stir-fry, cooking it until it starts to brown. Remove it from the wok and set aside.

2. Add the garlic, onion, and ginger and stir-fry for about 1 minute.

3. Add the squash and edamame and stir-fry about 2 minutes.

4. Add the bamboo shoots, chilis, and rice, stirring well to combine.

5. Add the soy sauce and cover the wok, cooking the mixture for about 5 minutes or until the squash becomes tender. During the cooking, check that the mixture does not get too dry and add stock as needed, stirring it in well. Serve hot.

PER SERVING Calories: 410 | Fat: 18g | Sodium: 830mg | Carbohydrates: 45g | Fiber: 9g | Protein: 19g

Why Chill the Rice?

If you don't chill cooked rice for stir-frying, the grains clump together and become mushy; also, it's likely to absorb too much oil during cooking. Besides, stir-frying is a great way to use up leftover rice. This recipe calls for short-grain brown rice, which is somewhat sticky, but it provides a delicious texture and flavor for this dish. Any leftover rice will work.

Risotto Curry

Combining Italian and Indian cuisines, this recipe is a delightful change of pace. You could add chicken or shrimp to it for extra lean protein.

INGREDIENTS | **SERVES 4**

2½ cups Chicken Stock (Chapter 3)
1 tablespoon olive oil
1 onion, chopped
1 cup chopped portabella mushrooms
1 cup arborio rice
2 teaspoons curry powder
¼ cup dry white wine

Arborio Rice

Risotto is a classic Italian dish that purists say must be made with arborio rice. Arborio is a short-grain rice that has a higher content of amylopectin, a branched starch molecule that is released from the rice when it is stirred, making the liquid creamy. You must stir risotto frequently as it cooks; be sure to cook only until the rice is al dente.

1. Place stock in small saucepan over low heat.

2. In large saucepan, heat olive oil over medium heat. Add onion and mushrooms; cook and stir until tender, about 7 minutes.

3. Add rice and curry powder to large saucepan; cook and stir until rice turns golden, about 3–4 minutes.

4. Add wine; cook and stir until wine is absorbed.

5. Add warm stock, about ½ cup at a time, stirring almost constantly, until liquid is absorbed. This should take about 20 minutes. When done, the rice should be tender but still slightly firm in the center, and the sauce creamy and thick. Serve immediately.

PER SERVING Calories: 200 | Fat: 5g | Sodium: 220mg | Carbohydrates: 28g | Fiber: 2g | Protein: 6g

Baked Rice Pilaf

For a vegetarian side dish, use vegetable broth or water instead of the chicken stock.

INGREDIENTS | SERVES 6

2 cups Chicken Stock (Chapter 3)
½ cup water
2 tablespoons olive oil
1 onion, chopped
½ cup shredded carrots
½ teaspoon salt
⅛ teaspoon black pepper
½ teaspoon dried marjoram leaves
1¼ cups long-grain white rice

1. Preheat oven to 350°F.

2. Combine chicken stock and water in a small saucepan and place over medium heat.

3. Meanwhile, heat olive oil in ovenproof, 2-quart skillet over medium heat. Add onion; cook and stir until crisp-tender, about 4 minutes.

4. Add carrots, salt, pepper, and marjoram; cook and stir 2 minutes longer.

5. Stir in rice; cook and stir 3 minutes longer. Pour hot Chicken Stock mixture over all and stir.

6. Cover and bake 35–45 minutes, or until rice is tender and liquid is absorbed. Fluff with fork and serve.

PER SERVING Calories: 230 | Fat: 6g | Sodium: 320mg | Carbohydrates: 37g | Fiber: 1g | Protein: 5g

Paella

Paella is a dish for a celebration! This delicious recipe is a cross between a soup and a stew. Serve it with lots of garlic bread to soak up the juices.

INGREDIENTS | SERVES 6

2 cups Chicken Stock (Chapter 3)

¼ teaspoon saffron threads

2 tablespoons olive oil

½ pound medium raw shrimp

1 pound boneless, skinless chicken breasts, chopped

½ teaspoon salt

⅛ teaspoon white pepper

1 onion, chopped

4 cloves garlic, minced

1 (14.5-ounce) can diced tomatoes, undrained

1 cup arborio rice

1 (8-ounce) can artichoke hearts, chopped

1 cup frozen peas, thawed

½ cup chopped jarred roasted red pepper

12 whole mussels, debearded

1. In microwave-safe glass measuring cup, combine chicken broth and saffron. Microwave on high for 1 minute, then set aside.

2. In a large skillet, heat olive oil over medium heat. Add shrimp; cook and stir until shrimp curl and turn pink; remove from skillet.

3. Add chicken to skillet and sprinkle with salt and pepper; cook and stir until chicken turns white; remove from skillet.

4. Add onion and garlic to drippings remaining in skillet; cook and stir for 3 minutes.

5. Add tomatoes and rice; cook and stir for 2–3 minutes.

6. Add the chicken broth mixture. Bring to a simmer, then reduce heat to low, cover, and cook for 20 minutes.

7. Add chicken, shrimp, artichoke hearts, peas, and red pepper to rice mixture; stir.

8. Arrange mussels over top and cover skillet. Cook, shaking skillet frequently, for 5 –7 minutes, or until mussels open. Serve immediately.

PER SERVING Calories: 370 | Fat: 9g | Sodium: 650mg | Carbohydrate: 29g | Fiber: 3g | Protein: 40g

Tomato Avocado Spaghetti

Serve this delicious dish when tomatoes and basil are in season.

INGREDIENTS | **SERVES 6**

2 tomatoes, chopped

2 cups grape tomatoes

¼ cup sliced green onion

2 avocados, peeled and diced

½ teaspoon salt

⅛ teaspoon black pepper

½ cup chopped fresh basil

2 tablespoons olive oil

1 (16-ounce) package whole-wheat spaghetti

1. Bring a large pot of water to a boil.

2. Meanwhile, in serving bowl, combine tomatoes, grape tomatoes, onion, avocado, salt, pepper, basil, and olive oil; mix gently.

3. Cook pasta according to package directions, until al dente; drain.

4. Immediately toss with tomato mixture. Serve at once.

PER SERVING Calories: 440 | Fat: 16g | Sodium: 210mg | Carbohydrates: 67g | Fiber: 15g | Protein: 13g

Breakfast and Brunch

Egg and Veggie Scramble

Use your favorite vegetables in this easy breakfast recipe.

INGREDIENTS | **SERVES 4**

2 tablespoons olive oil
½ cup chopped onion
1 cup sliced mushrooms
½ cup chopped red bell pepper
¼ teaspoon salt
⅛ teaspoon black pepper
½ teaspoon dried thyme leaves
8 eggs
2 tablespoons water
½ cup grated Cheddar cheese

1. In large skillet, heat olive oil over medium heat. Add onion, mushrooms, and red bell pepper; cook and stir 4–5 minutes, or until vegetables are tender. Sprinkle with salt, pepper, and thyme.

2. In medium bowl, combine eggs and water; beat until frothy. Add to skillet when vegetables are tender. Cook, stirring occasionally, until eggs are just set.

3. Sprinkle with cheese, remove from heat, and cover. Let stand 3–4 minutes, or until cheese melts. Serve immediately.

PER SERVING Calories: 280 | Fat: 22g | Sodium: 370mg | Carbohydrates: 5g | Fiber: <1g | Protein: 17g

Buckwheat Flax Pancakes

Pancakes are easy if you follow a few rules, such as: Don't overmix the batter!

INGREDIENTS | **SERVES 2**

¾ cup whole-wheat flour
½ cup buckwheat flour
1½ teaspoons baking powder
1 egg
¼ cup apple juice concentrate
¼ cup ground flax seeds
1¼–1½ cups milk

1. Sift flours and baking powder together.

2. Combine egg, apple juice concentrate, flax seeds, and 1¼ cups milk.

3. Add wet ingredients to dry ingredients; mix well, but do not overmix. Add remaining milk if necessary to reach desired consistency.

4. Cook pancakes in nonstick skillet or on griddle treated with nonstick spray over medium heat.

PER SERVING Calories: 510 | Fat: 15g | Sodium: 480mg | Carbohydrates: 76g | Fiber: 15g | Protein: 21g

Edamame Omelet

The addition of cheese turns this into a fusion dish; to add more Asian flavors, you might want to stir some shredded daikon and crushed chilis, to taste, into the mix.

INGREDIENTS | SERVES 2

2 tablespoons olive oil

1 teaspoon minced garlic

1 bunch scallions, trimmed and cut into 1" pieces

½ cup shelled edamame

1 tablespoon soy sauce, or to taste

3 large eggs

½ cup shredded Cheddar cheese

Fresh cilantro, for garnish

1. Heat 2 tablespoons oil in a small skillet over medium heat and sauté the garlic and scallion for about 2 minutes.

2. Add the edamame and soy sauce and sauté 1 minute more. Remove from the skillet and set aside.

3. Heat the remaining 1 tablespoon oil in the same skillet. Beat the eggs until mixed and pour into the hot oil. Scatter shredded cheese on top.

4. Lift up the edges of the omelet, tipping the skillet back and forth to cook the uncooked eggs. When the top looks firm, sprinkle the scallion mixture over one half of the omelet and fold the other half over top.

5. Carefully lift the omelet out of the skillet. Divide it in half, sprinkle with the cilantro, and serve.

PER SERVING Calories: 420 | Fat: 33g | Sodium: 800mg | Carbohydrates: 9g | Fiber: 3g | Protein: 22g

Veggie Frittata

Versatile and adaptable to whichever veggies are in season, this wholesome dish starts the day with a bang, and it makes a good light supper, too. It's easy to increase quantities to feed larger groups.

INGREDIENTS | **SERVES 4**

3 tablespoons olive oil

2 red potatoes, diced

6 asparagus spears, trimmed and cut into 2" lengths

½ zucchini or yellow summer squash, diced

2 teaspoons minced garlic

1 teaspoon seasoning salt

1 teaspoon smoked paprika

6 large eggs

1 cup shredded Cheddar cheese

½ cup chopped fresh Italian parsley

What's Smoked Paprika?

A Spanish seasoning made from slowly oak-smoked and ground pimentón, a variety of Spanish red pepper, smoked paprika imparts an earthy, woodsy taste to an infinite number of savory dishes. It's readily available in well-stocked supermarkets, specialty food stores, and online.

1. Preheat the broiler.

2. Heat oil in 8" or 9" skillet over medium heat. Add the potatoes and sauté for about 3 minutes or until the cubes begin to brown.

3. Add the asparagus, zucchini, garlic, and seasonings and cover the skillet, cooking for 2–3 minutes.

4. Meanwhile, beat the eggs until foamy. Stir in the cheese and parsley and pour over the vegetables.

5. Using a spatula, lift up the edges of the eggs and tip the skillet to all sides, allowing the uncooked eggs to flow underneath the vegetables and to cook.

6. When the eggs are almost firm, slide the skillet under the broiler and cook until the top is bubbly and brown. Cheese should be melted and runny.

7. Serve hot, sliced in wedges.

PER SERVING Calories: 350 | Fat: 23g | Sodium: 430mg | Carbohydrates: 20g | Fiber: 2g | Protein: 16g

Cheese Egg Casserole

*This is a strata, or casserole, made of bread, cheese, and vegetables
baked in an egg custard until puffed and golden.*

INGREDIENTS | **SERVES 4**

6 slices stale Whole-Grain Oatmeal
Bread (Chapter 13)

8 eggs

1 cup milk

⅛ teaspoon dry mustard

½ teaspoon salt

⅛ teaspoon black pepper

2 onions, chopped

3 cloves garlic, minced

1 tablespoon olive oil

1 cup shredded sharp Cheddar cheese

1. Arrange bread slices in a single layer in a shallow baking dish so they fit snugly.

2. In a small bowl, combine eggs, milk, mustard, salt, and pepper and beat well. Pour over bread.

3. In a small skillet, cook onion and garlic in olive oil until tender, about 5–6 minutes.

4. Sprinkle onion mixture and cheese over the bread in casserole. Cover and refrigerate overnight.

5. The next day, preheat oven to 350°F.

6. Bake casserole, uncovered, until golden brown and puffed, 25–35 minutes. Cut into squares and serve immediately.

PER SERVING Calories: 470 | Fat: 26g | Sodium: 880mg | Carbohydrates: 31g | Fiber: 3g | Protein: 26g

Salmon Soufflé

This dish may have more than 9 grams of fat per serving, but remember, it's the good omega-3 fats from salmon.

INGREDIENTS | SERVES 4

1 (7-ounce) can salmon, drained
1 tablespoon olive oil
½ cup finely chopped red onion
2 tablespoons fresh lemon juice
½ teaspoon dried dill weed
8 egg whites
¼ teaspoon cream of tartar
¼ cup mayonnaise
⅛ teaspoon cayenne pepper

Garnishing

Soufflés and omelets can be garnished for added color and nutrition. Use ingredients that are in the recipe as garnishes; this Salmon Soufflé would be delicious garnished with chopped chives.

1. Preheat oven to 400°F.

2. Remove skin and bones from salmon if necessary; flake salmon and set aside.

3. In small pan, heat olive oil over medium heat. Add onion; cook and stir until tender, about 5 minutes.

4. Remove from heat and add salmon, lemon juice, and dill weed; do not stir, but set aside.

5. In large bowl, combine egg whites with cream of tartar; beat until stiff peaks form.

6. Add mayonnaise and pepper to salmon mixture and mix gently.

7. Fold egg whites into salmon mixture.

8. Spray the bottom of a 2-quart casserole with nonstick cooking spray. Pour salmon mixture into dish.

9. Bake for 20 minutes, then lower heat to 350°F and bake for 20–30 minutes longer or until soufflé is puffed and deep golden brown. Serve immediately.

PER SERVING Calories: 250 | Fat: 18g | Sodium: 460mg | Carbohydrates: 3g | Fiber: 0g | Protein: 17g

Quinoa-Blueberry-Chia Pancakes

Serve these nutritious and hearty pancakes with melted butter and maple or fruit syrup or honey.

INGREDIENTS | SERVES 4

2 large eggs, well beaten

1 cup plain yogurt

2 tablespoons chia seeds, soaked

3 tablespoons melted butter

1 cup fresh or frozen blueberries

1 cup cooked quinoa

2–3 tablespoons maple or agave syrup

1–1¼ cups white or whole-wheat flour

2 teaspoons baking powder

1 teaspoon baking soda

½ teaspoon salt

Agave Syrup

Agave syrup is a low-glycemic sweetener made from the sap of the blue agave plant. Blue agave is considered to be the finest in the world. Quality-brand tequilas are also produced from the blue agave plant.

1. Stir together the eggs, yogurt, chia seeds, and melted butter.

2. Stir in the blueberries, quinoa and maple syrup.

3. Fold in the flour, baking powder, baking soda, and salt and mix until just blended.

4. Spray a nonstick griddle or large skillet with nonstick cooking spray and heat the griddle over medium-low to medium heat. Drop the batter by large spoonfuls onto the heated griddle and cook until the bottoms turn golden.

5. Flip the pancakes over, respraying the skillet as needed. Remove the pancakes from the skillet when both sides are golden and the centers are firm. Repeat with the remaining batter and serve immediately.

PER SERVING Calories: 490 | Fat: 17g | Sodium: 980mg | Carbohydrates: 70g | Fiber: 6g | Protein: 15g

Cornmeal Cranberry Pancakes

*Apple juice adds a nice bit of sweetness to these tender pancakes. Serve them
with cranberry sauce or warmed honey for a fabulous breakfast.*

INGREDIENTS	SERVES 6

¾ cup cornmeal

½ teaspoon salt

2 tablespoons maple or agave syrup

2 tablespoons butter

½ cup water

1 cup apple juice

1 egg

½ cup flour

¼ cup whole-wheat flour

1 teaspoon baking powder

½ teaspoon baking soda

1 cup dried cranberries

1 tablespoon canola oil

Making Pancakes

For the best pancakes, the griddle should
be hot enough that a drop of water skips
and steams as soon as it's dropped onto
the surface. Cook pancakes until the sides
look dry and bubbles form on the surface
and begin to break. Use a large spatula to
easily turn the pancakes. The second side
will never brown as much as the first, so
don't worry about it!

1. In large bowl, combine cornmeal, salt, syrup, and butter.

2. In microwave-safe glass measuring cup, combine water and apple juice. Microwave on high 1–2 minutes, or until mixture boils. Add to cornmeal mixture; stir and let stand for 5 minutes.

3. Beat in egg until mixed.

4. Add flours, baking powder, and baking soda and stir just until combined. Add cranberries.

5. Heat large skillet over medium heat. Brush the surface with oil. Pour batter onto skillet using ¼ cup measure. Cook until edges appear dry and bubbles form and just start to break on the surface, about 4 minutes. Gently turn pancakes and cook on second side until done. Serve immediately.

PER SERVING Calories: 280 | Fat: 8g | Sodium: 420mg | Carbohydrates: 51g | Fiber: 3g | Protein: 4g

Whole-Grain Waffles

Homemade waffles taste so much better than frozen. You can use them for breakfast with fresh fruit or serve them for dinner with some Turkey Chili (Chapter 8).

INGREDIENTS | SERVES 8

¾ cup all-purpose flour
¾ cup whole-wheat flour
¼ cup ground flax seeds
1 cup cornmeal
2 teaspoons baking powder
½ teaspoon baking soda
⅛ teaspoon salt
1 egg
2 tablespoons butter, melted
2 cups buttermilk
4 egg whites
¼ cup maple or agave syrup

Waffles

The first waffle you cook almost always sticks; you can consider it a test waffle. Be sure to lightly spray the waffle iron with nonstick cooking spray before you add the batter each time, and remove any bits of the previous waffle before adding batter. You might need nonstick cooking spray with flour as extra protection against sticking.

1. In medium bowl, combine flours, flax seeds, cornmeal, baking powder, baking soda, and salt, and mix well.

2. In small bowl, combine egg, butter, and buttermilk and mix well.

3. Add wet ingredients to dry ingredients; stir just until combined.

4. In large bowl, beat egg whites until foamy. Gradually add syrup, beating until stiff peaks form. Fold into flour mixture.

5. Spray waffle iron with nonstick cooking spray and heat according to directions. Pour about ¼ cup batter into the waffle iron, close, and cook until the steaming stops, or according to the appliance directions. Serve immediately.

PER SERVING Calories: 260 | Fat: 6g | Sodium: 360mg | Carbohydrates: 42g | Fiber: 4g | Protein: 10g

Banana Oat Bran Waffles

Use either a standard nonstick waffle iron or a Belgian nonstick one that makes waffles with deep indentations to hold pools of rich maple syrup. Be sure to use very ripe and soft bananas so they can blend into the batter.

INGREDIENTS | SERVES 4

2 large eggs

1 cup buttermilk

2 very ripe bananas

4 tablespoons melted butter plus extra for serving

1 cup all-purpose flour

½ cup oat bran

2 teaspoons baking powder

½ teaspoon salt

½ cup crushed pecans

Maple syrup or other fruit syrup for serving

1. Preheat the waffle iron. Spray both surfaces with nonstick cooking spray.

2. Beat together the eggs, buttermilk, bananas, and butter until well blended and smooth.

3. Fold in the flour, oat bran, baking powder, and salt, stirring until just combined and moistened. The batter should be stiff, not runny. Fold in the pecans.

4. Bake waffles according to manufacturer's directions. Serve hot with extra butter and syrup.

PER SERVING Calories: 470 | Fat: 26g | Sodium: 610mg | Carbohydrates: 52g | Fiber: 6g | Protein: 13g

What's Oat Bran?

Because it is so high in fiber, oat bran has become one of the darlings of the health food world and is often touted as one of the soluble-fiber foods that help lower cholesterol levels in the blood. It's also a welcome ingredient in the kitchen for its use in cereals, baked goods, soups, and stews, adding texture and a delicate nutty taste.

Double Corn Waffles

Cornmeal plus corn kernels equal whole-grain fiber heaven. You can use canned or frozen corn, but this is a real treat if you can get corn in season at the end of summer.

INGREDIENTS | **SERVES 6**

3 eggs
4 ounces canola oil
1½ cups plain yogurt
1¾ cups yellow cornbread mix
½ cup corn kernels

Good Company

Honey butter spread is a good partner for cornbread and cornmeal muffins. Whip 2 tablespoons of honey with ½ stick softened unsalted butter with an electric mixer for a delicious butter spread to accompany double corn waffles.

1. Whisk together eggs, canola oil, and yogurt.

2. Stir egg mixture into cornbread mix to combine. There will be lumps; be careful not to overmix.

3. Fold corn kernels into batter.

4. Pour or ladle about ½ cup waffle batter onto preheated waffle iron sprayed with oil; cook according to manufacturer's instructions.

5. Serve hot with honey butter spread.

PER SERVING Calories: 410 | Fat: 28g | Sodium: 640mg | Carbohydrates: 34g | Fiber: 0g | Protein: 9g

Fruity Stuffed French Toast

Serve this delicious toast with warmed maple syrup or a combination of powdered sugar and cinnamon.

INGREDIENTS | **SERVES 4–6**

4 slices Honey Wheat Sesame Bread, cut 1" thick (Chapter 13)
⅓ cup buttermilk
1 egg
3 tablespoons sugar, divided
½ cup ricotta cheese
½ teaspoon cinnamon
¾ cup frozen blueberries, unthawed
2 tablespoons butter

1. Cut a pocket in the center of each piece of bread, making sure to not cut through to the other side.

2. Combine buttermilk, egg, and 1 tablespoon of sugar in a shallow bowl and beat well.

3. In small bowl, combine remaining 2 tablespoons of sugar with ricotta and cinnamon and mix well. Fold in blueberries. Gently stuff into the bread slices.

4. In nonstick pan melt butter over medium heat. Dip bread into the egg mixture, turning to coat. Cook until crisp and browned, turning once, about 6–9 minutes.

PER SERVING Calories: 300 | Fat: 14g | Sodium: 135mg | Carbohydrates: 36g | Fiber: 3g | Protein: 9g

Breakfast Chia Salad

Mandarin oranges are a small citrus fruit that look more like a tangerine than an orange. High in vitamin C, you should always choose canned mandarin oranges without the heavy syrup.

INGREDIENTS | **SERVES 4**

2 cups Gala or Braeburn apples, cubed

1½ cups pears, cubed

1 cup mandarin orange slices

½ cup kiwi, sliced

¼ cup fresh blueberries

¼ cup fresh pomegranate seeds

1 tablespoon dried cranberries

2 tablespoons chia seeds, soaked

3 tablespoons sunflower seeds

1. Combine all ingredients in a large bowl.

2. Toss and serve.

PER SERVING Calories: 190 | Fat: 5g | Sodium: 0mg | Carbohydrates: 37g | Fiber: 8g | Protein: 3g

California English Muffin

Food referenced as "California" style is traditionally fresh, uncomplicated cuisine that makes the most of locally grown ingredients.

INGREDIENTS | **SERVES 2**

1 light multigrain English muffin

2 tablespoons cream cheese

2 thick slices tomato

¼ cup sprouts

Salt and black pepper, to taste

1. Split and toast English muffin.

2. Spread 1 tablespoon cream cheese on each English muffin half.

3. Top each half with 1 slice of tomato and sprouts.

4. Salt and pepper to taste.

PER SERVING Calories: 130 | Fat: 6g | Sodium: 130mg | Carbohydrates: 18g | Fiber: 2g | Protein: 4g

French Toast with Citrus Chia Compote

This citrus compote can be served with Buckwheat Pancakes (Chapter 5) or Whole-Grain Waffles (Chapter 5) or even Fruity Slow-Cooker Flax Oatmeal (Chapter 5).

INGREDIENTS | SERVES 4–6

1 orange
1 red grapefruit
½ cup maple syrup, divided
1 cup fresh orange juice, divided
2 tablespoons chia seeds, soaked
1 teaspoon vanilla
1 egg
2 tablespoons butter
6 slices Hearty-Grain French Bread (Chapter 13)

French Toast

When making French toast, it's important to let the bread soak up some of the liquid mixture it is dipped in before it's cooked. But if the bread is soaked too long, it will fall apart when you take it from the liquid. Place the bread into the liquid, push it down so the liquid covers the bread, and let sit for about 30 seconds. Cook immediately.

1. Peel and chop orange and grapefruit and place in small bowl.

2. In small saucepan, combine ¼ cup syrup with ½ cup orange juice and bring to a simmer. Simmer for 5–6 minutes, or until slightly thickened. Add chia seeds; pour over orange mixture. Set aside.

3. In shallow bowl, combine remaining ¼ cup maple syrup with ½ cup orange juice, vanilla, and egg, and beat well.

4. Heat a nonstick pan over medium heat and add butter.

5. Slice bread on an angle. Dip bread into egg mixture, turning to coat. Cook in hot butter over medium heat for 6–8 minutes, turning once, until bread is crisp and deep golden brown. Serve with citrus compote.

PER SERVING Calories: 370 | Fat: 10g | Sodium: 250mg | Carbohydrates: 66g | Fiber: 6g | Protein: 8g

Creamy Oatmeal

Applesauce adds creamy texture and nutrition to this simple oatmeal recipe.
Serve it hot with some warmed maple syrup or honey.

INGREDIENTS | SERVES 6

2 cups water

2 cups No-Sugar Apricot Applesauce
(Chapter 14)

1½ teaspoons cinnamon

¼ cup maple syrup

2 tablespoons honey

½ teaspoon salt

2 cups quick-cooking oatmeal

½ cup dried currants

Steel-Cut Oats

Steel-cut oats are really essential when cooking oatmeal in the slow cooker. They have a firmer texture and stand up to the long cooking time. They are made from the whole-oat grain, also known as groats, cut into pieces. All types of oatmeal have the same nutritional qualities, although instant oatmeal may have less fiber. In Scotland, oatmeal is called porridge and is a staple breakfast food.

1. In large saucepan, combine water, applesauce, cinnamon, syrup, honey, and salt and bring to a boil.

2. Stir in oatmeal and cook 2–4 minutes, or until mixture thickens.

3. Stir in currants; cover and remove from heat. Let stand 5 minutes.

4. Stir and serve immediately.

PER SERVING Calories: 250 | Fat: 2.5g | Sodium: 200mg | Carbohydrates: 56g | Fiber: 6g | Protein: 5g

Fruity Slow-Cooker Flax Oatmeal

Waking up to hot oatmeal in the slow cooker is very luxurious. Drizzle this with some maple syrup and top with fresh fruit.

INGREDIENTS | SERVES 4–6

1 cup steel-cut oats

2 tablespoons ground flax seeds

1¾ cups water

¼ cup frozen orange juice concentrate, thawed

1 cup mixed dried fruit

¼ teaspoon salt

2 tablespoons maple syrup

1 (13-ounce) can evaporated milk

Another Overnight Method

For another way to cook steel-cut oats, place 1 cup steel cut oats, 4 cups water, and dried fruit in medium saucepan; bring to a quick boil. Turn off the heat and cover saucepan. When cooled, place in covered container and refrigerate overnight. In morning, the oatmeal will have absorbed all of the water. Scoop 1 portion of the oatmeal into a bowl; microwave on high for 1 ½–2 minutes. Add milk and serve. Heat up refrigerated leftover portions as needed; use within 3 days.

1. Place oats in a dry, heavy saucepan over medium-low heat. Toast oats 5–7 minutes, stirring frequently, until oats are deeper golden brown and fragrant. Cool completely.

2. In 2 quart slow cooker, combine oats, ground flax seeds, water, orange juice concentrate, dried fruit, and salt; mix well. Cover and cook on low 7–9 hours.

3. In the morning, stir in the maple syrup and evaporated milk; cook for another 30 minutes until hot. Stir well and serve immediately.

PER SERVING Calories: 450 | Fat: 11g | Sodium: 260mg | Carbohydrates: 79g | Fiber: 7g | Protein: 14g

Oat Cakes

These are like a bowl of oatmeal to go. They're a great alternative to purchased energy bars. You get protein from the egg and yogurt and lots of fiber from the oatmeal and apricots.

INGREDIENTS | **SERVES 8**

3 cups rolled oats

2 cups flour

1 tablespoon chia seeds

¼ teaspoon baking powder

1 egg white

⅓ cup plain yogurt

½ cup maple or agave syrup

½ cup honey

½ teaspoon vanilla extract

½ cup dried apricots, chopped

1. Preheat oven to 325°F.

2. Pulse the oats in a food processor 10 times, then add the flour, chia seeds, and baking powder and pulse to mix.

3. In a bowl, whisk the egg white until frothy, then add the yogurt, maple syrup, honey, and vanilla.

4. Add the oat mixture and dried apricots to the yogurt mixture. Mix with a wooden spoon.

5. Roll the mixture into 8 balls and flatten them into thick, cylindrical patties.

6. Bake them on a parchment-lined baking sheet for 15–20 minutes. Let cool. Refrigerate unless eating right away.

PER SERVING Calories: 430 | Fat: 3.5g | Sodium: 40mg | Carbohydrates: 90g | Fiber: 6g | Protein: 10g

Country Style Omelet

Omelets don't have to be served exclusively at breakfast! Next time you need an easy dinner recipe, try this delicious twist on the classic omelet.

INGREDIENTS | **SERVES 2**

2 teaspoons olive oil
1 cup zucchini, diced
¼ cup red pepper, diced
1 cup plum tomatoes, skinned and cubed
⅛ teaspoon black pepper
4 eggs
1 tablespoon Parmesan cheese
1 teaspoon fresh basil, minced

1. Heat oil in nonstick skillet. Add zucchini and red pepper; sauté for 5 minutes.

2. Add tomatoes and pepper; cook uncovered for another 10 minutes, allowing fluid from tomatoes to cook down.

3. In small bowl, whisk together eggs, Parmesan, and basil; pour over vegetables in skillet.

4. Cook over low heat until browned, approximately 10 minutes on each side.

PER SERVING Calories: 230 | Fat: 16g | Sodium: 190mg | Carbohydrates: 8g | Fiber: 2g | Protein: 15g

Creamy Millet Porridge

Millet makes a delicious breakfast dish. Millet and tapioca are both eaten in many parts of Africa as a staple, like rice or corn here in the U.S.

INGREDIENTS | **SERVES 6**

1½ cups millet
½ cup dried chopped apricots
¼ cup agave syrup
2 cups apricot nectar
3 cups water
½ teaspoon salt
½ cup silken tofu

1. In large saucepan, combine millet, apricots, and agave syrup and stir to mix.

2. Add nectar, water, and salt. Bring to a boil over medium-high heat, then reduce heat to low. Cover saucepan and cook 20–30 minutes, until millet is tender.

3. Uncover and stir. Stir in tofu and serve immediately.

PER SERVING | Calories: 460 | Fat: 2.5g | Sodium: 210mg | Carbohydrates: 105g | Fiber: 5g | Protein: 7g

Maple Cinnamon Breakfast Quinoa

*Quinoa is a filling and healthy breakfast and has more protein than regular oatmeal.
This is a deliciously sweet and energizing way to kick off your day.*

INGREDIENTS | SERVES 2

1 cup quinoa

2–2½ cups water

1 teaspoon butter

⅔ cup milk

½ teaspoon cinnamon

2 tablespoons maple syrup

2 tablespoons raisins (optional)

2 bananas, sliced (optional)

1. Heat the quinoa and water in a small saucepan and bring to a boil. Reduce to a simmer and allow to cook, covered, for 15 minutes, until liquid is absorbed.

2. Remove from heat and fluff the quinoa with a fork. Cover, and allow to sit for 5 minutes.

3. Stir in the butter and milk, then remaining ingredients.

PER SERVING Calories: 440 | Fat: 9g | Sodium: 65mg | Carbohydrates: 76g | Fiber: 5g | Protein: 14g

Vanilla Flax Granola

Making your own granola allows you to create whatever flavors you desire. Crystallized ginger, chopped dates, a sprinkle of cinnamon, coconut flakes, dried papaya—the possibilities are endless!

INGREDIENTS | YIELDS 2½ CUPS

⅔ cup maple syrup

⅓ cup canola oil

1½ teaspoons vanilla

2 cups oats

½ cup ground flax seeds or wheat germ

¾ cup dried fruit, diced small

1. Preheat oven to 325°F.

2. Over low heat, melt and whisk together syrup, canola oil, and vanilla until margarine is melted.

3. On large baking tray in a single layer, toss together oats, flax seeds, and dried fruit. Drizzle maple syrup mixture over oats, gently tossing to combine as needed.

4. Bake for 25–30 minutes, carefully tossing once during cooking. Granola will harden as it cools.

PER ½ CUP | Calories: 490 | Fat: 22g | Sodium: 20mg | Carbohydrates: 70g | Fiber: 8g | Protein: 7g

Chicken and Apple Patties

Rather than eat sausages full of nitrates, try this easy recipe that is flavorful and good for you, too.

INGREDIENTS | **SERVES 8**

2 tablespoons olive oil
1 onion, finely chopped
3 cloves garlic, minced
1 cup finely chopped, peeled apple
1 tablespoon brown sugar
2 tablespoons fresh lemon juice
1½ pounds ground chicken
1 teaspoon salt
¼ teaspoon white pepper
1 teaspoon dried thyme leaves

1. In large saucepan, heat olive oil over medium heat. Add onion and garlic; cook and stir until tender, about 5 minutes.

2. Remove from heat and add apple, brown sugar, and lemon juice. Let cool for 20 minutes.

3. Place in large bowl and add chicken, salt, pepper, and thyme. Work with your hands until combined.

4. Form mixture into 16 patties. You can freeze the patties at this point, or cook them in more olive oil, turning once, until thoroughly cooked, about 3–4 minutes per side. To cook frozen patties, let thaw in refrigerator overnight, then proceed as directed.

PER SERVING Calories: 170 | Fat: 10g | Sodium: 340mg | Carbohydrates: 6g | Fiber: <1g | Protein: 14g

Corned Beef Hash

*Serve this delicious hash on toasted Hearty-Grain French Bread
(Chapter 13), topped with scrambled eggs.*

INGREDIENTS | **SERVES 6**

2 tablespoons olive oil

2 onions, chopped

4 cloves garlic, minced

8 fingerling potatoes, chopped

4 carrots, chopped

¼ cup water

½ pound deli corned beef, diced

⅛ teaspoon ground cloves

⅛ teaspoon white pepper

3 tablespoons chili sauce

Corned Beef

Corned beef is a high-sodium food, made of brisket that has been pickled or "corned" in a mixture of water, vinegar, sugars, and salt. When you use it, use a small amount (about an ounce per person), mainly for flavor. Adding lots of vegetables helps reduce the sodium count and makes this treat more healthy.

1. Place olive oil in large saucepan; heat over medium heat. Add onion and garlic; cook and stir for 3 minutes.

2. Add potatoes and carrots; cook and stir until potatoes are partially cooked, about 5 minutes.

3. Add water, corned beef, cloves, pepper, and chili sauce. Stir well, then cover, reduce heat to low, and simmer for 10–15 minutes, or until blended and potatoes are cooked. Serve immediately.

PER SERVING Calories: 220 | Fat: 6g | Sodium: 710mg | Carbohydrates: 33g | Fiber: 5g | Protein: 10g

CHAPTER 6

Fish

Baked Bread Crumb-Crusted Halibut with Lemon

Mildly flavored fish such as catfish, cod, halibut, orange roughy, rockfish, and snapper benefit from the distinctive flavor of lemon. Adding slices of lemon to top of fish allows the flavor to infuse into fish.

INGREDIENTS | **SERVES 6**

2 large lemons
¼ cup dried bread crumbs
1½ pounds (24 ounces) halibut fillets
Salt and white or black pepper, to taste (optional)

Making Bread Crumbs

There are several ways you can make your own bread crumbs. Tear the bread into tiny pieces with your fingers or cut the bread into cubes and process in a food processor with a bit of flour to prevent sticking. You can also let bread dry for a day or two, then grate it on a food grater.

1. Preheat oven to 375°F.

2. Wash 1 lemon; cut into thin slices. Grate 1 tablespoon of zest from the second lemon, then juice it.

3. Combine grated zest and bread crumbs in small bowl; stir to mix. Set aside.

4. Put lemon juice in shallow dish; arrange lemon slices in bottom of baking dish treated with nonstick spray. Dip fish pieces in lemon juice; set on lemon slices in baking dish.

5. Sprinkle bread crumb mixture evenly over fish pieces along with salt and pepper, if using; bake until crumbs are lightly browned and fish is just opaque, 10–15 minutes. (Baking time will depend on thickness of fish.) Serve immediately, using lemon slices as garnish.

PER SERVING Calories: 137 | Fat: 3g | Sodium: 73mg | Carbohydrates: 5g | Fiber: 2g | Protein: 24g

Curried Cod with Apricots

Cod, like other white fish, is very mild and adapts well to almost any flavoring.
Curry and apricots are a marvelous combination with this fish.

INGREDIENTS | SERVES 4

1 tablespoon olive oil
1 onion, chopped
3 cloves garlic, minced
1 tablespoon curry powder
1 cup dry white wine
½ teaspoon dried thyme leaves
1 pound cod fillets
¼ teaspoon salt
⅛ teaspoon white pepper
½ cup dried apricots, thinly sliced

White Wine

Adding wine to recipes is a wonderful way to reduce fat and add lots of flavor. Alcohol, like fat, is a flavor carrier, so wine spreads the flavors throughout the dish, but heat evaporates the alcohol, leaving the flavor behind.

1. Heat olive oil in large skillet over medium heat. Add onion and garlic; cook and stir for 3 minutes.

2. Add curry powder; cook and stir for 3 minutes longer until onion is tender.

3. Add wine and thyme and bring to a boil.

4. Reduce heat to medium. Sprinkle cod with salt and pepper and add to skillet with sauce. Simmer for 5 minutes, then turn and simmer for 5–6 minutes longer, until fish flakes when tested with fork. Remove fish to serving platter and cover to keep warm.

5. Add apricots to skillet and cook over high heat until they plump, about 2–3 minutes. Spoon apricots and sauce over fish and serve immediately.

PER SERVING Calories: 230 | Fat: 4.5g | Sodium: 240mg | Carbohydrates: 17g | Fiber: 3g | Protein: 22g

Cod and Potatoes

Thinly sliced potatoes are layered with olive oil and herbs and baked until crisp, then topped with cod and lemon juice. This makes a delicious, light, and easy-to-digest meal.

INGREDIENTS | SERVES 4

3 Yukon Gold potatoes
¼ cup olive oil
⅛ teaspoon white pepper
1½ teaspoons dried herbs de Provence, divided
4 (4-ounce) cod steaks
1 tablespoon butter
2 tablespoons fresh lemon juice

Yukon Gold Potatoes

This variety of potato is literally gold colored. The potato tastes buttery and rich even when cooked without fat. You can find it in specialty stores and in the produce aisle of many supermarkets. It was introduced into American grocery stores in 1980 after a Canadian researcher bred a wild South American potato with a North American variety.

1. Preheat oven to 350°F. Spray a 9" glass baking dish with nonstick cooking spray.

2. Thinly slice the potatoes. Layer in the baking dish, drizzling each layer with a tablespoon of olive oil, a sprinkle of pepper, and some of the herbs de Provence.

3. Bake for 35–45 minutes, or until potatoes are browned on top and tender when pierced with a fork.

4. Arrange cod steaks on top of potatoes. Dot with butter and sprinkle with lemon juice and remaining herbs de Provence.

5. Bake for 15–25 minutes longer, or until fish flakes when tested with fork.

PER SERVING Calories: 340 | Fat: 18g | Sodium: 105mg | Carbohydrates: 20g | Fiber: 1g | Protein: 23g

Baked Orange Roughy with Spicy Plum Sauce

Brown rice has a heartier taste than white, and it is better for you. Brown rice is made by removing just the outer covering, or hull, from the rice so it can absorb water as it cooks. It also has more B vitamins, iron, and fiber than white rice.

INGREDIENTS | SERVES 4

1 pound (16 ounces) orange roughy fillets

1 teaspoon paprika

1 bay leaf

1 clove garlic, crushed

1 apple, peeled, cored, and cubed

1 teaspoon grated fresh ginger

1 small red or Spanish onion, chopped

1 teaspoon olive oil

¼ cup Plum Sauce (Chapter 12)

¼ teaspoon Chinese five spice powder

1 teaspoon frozen unsweetened apple juice concentrate

½ teaspoon soy sauce

¼ teaspoon blackstrap molasses

1⅓ cups cooked brown rice

Cooking Rice

Rinse the rice before cooking to remove surface starch. Use double the amount of liquid than rice when cooking or leave at least an inch above the rice and don't lift the lid when the rice is cooking, and cook over a slow flame. If the heat is too high, you can always add a little more liquid and cover again. Tightly covering rice makes sure it doesn't dry out and stays light and fluffy. Shake occasionally while keeping the pan lid on as it is cooking. When cooked, usually about 8–10 minutes, let stand a few minutes, fluff with a fork, and serve.

1. Preheat oven to 400°F. Treat baking dish with nonstick spray.

2. Rinse orange roughy and pat dry between paper towels. Rub both sides of fish with paprika; set in prepared dish.

3. In covered microwave-safe bowl, mix bay leaf, garlic, apple, ginger, and onion in oil; microwave on high 3 minutes, or until apple is tender and onion is transparent. Stir; remove and discard bay leaf.

4. Top the fish fillets with the mixture. Bake uncovered 15–18 minutes, or until fish is opaque.

5. While fish bakes, add plum sauce, five spice, apple juice concentrate, soy sauce, and molasses to microwave-safe bowl; microwave on high 30 seconds. Stir, add a little water if needed to thin mixture, and microwave another 15 seconds. Cover until ready to serve. If necessary, bring back to temperature by microwaving mixture another 15 seconds just prior to serving.

6. To serve, equally divide cooked rice among 4 serving plates. Top each with an equal amount of baked fish and plum sauce, drizzling sauce atop fish.

PER SERVING Calories: 240 | Fat: 2.5g | Sodium: 115mg | Carbohydrates: 35g | Fiber: 3g | Protein: 19g

Jon's Fish Tacos

Fish tacos, a staple in California, are making their way to trendy restaurants across the country.

INGREDIENTS | SERVES 4

¼ cup mayonnaise
½ cup plain yogurt
¼ cup onion, chopped
2 tablespoons jalapeño pepper, minced
2 teaspoons fresh cilantro, minced
2 cups cabbage, shredded
¼ cup fresh lime juice
1 clove garlic, minced
1 tablespoon canola oil
1 pound tilapia fillets
4 whole-wheat tortillas, 6" diameter
1 cup tomato, chopped

1. In medium bowl, whisk together mayonnaise, yogurt, onion, jalapeño, and cilantro. Stir in shredded cabbage; chill.

2. In separate bowl, combine lime juice, garlic, and canola oil to make a marinade for fish. Pour over fish; cover and refrigerate at least 1 hour.

3. Place fish on aluminum-lined grill (spray aluminum with cooking spray); cook 6–7 minutes on each side, until fish is tender and beginning to flake.

4. While fish is cooking, loosely wrap whole-wheat tortilla in large piece of aluminum foil to heat.

5. To assemble tacos, cut fish into strips; divide into 4 portions. Place strips in center of each heated tortilla. Top with coleslaw mixture and chopped tomatoes. Add fresh ground pepper, if desired.

PER SERVING Calories: 410 | Fat: 19g | Sodium: 350mg | Carbohydrates: 30g | Fiber: 4g | Protein: 27g

A-Taste-of-Italy Baked Fish

Not satisfied with the fish at your local grocery store? There may be a fresh fish market closer than you think. This fish will be pricier, but much more fresh.

INGREDIENTS | **SERVES 4**

1 pound (16 ounces) cod fillets
1 (14½-ounce) can stewed tomatoes
¼ teaspoon dried minced onion
½ teaspoon dried minced garlic
¼ teaspoon dried basil
¼ teaspoon dried parsley
⅛ teaspoon dried oregano
⅛ teaspoon sugar
1 tablespoon grated Parmesan cheese

1. Preheat oven to 375°F.

2. Rinse cod with cold water and pat dry with paper towels.

3. In a 2–3-quart baking pan or casserole treated with nonstick cooking spray, combine all ingredients except fish; mix.

4. Arrange fillets over mixture, folding thin tail ends under; spoon mixture over fillets. For fillets about 1" thick, bake uncovered 20–25 minutes, or until fish is opaque and flaky.

PER SERVING | Calories: 128 | Fat: 1g | Sodium: 312mg | Carbohydrates: /g | Fiber: 1g | Protein: 22g

Grilled Haddock with Peach Mango Salsa

The fruit in the salsa complements the gentle taste of haddock nicely.

INGREDIENTS | **SERVES 4**

2 tablespoons olive oil
2 tablespoons fresh lime juice
¼ teaspoon salt
¼ teaspoon black pepper
1 pound haddock fillets
Fresh Peach Mango Salsa (Chapter 12)

1. Mix olive oil, lime juice, salt, and pepper in a shallow dish; add haddock. Turn and coat·fish with marinade.

2. Heat gas grill or broiler. Spray large piece of aluminum foil with nonstick cooking spray.

3. Place fillets on foil; cook 7–8 minutes on each side, or until fish is tender when pierced with a fork.

4. Top each piece of fish with ½ cup fresh Peach-Mango Salsa.

PER SERVING Calories: 204 | Fat: 8g | Sodium: 467mg | Carbohydrates: 11g | Fiber: 2g | Protein: 22g

Cumin and Coriander-Crusted Mahi-Mahi

This delicious entrée combines vibrant cumin, coriander, and cilantro for a potent rub on the mahi-mahi filet. Salmon could also be flavored with this rub.

INGREDIENTS | SERVES 6

1 tablespoon olive oil

1 clove fresh garlic, minced

½ teaspoon all-purpose seasoning

3 tablespoons fresh cilantro, finely chopped

2 tablespoons finely chopped onions

1 teaspoon ground cumin

½ teaspoon ground coriander

½ teaspoon black pepper

6 mahi-mahi fillets

1. Mix all ingredients expect mahi-mahi in a bowl to create a paste. Coat each fillet with paste.

2. Spray a 9" × 13" baking dish with nonstick spray. Place fillets in the dish without crowding and cover with foil.

3. Bake at 350°F for 10 minutes. Turn and bake uncovered for an additional 5 minutes or until fish flakes easily with a fork.

PER SERVING Calories: 144 | Fat: 3g | Sodium: 146mg | Carbohydrates: 1g | Fiber: 0g | Protein: 26g

Orange Teriyaki Salmon

This recipe creates its own teriyaki sauce, which makes for the perfect marinade when combined with fresh orange juice. This can also be used on beef or chicken.

INGREDIENTS | SERVES 6

2 tablespoons soy sauce

1 clove fresh garlic, minced

½ teaspoon all-purpose seasoning

1 tablespoon agave syrup

1 tablespoon rice vinegar

3 tablespoons fresh orange juice

½ cup green onions, sliced

6 (4- or 5-ounce) salmon fillets

1 cup orange slices

1. Preheat oven to 350°F.

2. Mix all ingredients except salmon fillets and orange slices in a bowl.

3. Spray a 9" × 13" baking dish with nonstick spray. Place salmon in the dish. Pour mixture over the fish and top with orange slices.

4. Cover with foil; bake 15 minutes, or until fish flakes easily.

PER SERVING Calories: 160 | Fat: 4g | Sodium: 470mg | Carbohydrates: 7g | Fiber: 1g | Protein: 24g

Fisherman's Stew

This hearty and flavorful stew can also be made with chicken or ham instead of seafood.
This makes a delicious meal when served with biscuits and a fruit salad.

INGREDIENTS | SERVES 6

1 tablespoon olive oil
1 onion, chopped
1 cup chopped celery
3 carrots, sliced
2 potatoes, peeled and cubed
⅓ cup long-grain rice
3 cups Chicken Stock (Chapter 3) or vegetable stock
2 cups water
½ teaspoon salt
⅛ teaspoon black pepper
1 teaspoon dried tarragon leaves
1 pound red snapper fillets
½ pound peeled shrimp
½ pound bay scallops
1 cup shredded Cheddar cheese
1 tablespoon arrowroot

Fish for Stew

You can pick and choose different varieties of fish to include in this recipe. Remember that some fish cook faster than others. The general rule is to cook for 10 minutes per inch of thickness. In a stew, shrimp cook in about 3–5 minutes; mussels and clams take 6–8; and white fish cooks in 5–9 minutes.

1. In large soup pot, heat olive oil over medium heat. Add onion and celery; cook and stir 5 minutes.

2. Add carrots and potatoes; cook and stir 3 minutes longer.

3. Add rice; cook and stir 2 minutes.

4. Add stock, water, salt, pepper, and tarragon and bring to a simmer. Reduce heat, cover, and simmer about 15 minutes, or until rice is almost tender.

5. Cut snapper into 1" pieces. Add to pot along with shrimp and scallops; stir to blend. Cover, and simmer for 5–8 minutes, until fish flakes and shrimp and scallops are opaque.

6. In small bowl, toss cheese with arrowroot. Stir into soup; cook and stir until cheese melts. Serve immediately.

PER SERVING Calories: 400 | Fat: 12g | Sodium: 680mg | Carbohydrates: 31g | Fiber: 3g | Protein: 40g

Fennel Grilled Haddock

Fennel is sweet and tastes like licorice, especially when grilled. It imparts its distinctive flavor to the mild fish using this grilling method.

INGREDIENTS | SERVES 4

2 bulbs fennel
4 (5-ounce) haddock or halibut steaks
3 tablespoons olive oil
Pinch salt
⅛ teaspoon cayenne pepper
1 teaspoon paprika
2 tablespoons fresh lemon juice

Purchasing Haddock

Haddock has a fine white flesh. Fresh haddock will hold together well and will be firm. Fillets should be translucent; if you notice the fillet has a chalky hue to it, it is old. Refrigerate your haddock as soon as possible after purchase, either in the original wrapping from the fishmonger or in an airtight container, and use it within 24 hours. If you freeze the fish it should last 3 months.

1. Prepare and preheat grill.

2. Slice fennel bulbs lengthwise into ½" slices, leaving the stalks and fronds attached.

3. Brush fennel and haddock with olive oil on all sides to coat. Sprinkle fish with salt, pepper, and paprika. Place fennel on grill 6" above medium coals, cut-side down. Arrange fish on top of fennel and close the grill.

4. Grill for 5–7 minutes or until fennel is deep golden brown and fish flakes when tested with fork.

5. Remove fish to serving platter, sprinkle with lemon juice, and cover.

6. Cut the root end and stems from the fennel and discard. Slice fennel and place on top of fish; serve immediately.

PER SERVING Calories: 260 | Fat: 12g | Sodium: 190mg | Carbohydrates: 9g | Fiber: 4g | Protein: 28g

Baked Sole Amandine

Almonds contain lots of healthy monounsaturated fat. Just a few add great flavor and crunch to this classic recipe.

INGREDIENTS | **SERVES 4**

1 egg
¼ cup milk
½ cup dried bread crumbs
¼ cup ground almonds
1 teaspoon dried basil leaves
¼ teaspoon salt
½ teaspoon dried thyme leaves
1 pound sole fillets
2 tablespoons fresh lemon juice
1 tablespoon water
1 tablespoon butter, melted
¼ cup sliced almonds
3 green onions, chopped

Almonds

Almonds are a delicious tree nut. We use them in various ways in cooking. Plain whole almonds come with the skin attached. Blanched almonds have had their skins removed. Sliced almonds are thinly sliced, unblanched whole almonds. Slivered almonds are blanched almonds cut into little sticks. If a recipe calls for ground almonds, slivered almonds are the best choice; grind them in a food processor.

1. Preheat oven to 425°F. Line a baking sheet with parchment paper and set aside.

2. In shallow dish, combine egg and milk; beat until combined.

3. On plate, combine bread crumbs, ground almonds, basil, salt, and thyme and mix well.

4. Dip the fish into the egg mixture, then in the crumb mixture to coat. Place on prepared baking sheet.

5. In a small bowl, combine lemon juice, water, and melted butter; sprinkle over the fish. Sprinkle sliced almonds over fish.

6. Bake for 8–10 minutes or until fish flakes easily when tested with fork. Sprinkle with green onions and serve immediately.

PER SERVING Calories: 290 | Fat: 13g | Sodium: 380mg | Carbohydrates: 14g | Fiber: 2g | Protein: 28g

Grilled Fish and Spinach Packets

This beautiful method of cooking delicate fish is perfect for entertaining.
The packets make a gorgeous presentation.

INGREDIENTS | **SERVES 4**

1 tablespoon olive oil

1 onion, chopped

2 cloves garlic, minced

¼ cup dry white wine

¼ teaspoon salt

⅛ teaspoon white pepper

1 tablespoon chopped fresh tarragon

1 (10-ounce) package fresh baby spinach

1 pound white fish fillets, such as haddock

1 green bell pepper, julienned

En Papillote

Food cooked in foil or parchment paper is called en papillote. This method of cooking keeps food moist and is an excellent way to cook delicate foods like greens and fish. The food steams in the packet, sealing in juices and flavor. Warn your guests to be careful opening these packets because steam will billow out.

1. Prepare and preheat grill.

2. In a small skillet, heat oil over medium heat. Add onion and garlic; cook and stir until tender, about 6–7 minutes. Remove from heat and stir in wine, salt, and pepper.

3. Return to high heat and boil until reduced by half, about 5 minutes. Remove from heat and stir in tarragon. Set aside.

4. Tear off four 12" × 18" pieces of heavy duty foil and place on work surface. Divide spinach into quarters and place on foil. Cut fish into 4 pieces and place on top of spinach. Spoon onion mixture on fish and top with green bell pepper.

5. Bring up long edges of foil and, leaving some space for steam expansion, seal with a double fold, then fold in short ends to seal.

6. Place on grill rack 6" from medium coals. Grill, turning packets twice and rearranging on grill, until fish flakes easily when tested with fork, about 15–20 minutes. Serve immediately.

PER SERVING Calories: 170 | Fat: 4.5g | Sodium: 320mg | Carbohydrates: 7g | Fiber: 3g | Protein: 23g

Grilled Salmon

Salmon is marinated for a while, then grilled to perfection in this delicious and easy recipe. Serve with roasted potatoes and steamed veggies.

INGREDIENTS | SERVES 4

¼ cup fresh orange juice

1 tablespoon fresh lemon juice

2 tablespoons olive oil

1 tablespoon Dijon mustard

2 cloves garlic, minced

½ teaspoon dried dill weed

4 (6-ounce) salmon steaks

Salmon

Salmon is so good for you; try to eat it two times a week. This oily fish contains long-chain omega-3 fatty acids EPA and DHA, thought to be especially valuable to cancer patients. The fats in salmon help reduce the risk of heart disease, cholesterol levels, and blood clotting ability, which can help prevent heart attacks. Omega-3s may also help cancer patients tolerate chemotherapy better, according to some new research in Italy.

1. In 13" × 9" glass baking dish, combine orange juice, lemon juice, olive oil, mustard, garlic, and dill. Add salmon steaks; turn to coat. Cover and refrigerate 1–2 hours.

2. Prepare and preheat grill. Make sure grill is clean. Lightly oil the grill rack with vegetable oil.

3. Add salmon and grill 6" from medium coals 9–12 minutes, turning once, until fish flakes easily when tested with fork. Discard remaining marinade.

PER SERVING Calories: 270 | Fat: 13g | Sodium: 210mg | Carbohydrates: 3g | Fiber: 0g | Protein: 34g

Salmon Vegetable Stir-Fry

Sturdy vegetables are used in this stir-fry because they can continue cooking while the salmon steams.

INGREDIENTS | SERVES 4

2 tablespoons rice vinegar

1 tablespoon honey or agave syrup

1 tablespoon grated gingerroot

1 tablespoon arrowroot

2 tablespoons hoisin sauce

⅛ teaspoon white pepper

2 tablespoons canola oil

1 onion, sliced

½ pound sugar-snap peas

3 carrots, sliced

1 red bell pepper, sliced

¾ pound salmon fillet

Hoisin Sauce

Hoisin sauce is used in Asian cooking. It's a rich, thick, dark, and sweet sauce that stands up to the rich flavors of salmon. It is used sparingly, usually mixed into a stir-fry sauce or marinade. Hoisin sauce is made from fermented soybeans, vinegar, sugar, garlic, and chili peppers. Look for a variety without MSG.

1. In small bowl, combine rice vinegar, honey, gingerroot, arrowroot, hoisin sauce, and pepper. Mix well and set aside.

2. In large skillet or wok, heat oil over high heat. Add onion, peas, and carrots. Stir-fry for 3–4 minutes or until vegetables begin to soften. Add red bell pepper.

3. Immediately place salmon fillet on top of vegetables. Reduce heat to medium, cover, and cook for 4–5 minutes or until salmon flakes when tested with fork.

4. Stir the vinegar mixture and add to skillet or wok. Turn heat to medium-high; stir-fry 2–3 minutes to break up the salmon until the sauce bubbles and thickens. Serve immediately over hot cooked rice.

PER SERVING Calories: 280 | Fat: 10g | Sodium: 220mg | Carbohydrates: 26g | Fiber: 5g | Protein: 20g

Baked Snapper with Orange Rice Dressing

This recipe combines two cancer-fighting foods: fish and almonds. And, it's delicious!

INGREDIENTS | SERVES 4

¼ cup chopped celery

½ cup chopped onion

½ cup fresh orange juice

1 tablespoon fresh lemon juice

1 teaspoon grated orange zest

1⅓ cups cooked rice

1 pound (16 ounces) red snapper fillets

Salt and white or black pepper, to taste (optional)

2 teaspoons butter

2 tablespoons ground raw almonds

1. Preheat oven to 350°F.

2. In a microwave-safe bowl, mix celery and onion with juices and orange zest; microwave on high 2 minutes, or until mixture comes to a boil. Add rice; stir to moisten, adding water 1 tablespoon at a time if necessary to thoroughly coat rice. Cover and let stand 5 minutes.

3. Rinse fillets and pat dry between paper towels.

4. Prepare baking dish with nonstick spray. Spread rice mixture in dish; arrange fillets on top. Season fillets with salt and pepper, if using.

5. Combine butter and almonds in a microwave-safe bowl; microwave on high 30 seconds, or until butter is melted. Stir; spoon over top of fillets.

6. Cover and bake 10 minutes. Remove cover and bake another 5–10 minutes, or until fish flakes easily when tested with a fork and almonds are lightly browned.

PER SERVING Calories: 240 | Fat: 5g | Sodium: 95mg | Carbohydrates: 21g | Fiber: 1g | Protein: 26g

Seared Scallops with Fruit

Serve this super-quick and colorful dish with brown-rice pilaf and a green salad.

INGREDIENTS	SERVES 3–4

1 pound sea scallops

Pinch salt

⅛ teaspoon white pepper

1 tablespoon olive oil

1 tablespoon butter

2 peaches, sliced

¼ cup dry white wine

1 cup blueberries

1 tablespoon fresh lime juice

Scallops

Scallops are shellfish that are very low in fat. Sea scallops are the largest, followed by bay scallops and calico scallops. They should smell very fresh and slightly briny, like the sea. If they smell fishy, do not buy them. There may be a small muscle attached to the side of each scallop; pull that off and discard it because it can be tough.

1. Rinse scallops and pat dry. Sprinkle with salt and pepper. Set aside.

2. In large skillet, heat olive oil and butter over medium-high heat. Add the scallops and don't move them for 3 minutes. Carefully check to see if the scallops are deep golden brown. If they are, turn and cook for 1–2 minutes on the second side. Remove to serving plate.

3. Add peaches to skillet and brown quickly on one side, about 2 minutes. Turn peaches and add wine to skillet; bring to a boil.

4. Remove from heat and add blueberries. Pour over scallops, sprinkle with lime juice, and serve immediately.

PER SERVING Calories: 280 | Fat: 10g | Sodium: 320mg | Carbohydrates: 18g | Fiber: 3g | Protein: 26g

Stir-Fried Ginger Scallops with Vegetables

Some people avoid scallops due to their texture. If you're having texture issues with eating due to treatment, you may want to avoid them.

INGREDIENTS | **SERVES 4**

1 pound (16 ounces) scallops
1 teaspoon canola or sesame oil
1 tablespoon chopped fresh ginger
2 cloves garlic, minced
4 scallions, thinly sliced (optional)
1 teaspoon rice wine vinegar
2 teaspoons soy sauce
½ cup Chicken Stock (Chapter 3)
2 cups broccoli florets
1 teaspoon arrowroot
¼ teaspoon toasted sesame oil

1. Rinse scallops and pat dry between layers of paper towels. If necessary, slice scallops so they're uniform size. Set aside.

2. Add oil to heated nonstick deep skillet or wok; sauté ginger, garlic, and scallions 1–2 minutes, being careful ginger doesn't burn. Add vinegar, soy sauce, and stock; bring to a boil. Remove from heat.

3. Place broccoli in large, covered microwave-safe dish; pour chicken broth mixture over top. Microwave on high 3–5 minutes, depending on preference. (Keep in mind that vegetables will continue to steam for a minute or so if cover remains on dish.)

4. Heat skillet or wok over medium-high temperature. Add scallops; sauté 1 minute on each side. (Do scallops in batches if necessary; be careful not to overcook.) Remove scallops from pan when done; set aside.

5. Drain (but do not discard) liquid from broccoli; return liquid to bowl and transfer broccoli to heated skillet or wok. Stir-fry to bring up to serving temperature.

6. Meanwhile, in small cup or bowl, add enough water to arrowroot to make a slurry or roux. Whisk slurry into reserved broccoli liquid; microwave on high 1 minute. Add toasted sesame oil; whisk again.

7. Pour thickened broth mixture over broccoli; toss to mix. Add scallops back to broccoli mixture; stir-fry over medium heat to return scallops to serving temperature. Serve over rice or pasta.

PER SERVING Calories: 150 | Fat: 3g | Sodium: 410mg | Carbohydrates: 8g | Fiber: 2g | Protein: 22g

Scallops and Shrimp with White Bean Sauce

The beans in this recipe add an extra punch of protein to the fish.

INGREDIENTS | SERVES 4

½ cup finely chopped onion, steamed

2 cloves garlic, minced

2 teaspoons olive oil, divided

¼ cup dry white wine

¼ cup tightly packed fresh parsley leaves

¼ cup tightly packed fresh basil leaves

1⅓ cups canned cannellini (white) beans, drained and rinsed

¼ cup Chicken Stock (Chapter 3)

½ pound (8 ounces) shrimp, shelled and deveined

½ pound (8 ounces) scallops

1. In nonstick saucepan, sauté onion and garlic in 1 teaspoon of oil over moderately low heat, for about 5 minutes until onion is soft.

2. Add wine; simmer until wine is reduced by ½.

3. Add parsley, basil, ⅓ cup of beans, and chicken stock; simmer, stirring constantly, 1 minute.

4. Transfer bean mixture to blender or food processor; purée. Pour purée back into saucepan; add remaining beans. Simmer 2 minutes.

5. In nonstick skillet, heat remaining 1 teaspoon of oil over moderately high heat until it is hot but not smoking. Sauté shrimp 2 minutes on each side, or until cooked through.

6. Using slotted spoon, transfer shrimp to plate; cover to keep warm.

7. Add scallops to skillet; sauté 1 minute on each side, or until cooked through. To serve, divide bean sauce between 4 shallow bowls and arrange shellfish over top.

PER SERVING Calories: 230 | Fat: 4.5g | Sodium: 380mg | Carbohydrates: 17g | Fiber: 4g | Protein: 25g

Curried Shrimp and Vegetables

Adding lots of vegetables to seafood not only enhances the flavor, it increases the nutrition of a dish and lowers the fat and cholesterol content.

INGREDIENTS | SERVES 6

1 tablespoon olive oil
1 onion, chopped
3 cloves garlic, minced
1 tablespoon curry powder
½ teaspoon cinnamon
1½ cups water
2 carrots, sliced
2 russet potatoes, peeled and cubed
1 zucchini, sliced
1 (14.5-ounce) can diced tomatoes
1 pound raw shrimp
4 cups hot cooked brown rice

1. In a large skillet, heat oil over medium heat. Add onion and garlic; cook and stir until crisp-tender, about 4 minutes.

2. Add curry powder and cinnamon; cook and stir for 1 minute longer.

3. Add water, carrots, and potatoes; bring to a simmer. Reduce heat to low, cover, and cook for 8–10 minutes or until carrots are crisp-tender.

4. Add zucchini, tomatoes, and shrimp; cover and simmer for 5–8 minutes or until shrimp are pink.

5. Spoon rice onto individual plates and top with shrimp and vegetables. Serve immediately.

PER SERVING Calories: 350 | Fat: 5g | Sodium: 160mg | Carbohydrates: 54g | Fiber: 7g | Protein: 22g

Cooking with Curry

The flavors in curry powder are enhanced when they are heated, which is why the powder is often cooked in the first step of many Indian recipes, but it's still good when uncooked. You can buy curry powder in many blends, from hot to mild. Curry powder is a blend of spices, and each blend is usually unique to a particular area of India.

Festive Scallops

This dish goes great when served over steamed broccoli. The term "festive" comes from the colorful and flavorful combination of ingredients.

INGREDIENTS | SERVES 6

1 cup bell peppers, diced
2 cups tomatoes, diced
2 tablespoons fresh cilantro, chopped
½ teaspoon all-purpose seasoning
1 clove garlic, minced
2 cups Chicken Stock (Chapter 3)
½ cup cooking wine
1 cup carrots, chopped
1 teaspoon oregano
1 cup yellow onions, sliced
1½ pounds scallops, cleaned

1. Coat a deep skillet with nonstick spray. Add all ingredients except scallops. Cook on medium-high for 5–8 minutes, stirring often.

2. Add scallops to skillet, cover, and simmer for 10 minutes, stirring often.

PER SERVING Calories: 180 | Fat: 2g | Sodium: 490mg | Carbohydrates: 15g | Fiber: 2g | Protein: 22g

Sesame Shrimp and Asparagus

To clean shrimp, remove the legs and carefully peel off the shell. Then make a shallow cut into the curled back of the shrimp and rinse to remove the vein. If you are serving the shrimp in a dish like this, remove the tails, too.

INGREDIENTS | SERVES 4

2 teaspoons canola oil
2 cloves garlic, chopped
1 tablespoon gingerroot, grated
1 pound medium shrimp
2 tablespoons dry white wine
½ pound asparagus, cut diagonally into 1" pieces
2 cups whole-grain pasta, cooked
½ teaspoon sesame seeds
¼ cup scallions, thinly sliced
1 teaspoon sesame oil

1. Heat oil in wok or large nonstick skillet. Stir fry garlic, gingerroot, and shrimp over high heat until shrimp begins to turn pink, about 2 minutes.

2. Add white wine and asparagus; stir fry an additional 3–5 minutes.

3. Add pasta, sesame seeds, scallions, and sesame oil; toss lightly and serve.

PER SERVING | Calories: 257 | Fat: 6g | Sodium: 173mg | Carbohydrates: 23g | Fiber: 3g | Protein: 28g

CHAPTER 7

Meat

Cabbage Rolls

Also known as stuffed cabbage, depending upon where you come from, high-fiber cabbage is stuffed with lean meat, with more fiber in the whole grains and brown rice.

INGREDIENTS | **SERVES 4; SERVING SIZE: 3 ROLLS**

12 large cabbage leaves
1 cup cooked brown rice
¼ cup currants
¼ cup toasted hazelnuts
¼ cup minced onion
¾ teaspoon salt
Black pepper, to taste
¾ pound ground pork
½ pound ground beef
1 tablespoon olive oil
2 cups tomato sauce
2 garlic cloves, finely minced
1 tablespoon agave syrup

Vegetarian Cabbage Rolls

For a meatless version, substitute chopped mushrooms for the ground beef and pork. You will also have to double the quantity of rice, add extra currants, and perhaps toss in some chopped celery and nuts. You can also up the amount of onions in this recipe for a vegetarian version. Heighten the protein by adding an egg or two to the filling.

1. Blanch the cabbage leaves in boiling water for 4 minutes. Remove and lay flat on a tray. Chill in the refrigerator.

2. Combine the cooked brown rice, currants, hazelnuts, onion, salt, and pepper in a bowl. Add ground pork and beef and mix well.

3. Remove cabbage leaves from the refrigerator and blot with paper towels. Place about ¼ cup meat mixture on each cabbage leaf. Fold in sides and then roll up leaf to completely enclose filling.

4. Heat the olive oil in a skillet. Add the tomato sauce, garlic, and brown agave syrup and stir to combine.

5. Place the cabbage rolls in the tomato sauce, seam sides down. Spoon some of the sauce over the rolls, cover.

6. Cook over medium-low heat for 60 minutes. Reduce heat to low and simmer for an additional 20 minutes, adding a little water if needed. Serve hot.

PER SERVING | Calories: 460 | Fat: 24g | Carbohydrates: 39g | Fiber: 7g | Protein: 28g

Savory Grilled Steaks

Marinating steaks adds to their flavor and helps tenderize the meat by breaking down fibers with acidic ingredients.

INGREDIENTS | **SERVES 6**

2 garlic cloves, minced

2 tablespoons tomato paste

1 tablespoon olive oil

3 tablespoons balsamic vinegar

¼ teaspoon black pepper

1 tablespoon soy sauce

6 (6-ounce) sirloin steaks

Cook Once, Eat Twice

When you're cooking steaks on the grill, make two or three extra and refrigerate them. Then you can use them in recipes from Grilled Steak Salad (Chapter 11) to Mustard Steak Wraps (Chapter 7). The steaks will keep in the refrigerator up to 3 days. Slice the meat thinly against the grain for best taste and texture.

1. In large zip-top, heavy-duty food storage bag, combine all ingredients except steaks; seal and knead to blend. Add steaks and turn to coat. Place bag in glass bowl; refrigerate 3–4 hours.

2. When ready to eat, prepare and preheat grill.

3. Remove steaks from marinade; discard marinade. Grill steaks 6" from medium coals 4–8 minutes on each side, until food thermometer registers at least 145°F, turning once.

4. Remove steaks from grill and cover with foil. Let stand 5–10 minutes before serving.

PER SERVING Calories: 280 | Fat: 14g | Sodium: 260mg | Carbohydrates: 4g | Fiber: 0g | Protein: 31g

Kasha-Stuffed Red Peppers

Most canned tomatoes are packed in juice or puréed tomato. When you open a can, save juices and add to recipes when liquids are called for. In this recipe, tomato juice from the can could substitute some water used to cook the peppers in.

INGREDIENTS | SERVES 4

2 pounds (4 large) red peppers

1 cup kasha

1 egg white, lightly beaten

2 cups Beef Stock (Chapter 3)

4 ounces lean ground beef

1 cup onion, finely chopped

5 ounces (½ package) frozen chopped spinach, thawed and drained

½ cup feta cheese, crumbled

½ cup canned diced tomatoes

1 teaspoon oregano

⅛ teaspoon crushed red pepper

1½ cups water

1. Preheat oven to 375°F.

2. Remove tops of red peppers and remove seeds. Set aside.

3. Mix kasha and egg white together in small bowl.

4. In a large nonstick saucepan sprayed with nonstick cooking spray, add kasha; cook over high heat 2–3 minutes, stirring constantly, until kasha kernels are separated.

5. Add beef stock slowly. Reduce heat; cover and cook 7–10 minutes, until kasha kernels are tender. Transfer to large bowl.

6. Brown beef in small nonstick skillet. Add onions; cook 2–3 minutes, until slightly softened.

7. Add beef mixture and chopped spinach to cooked kasha; mix well. Stir in feta cheese, diced tomato, oregano, and crushed red pepper.

8. Divide mixture equally; stuff each red pepper. Place peppers in 9" × 9" baking dish. Pour water around peppers.

9. Cover with foil; bake 60–75 minutes, or until peppers are cooked.

PER SERVING | Calories: 350 | Fat: 8g | Sodium: 340mg | Carbohydrates: 54g | Fiber: 11g | Protein: 20g

Mustard Steak Wraps

Mustard is a natural partner to steak. Combine that with some fresh vegetables, and you have a wonderful, easy-to-make sandwich.

INGREDIENTS | SERVES 4

2 Savory Grilled Steaks (Chapter 7)

1 yellow bell pepper, cut into thin strips

1 green bell pepper, cut into thin strips

½ cup red onion, chopped

2 tomatoes, chopped

6 (6") corn tortillas

3 tablespoons Dijon mustard

1 (3-ounce) package cream cheese, softened

6 lettuce leaves

1. If steaks are cold, let stand at room temperature 30 minutes, no longer. Then slice thinly across the grain.

2. Combine bell peppers in medium bowl with steak, onion, and tomatoes; toss to mix.

3. Place tortillas on work surface. In small bowl, combine mustard and cream cheese and spread onto tortillas.

4. Top with lettuce leaves, then steak mixture. Roll up. Serve immediately.

PER SERVING Calories: 360 | Fat: 17g | Sodium: 500mg | Carbohydrates: 31g | Fiber: 5g | Protein: 22g

Filet Mignon with Vegetables

This is a wonderful dish for entertaining. The roasted vegetables are tender and sweet, and the meat is juicy.

INGREDIENTS | SERVES 8–10

1 (16-ounce) package baby carrots, halved lengthwise

1 (8-ounce) package frozen pearl onions

16 new potatoes, halved

2 tablespoons olive oil

2 pounds filet mignon

⅛ teaspoon salt

⅛ teaspoon white pepper

½ cup dry red wine

1. Preheat oven to 425°F.

2. Place carrots, onions, and potatoes in large roasting pan and drizzle with olive oil; toss to coat. Spread in an even layer. Roast for 15 minutes, remove from oven.

3. Top vegetables with filet mignon; sprinkle the meat with salt and pepper. Pour wine over meat and vegetables. Return to oven; roast for 20–30 minutes longer, until beef registers 150°F for medium.

4. Remove from oven, tent with foil, and let stand for 5 minutes. Carve to serve.

PER SERVING Calories: 250 | Fat: 8g | Sodium: 500mg | Carbohydrates: 21g | Fiber: 3g | Protein: 24g

Sirloin Meatballs in Sauce

Cooking meatballs in a sauce keeps them moist and tender.
Serve this with hot cooked pasta or brown rice.

INGREDIENTS | SERVES 6; SERVING SIZE: 2 MEATBALLS

1 tablespoon olive oil
3 cloves garlic, minced
½ cup minced onion
2 egg whites
½ cup dry breadcrumbs
¼ cup grated Parmesan cheese
½ teaspoon crushed fennel seeds
½ teaspoon dried oregano leaves
2 teaspoons Worcestershire sauce
⅛ teaspoon black pepper
⅛ teaspoon crushed red pepper flakes
1 pound ground sirloin
1 recipe Spaghetti Sauce (Chapter 12)

1. In small saucepan, heat olive oil over medium heat. Add garlic and onion; cook and stir until tender, about 5 minutes. Remove from heat and place in large mixing bowl.

2. Add egg whites, breadcrumbs, Parmesan, fennel, oregano, Worcestershire sauce, pepper, and pepper flakes and mix well. Add sirloin; mix gently but thoroughly until combined. Form into 12 meatballs.

3. In a large nonstick saucepan, bring spaghetti sauce to simmer. Carefully add meatballs; return to simmer. Partially cover and simmer for 15–25 minutes, or until meatballs are thoroughly cooked.

PER SERVING Calories: 310 | Fat: 12g | Sodium: 530mg | Carbohydrates: 27g | Fiber: 6g | Protein: 23g

Baking Meatballs

You can also bake these meatballs and freeze them plain to use in other recipes. Place meatballs on a cookie sheet. Bake at 375°F for 15–25 minutes, or until meatballs are browned and cooked through. Cool for 30 minutes, then chill until cold. Freeze individually, then pack into freezer bags. To thaw, let stand in refrigerator overnight.

Beef Risotto–Stuffed Peppers

You can use any leftover cooked rice dish in this simple recipe. Just add some chopped cooked roast beef from the deli, an egg, and some cheese.

INGREDIENTS | SERVES 4

1 tablespoon olive oil
1 onion, chopped
2 cups Beef Risotto (Chapter 7)
1 egg
1 egg white
1 tomato, chopped
2 slices Whole-Grain Oatmeal Bread (Chapter 13), made into crumbs
4 bell peppers
1 cup Spaghetti Sauce (Chapter 12)
¼ cup water

Peppers for Stuffing

For stuffing, choose bell peppers that are short and wide, preferably those that will stand upright unaided. Reserve the tops; after stuffing the peppers, you can put the tops back on. For a nice presentation, think about using four different colors of peppers in this dish; choose red, green, yellow, and orange.

1. Preheat oven to 350°F. Spray a 9" square baking pan with nonstick cooking spray and set aside.

2. In medium saucepan, heat olive oil over medium heat. Add onion; cook and stir until tender, about 5 minutes.

3. Remove from heat and stir in risotto, egg, egg white, and tomato and mix well. Add bread crumbs.

4. Cut off the pepper tops and remove membranes and seeds. Stuff with risotto mixture. Place in prepared baking dish.

5. In small bowl, combine Spaghetti Sauce and water; pour over and around peppers.

6. Cover with foil and bake for 45–55 minutes, or until peppers are tender. Serve immediately.

PER SERVING Calories: 330 | Fat: 13g | Sodium: 250mg | Carbohydrates: 40g | Fiber: 6g | Protein: 14g

Beef Risotto

This elegant recipe is perfect for a spring dinner. It is a last-minute recipe,
so don't start it until after your guests have arrived.

INGREDIENTS | SERVES 6

2 cups water

2 cups Beef Broth (Chapter 3)

2 tablespoons olive oil

½ pound sirloin steak, chopped

1 onion, minced

2 cloves garlic, minced

1½ cups arborio rice

2 tablespoons steak sauce

¼ teaspoon pepper

1 pound asparagus, cut into 2" pieces

¼ cup grated Parmesan cheese

1 tablespoon butter

1. In medium saucepan, combine water and broth. Heat over low heat until warm; keep on heat.

2. In large saucepan, heat olive oil over medium heat. Add beef; cook and stir until browned. Remove from pan with slotted spoon and set aside.

3. Add onion and garlic to pan; cook and stir until crisp-tender, about 4 minutes.

4. Add rice; cook and stir for 2 minutes. Add the broth mixture 1 cup at a time, stirring until the liquid is absorbed, about 15 minutes.

5. When there is 1 cup broth remaining, return the beef to the pot and add the steak sauce, pepper, and asparagus.

6. Cook and stir until rice is tender, beef is cooked, and asparagus is tender, about 5 minutes. Stir in Parmesan and butter and serve immediately.

PER SERVING Calories: 250 | Fat: 11g | Sodium: 180mg | Carbohydrates: 26g | Fiber: 3g | Protein: 13g |

Pastitsio

This is a casserole to serve a crowd! Make it ahead of time and store it, unbaked, in the fridge, then add 10–15 minutes to the baking time.

INGREDIENTS | SERVES 10

1½ pounds lean ground beef
1 onion, finely chopped
3 cloves garlic, minced
2 cups Beef Stock (Chapter 3), divided
¾ cup dry white wine
1 (6-ounce) can tomato paste
½ cup bulgur wheat
1 teaspoon cinnamon
½ teaspoon nutmeg
½ teaspoon allspice
½ teaspoon salt
½ teaspoon black pepper
2 tablespoons arrowroot
1 (13-ounce) can evaporated milk
¾ cup grated Parmesan cheese, divided
2 cups cottage cheese, puréed
1 pound elbow macaroni

1. Preheat oven to 350°F.

2. In a large skillet, brown beef, stirring to break up beef, until partially cooked. Add onion and garlic; cook and stir until beef is done and vegetables are tender. Drain thoroughly.

3. Add 1 cup beef stock, wine, and tomato paste and stir until tomato paste is blended. Add bulgur, cinnamon, nutmeg, allspice, salt, and pepper and bring to a boil. Reduce heat and simmer for 20 minutes.

4. Bring a large pot of salted water to a boil.

5. In a medium saucepan, combine arrowroot and remaining 1 cup beef broth; stir to blend.

6. Add evaporated milk and bring to a boil over medium heat. Cook and stir with wire whisk until thickened, about 5–6 minutes. Remove from heat and stir in ½ cup Parmesan cheese and the cottage cheese.

7. Cook pasta until al dente; drain and add to cheese mixture.

8. Spray 9" × 13" glass baking dish with nonstick cooking spray. Layer half of the pasta mixture and half of the meat mixture in pan. Repeat layers, then sprinkle with remaining ¼ cup Parmesan cheese.

9. Bake for 45–50 minutes or until casserole is bubbling and cheese is melted and beginning to brown. Let stand for 10 minutes, then serve.

PER SERVING Calories: 450 | Fat: 11g | Sodium: 640mg | Carbohydrates: 52g | Fiber: 4g | Protein: 35g

Steak Stroganoff

Stroganoff is the perfect recipe for entertaining. Serve it with a spinach salad, some dinner rolls warm from the oven, and an apple pie.

INGREDIENTS | SERVES 6

1 pound boneless round steak

2 tablespoons olive oil

1 onion, chopped

1 (8-ounce) package sliced mushrooms

3 tablespoons tomato paste

3 tablespoons water

½ teaspoon basil leaves

1 tablespoon arrowroot

1 cup plain yogurt

¼ cup Beef Stock (Chapter 3)

3 cups hot cooked noodles

Tomato Paste

Tomato paste is an excellent ingredient to add lots of flavor to a dish without extra fat. If you can find tomato paste in a tube, just store it in the refrigerator and use it as you need it. If you can only find it in a can, remove the paste from the can and freeze it in a small freezer bag and cut off the amount you need.

1. Trim excess fat from the steak and slice against the grain into ¼" strips.

2. In a large skillet, heat olive oil over medium heat. Add onion and mushrooms; cook and stir until tender, about 5 minutes.

3. Add beef and cook, stirring frequently, until browned, about 4 minutes longer.

4. Meanwhile, in small bowl combine tomato paste, water, basil, arrowroot, yogurt, and stock and mix with wire whisk until blended.

5. Add to skillet and bring to a simmer. Simmer for 3–4 minutes or until sauce thickens. Serve immediately over hot cooked noodles.

PER SERVING Calories: 320 | Fat: 13g | Sodium: 135mg | Carbohydrates: 28g | Fiber: 2g | Protein: 23

Spicy Beef and Cabbage

Cabbage is delicious when lightly cooked. It adds color, crunch, and fiber to this simple dish.

INGREDIENTS | SERVES 4

¾ pound top round beef steak

½ cup fresh orange juice

2 tablespoons hoisin sauce

2 tablespoons rice vinegar

1 tablespoon arrowroot

⅛ teaspoon cayenne pepper

1 tablespoon canola oil

1 tablespoon minced gingerroot

1 onion, chopped

1 (10-ounce) package shredded cabbage

1½ cups shredded carrots

3 green onions, julienned

1. Trim excess fat from steak and cut into ⅛" × 3" strips against the grain.

2. In a small bowl, combine orange juice, hoisin sauce, rice vinegar, arrowroot, and pepper and mix well. Set aside.

3. In a large skillet, heat vegetable oil over medium high heat. Add gingerroot and onion; cook and stir for 3–4 minutes until onion is crisp-tender.

4. Add beef and cook for 2–3 minutes or until browned. Remove beef and onion from skillet with slotted spoon. Set aside.

5. Add cabbage, carrots, and green onion to skillet; stir-fry for 3 minutes.

6. Stir orange juice mixture and add to skillet along with beef. Stir-fry until sauce thickens slightly and beef and vegetables are tender. Serve immediately over hot cooked rice.

PER SERVING Calories: 270 | Fat: 11g | Sodium: 230mg | Carbohydrates: 22g | Fiber: 4g | Protein: 22g

Marinated Steak Kebabs

You can marinate the beef for up to 4 hours in the refrigerator. Don't marinate longer than that or the texture may soften too much.

INGREDIENTS | SERVES 4

1 tablespoon fresh lemon juice

1 tablespoon olive oil

½ teaspoon dried tarragon leaves

⅛ teaspoon Tabasco sauce

¼ teaspoon salt

⅛ teaspoon black pepper

1 clove garlic, minced

1 pound round steak

1 red bell pepper, cut into strips

2 zucchini, sliced

1. In a medium bowl, combine lemon juice, olive oil, tarragon, Tabasco, salt, pepper, and garlic; mix well.

2. Trim excess fat from steak and cut into 1" cubes. Add to lemon mixture and toss to coat; let stand for 20 minutes at room temperature.

3. Prepare and preheat grill.

4. Thread marinated beef, bell pepper strips, and zucchini slices on metal skewers.

5. Cook 6" from medium coals for 6–8 minutes, turning once and brushing with any remaining lemon juice mixture, until beef is desired doneness and vegetables are tender. Serve immediately.

PER SERVING Calories: 250 | Fat: 13g | Sodium: 230mg | Carbohydrates: 6g | Fiber: 2g | Protein: 27g

Orange Beef and Broccoli Stir-Fry

The essential oils in citrus peels add lots of flavor and provide highly beneficial nutritional properties thought to help reduce inflammation and possibly fight cancer. This recipe is very high in vitamin C as well as low in fat.

INGREDIENTS | SERVES 6

2 oranges
3 tablespoons soy sauce
1 tablespoon rice wine vinegar
1 tablespoon arrowroot
1 teaspoon agave syrup
1 pound beef sirloin
1 tablespoon sesame oil
6 cloves garlic, minced
2 tablespoons minced ginger root
2 pounds broccoli, broken into small florets
⅓ cup water
1 red bell pepper, sliced
½ cup chopped green onion

1. Thinly peel skin from oranges in wide strips, taking care not to include white pith. Julienne zest into thin strips.

2. Squeeze orange juice and combine with soy sauce, vinegar, arrowroot, and agave syrup in small bowl.

3. Trim excess fat from beef and cut across the grain into ⅛" × 3" slices.

4. Heat half of the sesame oil in large wok or skillet over medium-high heat. Add garlic and ginger root; stir-fry for 2 minutes.

5. Add beef; stir-fry for 3–4 minutes until browned. Remove beef from wok with slotted spoon and set aside.

6. Add remaining oil to wok and add broccoli. Stir-fry for 1 minute, then add water. Cover and simmer, stirring occasionally, until water evaporates and broccoli is tender.

7. Add bell pepper and onion to wok; stir-fry for 2 minutes.

8. Return beef to skillet along with orange juice mixture. Stir-fry until sauce has thickened, about 2–3 minutes. Serve immediately over hot cooked rice.

PER SERVING Calories: 290 | Fat: 15g | Sodium: 580mg | Carbohydrates: 21g | Fiber: 8g | Protein: 22g

Teppanyaki Beef Stir-Fry

This dish should be served immediately after it is cooked to prevent the beef from toughening up. Serve it with cellophane noodles.

INGREDIENTS | SERVES 6

1½ pounds top sirloin, cut in strips

1 clove garlic, minced

4 tablespoons vinegar

½ cup green onions, sliced

½ teaspoon all-purpose seasoning

½ cup bell peppers, sliced

½ cup yellow onions, sliced

½ cup broccoli florets

½ cup carrot sticks

½ cup baby corn

1 tablespoon dry ginger or 2 tablespoons fresh minced ginger root

¼ cup soy sauce

1. Heat nonstick skillet to medium-high and spray with cooking spray. Add beef and garlic to skillet. Cook on medium-high heat for 5 minutes, stirring often.

2. Add remaining ingredients to skillet. Lower heat to medium and cook for 10 minutes, stirring often.

PER SERVING Calories: 271 | Fat: 15g | Sodium: 790mg | Carbohydrates: 8g | Fiber: 2g | Protein: 25g

Beef for Stir-Fry

For stir-frying, cut beef into ¼" strips about 3" long. Cut against the grain for the most tender results. Make sure you trim off any excess fat before you begin. Beef sliced this thin must be cooked quickly; do not overbrown in the first step.

Texan Rice

This simple one-dish meal is a good choice for a busy weeknight dinner.

INGREDIENTS | SERVES 6

½ pound lean ground beef

1 onion, chopped

2 cloves garlic, minced

1 jalapeño pepper, minced

3 cups hot cooked brown rice

2 cups frozen corn, thawed

½ cup barbecue sauce

¼ cup ketchup

¼ teaspoon salt

⅛ teaspoon cayenne pepper

1. In a large nonstick skillet, cook the beef over medium heat until browned, about 5 minutes. Drain off any fat.

2. Add the onion, garlic, and jalapeño pepper and continue to cook until vegetables are tender, about 7 minutes longer. Drain again.

3. Add the rice, corn, barbecue sauce, ketchup, salt, and pepper and mix well.

4. Cook over low heat, stirring frequently, until food is hot. Serve immediately.

PER SERVING Calories: 250 | Fat: 3.5g | Sodium: 410mg | Carbohydrates: 44g | Fiber: 4g | Protein: 13g

Mustard Pork Tenderloin

Mustard and sour cream coat pork tenderloin to keep in moisture while it slowly roasts to perfection.

INGREDIENTS | SERVES 6

2 tablespoons red wine

1 tablespoon agave syrup

1 tablespoon olive oil

1¼ pounds pork tenderloin

¼ cup sour cream

3 tablespoons Dijon mustard

1 tablespoon minced fresh chives

1. Preheat oven to 325°F. In glass baking dish, combine red wine, agave syrup, and olive oil. Add pork tenderloin; turn to coat. Cover and refrigerate for 8 hours.

2. Let pork stand at room temperature for 20 minutes. Roast for 30 minutes, basting with the marinade.

3. In small bowl, combine sour cream, mustard, and chives. Spread over the tenderloin.

4. Continue roasting for 25–35 minutes or until pork registers 160°F. Let stand for 5 minutes, and slice to serve.

PER SERVING Calories: 170 | Fat: 8g | Sodium: 240mg | Carbohydrates: 3g | Fiber: 0g | Protein: 21g

Pork Medallions

Medallions are simply thin pieces of tender, lean meat. They must be cooked quickly so they stay tender and juicy.

INGREDIENTS | SERVES 4

4 (3-ounce) boneless lean pork chops
¼ teaspoon salt
⅛ teaspoon black pepper
2 tablespoons olive oil, divided
1 cup sliced mushrooms
¼ cup shredded carrot
2 tablespoons sliced green onions
2 tablespoons diced celery
1 tablespoon fresh lemon juice
½ teaspoon dried thyme leaves
1 tomato, chopped
1 cup Chicken Stock (Chapter 3) or Beef Stock (Chapter 3)
3 tablespoons arrowroot, divided
¼ cup skim milk

1. Place pork chops between 2 sheets of waxed paper. Gently pound with a meat mallet or rolling pin to ⅛" thickness. Sprinkle with salt and pepper and set aside.

2. In a large saucepan, heat 1 tablespoon olive oil over medium heat. Add mushrooms, carrot, green onion, and celery; cook and stir until tender, about 5 minutes.

3. Drain and remove to medium bowl; stir in lemon juice, thyme, and tomato.

4. Divide vegetable mixture among pork. Roll up, folding in sides, and secure with toothpicks or kitchen string. Sprinkle with 2 tablespoons arrowroot.

5. In same skillet, heat remaining 1 tablespoon olive oil. Brown the pork bundles for 3–4 minutes. Pour stock over pork, cover pan, and simmer until tender, about 10–15 minutes.

6. In a small bowl, combine remaining 1 tablespoon arrowroot and milk, mix well.

7. Remove pork from skillet and place on heated serving platter.

8. Add arrowroot mixture to skillet; cook and stir over medium heat until thickened and bubbly, about 5–6 minutes.

9. Remove toothpicks or string; slice pork into 1" slices. Arrange on serving platter; pour sauce over medallions. Serve immediately.

PER SERVING Calories: 320 | Fat: 19g | Sodium: 300mg | Carbohydrates: 12g | Fiber: <1g | Protein: 24g

Apricot Pork Pinwheels

This elegant dish is perfect for company. Serve with a spinach salad and cooked carrots.

INGREDIENTS | **SERVES 6**

1 pound pork tenderloin
⅓ cup chopped dried apricots
⅔ cup boiling Chicken Stock (Chapter 3)
1 tablespoon olive oil
1 medium onion, chopped
2 tablespoons chopped celery
⅛ teaspoon cinnamon
2 cups small whole-wheat bread cubes
2 tablespoons arrowroot
Dash nutmeg
1½ cups apricot nectar

Dried Apricots

Dried apricots are a great source of vitamin A, calcium, and iron. They are sweet and chewy and are good for snacking out of hand, in addition to being delicious when added to salads and sandwich spreads. The apricots are not peeled before drying; the peel helps hold in some of the moisture.

1. Using a sharp knife, cut the tenderloin in half lengthwise; do not cut all the way through. Open the meat like a book, and pound with meat mallet to a 10" × 6" rectangle that is about ⅓" thick. Set aside.

2. In a small bowl, combine apricots with stock; let stand for 5 minutes.

3. In a medium skillet, heat olive oil over medium heat. Add onion and celery; cook until tender, about 5 minutes. Remove pan from heat and add apricot mixture and cinnamon. Then add the bread crumbs, tossing to moisten.

4. Spread stuffing over pork. Roll up jelly-roll style, starting from the short edge. Secure with toothpicks or tie with kitchen string at 1" intervals. Cut into 6 slices.

5. Preheat broiler. Place meat slices on broiler pan. Broil 6" from the heat for 10 minutes, then carefully turn and broil for 8–12 minutes longer until pork is cooked and tender. Remove string or toothpicks.

6. While meat is broiling, combine arrowroot, nutmeg, and nectar in medium skillet; bring to a boil over medium-high heat. Boil until thickened and reduced, about 6–7 minutes. Pour over meat and serve immediately.

PER SERVING Calories: 230 | Fat: 6g | Sodium: 170mg | Carbohydrates: 27g | Fiber: 2g | Protein: 18g

Curried Pork Chops

Pork is such a mild meat it can be seasoned many ways. Curry powder, garlic, and onion make this dish special.

INGREDIENTS | SERVES 6

⅓ cup flour

¼ teaspoon salt

¼ teaspoon black pepper

6 (6-ounce) boneless loin pork chops

2 tablespoons olive oil

1 onion, chopped

1 green bell pepper, chopped

2 cloves garlic, minced

1 tablespoon curry powder

1 (6-ounce) can tomato paste

1½ cups water

½ cup raisins

½ cup Mango Chutney (Chapter 12)

Curry Powder

Curry powder is actually a mixture of spices that varies according to regional preferences or traditions. Most producers of curry powder usually include coriander, turmeric, cumin, and fenugreek in their blends. Other spices such as garlic, fennel, ginger, cinnamon, clove, cardamom, mustard, or varieties of peppers can also be added. You'll also notice a difference in taste between "raw" curry powder and curry that has been toasted or sautéed. Sautéing curry powder boosts the flavors, releasing the natural aromatic cancer-fighting oils in the spices.

1. In shallow bowl, combine flour, salt, and pepper, mixing well. Coat pork chops with the seasoned flour.

2. In a large skillet, heat oil over medium heat. Add pork; brown on both sides, about 5 minutes total. Remove from the skillet and set aside.

3. Add onion, bell pepper, and garlic to skillet and cook until tender, about 7 minutes. Drain fat.

4. Add curry powder, tomato paste, and water to skillet; bring to a simmer. Return pork to skillet and stir. Simmer, uncovered, over medium heat, until pork is tender, about 15–20 minutes.

5. Add the raisins and chutney, heat through for another 5 minutes, and serve.

PER SERVING Calories: 570 | Fat: 19g | Sodium: 480mg | Carbohydrates: 44g | Fiber: 5g | Protein: 54g

Pork and Garbanzo Bean Curry

If you love curry, increase the curry powder to 1 tablespoon.
You could also increase the amount of ginger you use.

INGREDIENTS | SERVES 4

1 pound pork tenderloin, cubed

1 tablespoon olive oil

2 cloves garlic, minced

1 onion, chopped

1 tablespoon minced ginger root

1 tablespoon arrowroot

2 teaspoons curry powder

¼ teaspoon salt

⅛ teaspoon black pepper

½ cup grated carrots

2 potatoes, peeled and cubed

½ cup water

1 (15-ounce) can garbanzo beans, drained

1. In a large skillet, brown pork in olive oil over medium heat for 5 minutes. Add the garlic, onion, and ginger and cook for 2 minutes.

2. Stir in the arrowroot, curry powder, salt, pepper, carrots, potatoes, and water and bring to a boil. Reduce the heat to low, cover, and cook for 10 minutes, adding more water if the mixture begins to dry.

3. Add garbanzo beans, cover, and cook over medium heat until the vegetables are cooked through, about 10 minutes longer. Serve immediately.

PER SERVING Calories: 380 | Fat: 9g | Sodium: 530mg | Carbohydrates: 45g | Fiber: 8g | Protein: 32g

Garbanzo Beans

Garbanzo beans, also called chick peas, are a wonderful source of high-quality protein and insoluble and soluble fiber. You need both types of fiber in your diet to help reduce cholesterol and prevent digestive diseases.

Pork Chops and Fruited Veggies Bake

These homemade pork chops are tender and juicy. They are easy to cook and pack a ton of fiber.

INGREDIENTS | SERVES 4

1 cup baby carrots, washed and peeled

1 (10-ounce) package frozen organic sliced peaches, thawed

2 teaspoons brown sugar

¼ teaspoon ground cinnamon

Pinch ground cloves

¼ teaspoon black pepper

¼ teaspoon dried thyme

¼ teaspoon dried rosemary

⅛ teaspoon dried oregano

1 teaspoon lemon zest

4 (6-ounce) bone-in pork loin chops

8 cloves garlic, crushed

4 large Yukon Gold potatoes, washed and sliced

1 (10-ounce) package frozen whole green beans, thawed

Fruit Swaps

You can substitute 4 peeled and sliced apples or pears for the peaches in the Pork Chops and Fruited Veggies Bake recipe. If you do, toss the slices with 1 tablespoon of lemon juice before mixing them with the brown sugar, cinnamon, and cloves.

1. Preheat oven to 425°F. Treat a large roasting pan or jelly roll pan with nonstick spray.

2. Place the carrots, peaches, brown sugar, cinnamon, and cloves in a medium-size bowl; stir to mix. Set aside.

3. Mix the pepper, thyme, rosemary, oregano, and lemon zest together and use a mortar and pestle or the back of a spoon to crush them.

4. Rub the pork chops with the garlic.

5. Evenly spread the sliced potatoes and green beans across the prepared baking pan. Place the garlic cloves and pork chops atop the vegetables. Spray lightly with the spray oil. Sprinkle with the herb mixture.

6. Spread the carrot and peach mixture atop the pork chops and vegetables.

7. Bake for 30 minutes or until the meat is tender and the potatoes and carrots are tender.

PER SERVING Calories: 610 | Fat: 23g | Sodium: 140mg | Carbohydrates: 53g | Fiber: 6g | Protein: 49g

Slow-Cooker Pork with Plum Sauce

A slow cooker can be a lifesaver for busy cooks, and come in a variety of sizes and prices.

INGREDIENTS | SERVES 4

½ pound (8 ounces) cooked shredded pork

1 clove garlic, crushed

½ teaspoon grated ginger root

⅛ cup apple juice

¼ teaspoon dry mustard

2 teaspoons soy sauce

⅛ teaspoon dried thyme

⅛ cup Plum Sauce (Chapter 12)

½ teaspoon arrowroot

1. In nonstick skillet treated with nonstick spray, stir-fry pork, garlic, and ginger for approximately 2 minutes.

2. In small bowl or measuring cup, combine remaining ingredients to make a slurry; pour over the heated pork, mixing well.

3. Cook in a slow cooker over low to medium heat until mixture thickens and juice is absorbed into pork, approximately 15 minutes.

PER SERVING Calories: 150 | Fat: 5g | Sodium: 200mg | Carbohydrates: 7g | Fiber: 0g | Protein: 17g

Pork Quesadillas

You can serve these toasty sandwiches with some salsa for dipping.

INGREDIENTS | SERVES 6

⅓ cup sour cream

1 cup shredded mozzarella cheese

1 cup chopped Mustard Pork Tenderloin (Chapter 7)

1 avocado, chopped

1 jalapeño pepper, minced

10 (6") corn tortillas

2 tablespoons olive oil

1. In a medium bowl, combine sour cream, cheese, pork tenderloin, avocado, and jalapeño pepper and mix gently.

2. Divide mixture among half the tortillas, placing the remaining half of tortillas on top to make sandwiches.

3. Heat griddle and brush with olive oil.

4. Place quesadillas on the griddle; cover and grill for 2–3 minutes on each side until tortillas are crisp and cheese is melted. Cut into quarters and serve.

PER SERVING Calories: 300 | Fat: 19g | Sodium: 190mg | Carbohydrates: 24g | Fiber: 5g | Protein: 11g

Skillet Chops and Veggies

This easy one-dish meal is pure comfort food. Serve with a butter lettuce salad mixed with mushrooms and green peppers.

INGREDIENTS | SERVES 4

4 (4-ounce) boneless loin pork chops

2 tablespoons arrowroot

½ teaspoon salt

⅛ teaspoon black pepper

2 tablespoons olive oil

1 onion, chopped

3 cloves garlic, minced

4 russet potatoes, thinly sliced

3 carrots, sliced

1 cup Chicken Stock (Chapter 3)

1 tablespoon fresh lemon juice

1. Sprinkle chops with arrowroot, salt, and pepper; set aside.

2. In large skillet, heat olive oil over medium heat. Add chops; brown 2–3 minutes on each side. Remove from heat and set aside.

3. Add onion and garlic to skillet; cook and stir until crisp-tender, about 5 minutes.

4. Add potatoes to pan; cook and stir until potatoes are coated. Top with carrots, then add browned pork chops.

5. Add stock and lemon juice and bring to a simmer. Cover skillet tightly, reduce heat to medium-low, and simmer 35–45 minutes, or until potatoes are tender and chops are cooked, shaking pan occasionally. Serve immediately.

PER SERVING Calories: 570 | Fat: 23g | Sodium: 490mg | Carbohydrates: 53g | Fiber: 6g | Protein: 36g

CHAPTER 8

Poultry

Chicken Breasts with Curried Stuffing

If you love curry powder, this is the recipe for you! Add curry powder to the yogurt topping as well for even more flavor.

INGREDIENTS | SERVES 4

1 tablespoon butter

½ cup shredded carrot

¼ cup sliced green onions

2 teaspoons curry powder

½ cup fresh bread crumbs

3 tablespoons dried currants

1 tablespoon Chicken Stock (Chapter 3)

4 (4-ounce) boneless, skinless chicken breasts

¼ teaspoon salt

⅛ teaspoon black pepper

½ teaspoon paprika

⅓ cup plain yogurt

2 teaspoons arrowroot

2 tablespoons orange marmalade

1. Preheat oven to 350°F.

2. In a small saucepan, melt butter over medium heat. Add carrot, green onions, and curry powder, and cook, stirring, until tender, about 5 minutes. Remove from the heat and stir in the bread crumbs, currants, and broth.

3. Place 1 chicken breast half, boned-side up, between 2 sheets of plastic wrap. Working from the center to the edges, pound lightly with a meat mallet or rolling pin until ¼" thick. Repeat with remaining chicken.

4. Sprinkle chicken with salt and pepper. Place ¼ of the stuffing mixture on each piece of chicken. Fold chicken over the filling and secure with a toothpick. Place chicken in an 8" square baking dish with 2" sides. Sprinkle with the paprika and cover with foil.

5. In a small bowl, combine yogurt, arrowroot, and marmalade; spread over chicken.

6. Bake until chicken is tender and the juices run clear when a piece is pierced, about 25–35 minutes.

PER SERVING Calories: 730 | Fat: 16g | Sodium: 540mg | Carbohydrates: 26g | Fiber: 2g | Protein: 113g

Walnut Chicken with Plum Sauce

Walnuts are an excellent source of B vitamins, magnesium, and antioxidants like vitamin E.

INGREDIENTS | **SERVES 4**

¾ pound (12 ounces) raw boneless, skinless chicken breast

1 teaspoon sherry

1 egg white

2 teaspoons canola oil

2 drops toasted sesame oil (optional)

⅓ cup ground walnuts

Health Benefits of Walnuts

Studies show that a diet rich in walnuts helps reduce the risk of heart disease by improving blood vessel elasticity, plaque accumulation, and lowering LDL cholesterol. Walnuts are high in calories, though, so eat them in moderation or use them as replacements for higher fat items in your diet.

1. Preheat oven to 350°F.

2. Cut chicken into bite-sized pieces; sprinkle with sherry and set aside.

3. In a small bowl, beat egg white and oils until frothy.

4. Fold chicken pieces into egg mixture; roll individually in chopped walnuts.

5. Arrange chicken pieces on baking sheet treated with nonstick cooking spray.

6. Bake 10–15 minutes, or until walnuts are lightly browned and chicken juices run clear. (Walnuts make the fat ratio of this dish high, so serve it with steamed vegetables and rice to bring the ratios into balance.)

PER SERVING Calories: 200 | Fat: 9g | Sodium: 70mg | Carbohydrates: 1g | Fiber: 0g | Protein: 27g

Chicken Kalamata

The health benefits of olives (and olive oil) come from the monounsaturated fats they contain. Olives are usually cured in a brine, salt, or olive oil, so if you must watch your salt intake, be careful how many you eat.

INGREDIENTS | SERVES 4

2 tablespoons olive oil

1 cup onion, chopped

1 teaspoon garlic, minced

1½ cups green peppers, chopped

1 pound boneless, skinless chicken breast, cut into 4 pieces

2 cups tomatoes, diced

1 teaspoon oregano

½ cup pitted kalamata olives, chopped

1. Heat olive oil over medium heat in large skillet. Add onions, garlic, and peppers; sauté for about 5 minutes until onions are translucent.

2. Add chicken pieces; cook for about 5 minutes each side until lightly brown.

3. Add tomatoes and oregano. Reduce heat and simmer 20 minutes.

4. Add olives; simmer an additional 10 minutes before serving.

PER SERVING | Calories: 311 | Fat: 11g | Sodium: 787mg | Carbohydrates: 25g | Fiber: 6g | Protein: 31g

Moroccan Tagine of Chicken and Chickpeas

In Morocco, a traditional tagine is a stew cooked at very low temperatures so the meat has time to become very tender.

INGREDIENTS | SERVES 6

1 clove garlic, minced

½ teaspoon all-purpose seasoning

2 teaspoons paprika

1 teaspoon ground ginger

½ teaspoon turmeric

1 cup yellow onions, chopped

2 cups tomatoes, diced

2 cups chickpeas, cooked

¼ cup cilantro, chopped

2 cups Chicken Stock (Chapter 3)

6 boneless, skinless chicken breasts, cut in chunks

1. Add all ingredients to a large saucepan.

2. Cook on medium-high for 10–12 minutes, stirring often.

3. Turn heat down; simmer for 8–10 minutes.

PER SERVING Calories: 290 | Fat: 5g | Sodium: 470mg | Carbohydrates: 27g | Fiber: 5g | Protein: 34g

Chicken Thighs Cacciatore

Top each portion with 1 tablespoon freshly grated Parmesan cheese. This adds only 30 calories but 2 more grams of protein, which is helpful when you are looking for dishes that provide protein.

INGREDIENTS | **SERVES 4**

2 teaspoons olive oil

½ cup chopped onion

2 cloves garlic, minced

4 chicken thighs, skin removed

½ cup dry red wine

1 (14½-ounce) can diced tomatoes, undrained

1 teaspoon dried parsley

½ teaspoon dried oregano

¼ teaspoon black pepper

⅛ teaspoon sugar

¼ cup grated Parmesan cheese

4 cups cooked spaghetti

2 teaspoons olive oil

1. Heat deep, nonstick skillet over medium-high heat; add 2 teaspoons olive oil. Add onion; sauté until transparent.

2. Add garlic and chicken thighs; sauté 3 minutes on each side, or until lightly browned. Remove from pan.

3. Add wine, tomatoes and juices, parsley, oregano, pepper, and sugar. Stir well, bring to a boil.

4. Add chicken back to pan; sprinkle Parmesan cheese over top. Cover, reduce heat, and simmer 10 minutes. Uncover and simmer 10 more minutes.

5. To serve, put 1 cup of cooked pasta on each of 4 plates. Top each serving with a chicken thigh; divide sauce between dishes. Drizzle ½ teaspoon olive oil over top of each dish, and serve.

PER SERVING | Calories: 370 | Fat: 9g | Sodium: 166mg | Carbohydrates: 48g | Fiber: 4g | Protein: 19g

Chicken with Portobello Mushrooms and Roasted Garlic

Serve this with a whole-grain side dish such as quinoa or brown rice.

INGREDIENTS | SERVES 4

1 tablespoon olive oil

4 (4-ounce) boneless, skinless chicken breasts

1 cup chicken broth

1 bulb Roasted Garlic (Chapter 2)

2 cups portobello mushrooms, chopped

½ teaspoon dried thyme leaves

1 tablespoon butter

2 tablespoons feta cheese, crumbled

1. Heat olive oil in large nonstick skillet; brown chicken breasts on both sides over medium heat, about 5 minutes per side.

2. Add chicken broth and roasted garlic paste to pan; cover and simmer on low 10 minutes.

3. Meanwhile, sauté mushrooms and thyme in butter in separate, smaller saucepan. Simmer 2 minutes.

4. Add the mushrooms and thyme mixture to the chicken and simmer for an additional 2 minutes.

5. When serving, top each chicken breast with 1½ teaspoons feta cheese and pour sauce over the top.

PER SERVING Calories: 270 | Fat: 13g | Sodium: 320mg | Carbohydrates: 8g | Fiber: 1g | Protein: 30g

Spanish Chicken Fricassee

Fricassees are Spanish stews that typically involve some sort of poultry, although other types of white meat can be used. Its base is usually created with wine or dry vermouth.

INGREDIENTS | **SERVES 6**

1½ pounds boneless, skinless chicken breasts, cut in large chunks

½ tablespoon olive oil

1 clove garlic, minced

½ teaspoon all-purpose seasoning

2 teaspoons paprika

1 teaspoon black pepper

½ cup bell pepper, diced

½ cup white onion, diced

½ cup celery, sliced

1 cup Chicken Stock (Chapter 3)

½ cup wine

1 cup carrots, sliced

1 cup tomatoes, diced

2 tablespoons fresh minced parsley

3 bay leaves

1 cup Yukon Gold potatoes, cubed

1. Add all ingredients except potatoes to large saucepan.

2. Cook on medium-high for 10 minutes, stirring often.

3. Add potatoes and simmer for another 15 minutes, or until sauce thickens, stirring occasionally.

PER SERVING Calories: 260 | Fat: 5g | Sodium: 210mg | Carbohydrates: 13g | Fiber: 2g | Protein: 36g

Green Chili Chicken

Cooking in parchment paper ensures the chicken will be tender and juicy. Parchment paper also holds in all the flavors.

INGREDIENTS | SERVES 6

6 boneless, skinless chicken breasts

1 (4-ounce) can chopped green chilis, drained

1 cup frozen corn

2 tomatoes, chopped

2 tablespoons fresh lime juice

¼ cup chopped fresh cilantro

½ teaspoon salt

⅛ teaspoon cayenne pepper

1 teaspoon ground cumin

1. Preheat oven to 375°F. Cut six 12" squares of parchment paper and place on work surface. Place one chicken breast in center of each.

2. In medium bowl, combine chilis, corn, tomatoes, lime juice, cilantro, salt, pepper, and cumin and mix well. Divide on top of chicken.

3. Fold edges of parchment paper over chicken and crimp to close. Place on cookie sheet.

4. Bake until chicken is cooked and parchment paper is browned, about 25–35 minutes. Serve immediately.

PER SERVING Calories: 190 | Fat: 3.5g | Sodium: 330mg | Carbohydrates: 10g | Fiber: 2g | Protein: 29g

Chicken Breasts with Salsa

Whole-grain cereal provides lots of folic acid, which helps reduce homocysteine levels. It makes a nice crunchy coating on chicken breasts.

INGREDIENTS | SERVES 4

2 tablespoons fresh lime juice, divided

1 egg white

1 cup whole-grain cereal, crushed

1 teaspoon dried thyme leaves

¼ teaspoon black pepper

4 (4-ounce) boneless, skinless chicken breasts

1 cup Super Spicy Salsa (Chapter 12)

1 jalapeño pepper, minced

1. Preheat oven to 375°F. Line a cookie sheet with a wire rack and set aside.

2. In small bowl, combine 1 tablespoon lime juice and egg white; beat until frothy. On shallow plate, combine crushed cereal, thyme, and pepper.

3. Dip chicken into egg white mixture, then into cereal mixture to coat. Place on prepared cookie sheet.

4. Bake for 20–25 minutes or until chicken is thoroughly cooked and coating is crisp.

5. Meanwhile, in small saucepan combine remaining 1 tablespoon lime juice, salsa, and jalapeño pepper. Heat through, stirring occasionally. Serve with chicken.

PER SERVING Calories: 250 | Fat: 4g | Sodium: 140mg | Carbohydrates: 16g | Fiber: 3g | Protein: 36g

Chicken Paillards with Zucchini

This simple chicken dish is healthy and beautiful, too. Serve with a green salad drizzled with Tangy Lemon Garlic Tomato Dressing (Chapter 12).

INGREDIENTS | SERVES 4

4 boneless, skinless chicken breasts

2 tablespoons arrowroot

½ teaspoon salt

⅛ teaspoon black pepper

½ teaspoon dried thyme leaves

2 tablespoons olive oil

1 onion, chopped

1 zucchini, sliced

3 tablespoons torn fresh basil leaves

¼ cup Chicken Stock (Chapter 3)

2 cups grape tomatoes

Zucchini

Zucchini is a mild vegetable with high water and fiber contents. It is delicious eaten raw with appetizer dips and on sandwiches, and good in stir-fries and soups. Look for smaller zucchini with tender skin and those that are heavy for their size. Zucchini will keep in the refrigerator for 3–4 days after purchase.

1. Place chicken, smooth-side down, between sheets of plastic wrap. Using a rolling pin or meat mallet, pound chicken until about ⅓" thick. Remove plastic wrap; sprinkle chicken with arrowroot, salt, pepper, and thyme.

2. In large saucepan, heat olive oil over medium-high heat. Add chicken; cook, turning once, until cooked through, about 4–5 minutes per side. Remove chicken from pan and keep warm.

3. Add onion to saucepan; cook and stir until crisp-tender, about 4 minutes.

4. Add zucchini; cook and stir 4 minutes longer.

5. Return chicken to pan and add basil, Stock, and grape tomatoes. Bring to a simmer; cook 2–3 minutes. Serve immediately.

PER SERVING Calories: 260 | Fat: 10g | Sodium: 380mg | Carbohydrates: 12g | Fiber: 2g | Protein: 30g

Sautéed Chicken with Roasted Garlic Sauce

When roasted, garlic turns sweet and nutty. Combined with tender sautéed chicken, this makes a memorable meal.

INGREDIENTS	SERVES 4

1 head Roasted Garlic (Chapter 2)
⅓ cup Chicken Stock (Chapter 3)
½ teaspoon dried oregano leaves
¼ cup arrowroot
⅛ teaspoon salt
⅛ teaspoon black pepper
¼ teaspoon paprika
4 (4-ounce) boneless, skinless chicken breasts
2 tablespoons olive oil

1. Squeeze garlic cloves from the skins and combine in small saucepan with chicken stock and oregano leaves.

2. On shallow plate, combine arrowroot, salt, pepper, and paprika. Coat chicken in this mixture.

3. In large skillet, heat 2 tablespoons olive oil. At the same time, place the saucepan with the garlic mixture over medium heat.

4. Add the chicken to the hot olive oil; cook for 5 minutes without moving. Then carefully turn chicken and cook for 4–7 minutes longer until chicken is thoroughly cooked.

5. Stir garlic sauce with wire whisk until blended. Serve with the chicken.

PER SERVING Calories: 320 | Fat: 13g | Sodium: 210mg | Carbohydrates: 14g | Fiber: <1g | Protein: 35g

Chicken Breasts with New Potatoes

This easy one-dish meal has the best combination of flavors; mustard adds a nice bit of spice to tender chicken and crisp potatoes.

INGREDIENTS | SERVES 6

12 small new red potatoes

2 tablespoons olive oil

⅛ teaspoon white pepper

4 cloves garlic, minced

1 teaspoon dried oregano leaves

2 tablespoons Dijon mustard

4 (4-ounce) boneless, skinless chicken breasts

1 cup cherry tomatoes

1. Preheat oven to 400°F. Line a roasting pan with parchment paper and set aside.

2. Scrub potatoes and cut in half. Place in prepared pan.

3. In small bowl, combine oil, pepper, garlic, oregano, and mustard and mix well. Drizzle half of this mixture over the potatoes and toss to coat. Roast for 20 minutes.

4. Cut chicken breasts into quarters. Remove pan from oven and add chicken to potato mixture. Using a spatula, mix potatoes and chicken together. Drizzle with remaining oil mixture. Return to oven and roast for 15 minutes longer.

5. Add tomatoes to pan. Roast for 5–10 minutes longer, or until potatoes are tender and browned and chicken is thoroughly cooked.

PER SERVING Calories: 420 | Fat: 8g | Sodium: 200mg | Carbohydrates: 56g | Fiber: 5g | Protein: 29g

Chicken Stir-Fry with Napa Cabbage

The combination of cabbage, bell pepper, and edamame is delicious and very healthy.

INGREDIENTS | SERVES 4

2 (5-ounce) boneless, skinless chicken breasts

2 tablespoons arrowroot

2 tablespoons lemon juice

1 tablespoon soy sauce

1 cup Chicken Stock (Chapter 3)

2 tablespoons canola oil

4 cups shredded Napa cabbage

4 green onions, sliced

1 green bell pepper, sliced

1½ cups frozen edamame, thawed

Stir-Frying

Stir-frying is one of the healthiest ways to cook. Once all the ingredients are prepared, the method takes 10 minutes or less. But all of the food must be prepared before the actual cooking begins; there is no time to chop or slice vegetables once the wok is hot and you start to stir-fry.

1. Cut chicken into 1" pieces.

2. In small bowl, combine arrowroot, lemon juice, soy sauce, and stock. Add chicken and let stand for 15 minutes.

3. Heat oil in large skillet or wok.

4. Drain chicken, reserving marinade. Add chicken to skillet; stir-fry until almost cooked, about 4 minutes. Remove to a plate.

5. Add cabbage and green onions to skillet; stir-fry until cabbage wilts, about 4 minutes.

6. Add bell pepper and edamame; stir-fry for 3–5 minutes longer until hot.

7. Stir marinade and add to skillet along with chicken. Stir-fry until sauce bubbles and thickens and chicken is thoroughly cooked. Serve over hot cooked brown rice.

PER SERVING Calories: 310 | Fat: 12g | Sodium: 420mg | Carbohydrates: 19g | Fiber: 5g | Protein: 30g

Chicken and Bean Tacos

Let your family assemble their own tacos so they can pick the toppings they like.

INGREDIENTS | SERVES 8

1 pound boneless, skinless chicken breasts

½ teaspoon salt

⅛ teaspoon black pepper

1 tablespoon arrowroot

2 tablespoons olive oil

1 onion, chopped

1 yellow bell pepper, chopped

1 (15-ounce) can Great Northern beans, drained

1 cup Super Spicy Salsa (Chapter 12)

8 corn taco shells

2 cups shredded lettuce

1 cup grape tomatoes

½ cup sour cream

1 cup shredded Cheddar cheese

1. Heat oven to 350°F.

2. Cut chicken into 1" cubes and sprinkle with salt, pepper, and arrowroot.

3. Heat olive oil in large skillet and add chicken. Cook and stir until almost cooked, about 4 minutes; remove from skillet.

4. Add onion and bell pepper to skillet; cook and stir 4–5 minutes, or until crisp-tender.

5. Return chicken to skillet along with beans and salsa; bring to a simmer. Simmer until chicken is cooked, about 3–5 minutes longer.

6. Meanwhile, heat taco shells as directed on package. When shells are hot, make tacos with chicken mixture, lettuce, tomatoes, sour cream, and cheese. Serve immediately.

PER SERVING Calories: 360 | Fat: 16g | Sodium: 360mg | Carbohydrates: 28g | Fiber: 5g | Protein: 26g

Sweet and Sour Turkey Burgers

Sweet and sour is an excellent flavor combination to use in low-fat cooking because the main ingredients are fat free. These tender and juicy burgers are really delicious.

INGREDIENTS | **SERVES 4**

1 tablespoon soy sauce

1 tablespoon honey

1 tablespoon apple cider vinegar

¼ cup dried bread crumbs

1 pound ground turkey breast

¼ cup chopped green onions

¼ cup chili sauce

6 Whole-Wheat Hamburger Buns (Chapter 13), split

6 slices canned pineapple, drained

6 butter lettuce leaves

Ground Turkey

When you buy ground turkey, look for an evenly colored product that has very little liquid in the package. If there is a lot of liquid, the meat will be dry when cooked. Ground turkey freezes very well, so purchase a lot when there's a sale. You can also grind your own turkey in a food processor using the pulse function.

1. In a medium bowl, combine soy sauce, honey, vinegar, and bread crumbs until blended.

2. Add ground turkey and green onions and mix well. Shape into 4 patties.

3. In a nonstick skillet over medium heat, fry patties, turning once, until done, about 8–10 minutes.

4. To serve, spread chili sauce on hamburger buns and top with a patty, pineapple ring, and lettuce. Complete with top half of the bun and serve immediately.

PER SERVING Calories: 430 | Fat: 10g | Sodium: 880mg | Carbohydrates: 59g | Fiber: 6g | Protein: 30g

Turkey with Couscous

*This easy recipe can be doubled to serve 6. You could also add
a chopped apple or some sliced mushrooms.*

INGREDIENTS | SERVES 3

1 (8-ounce) box instant couscous
½ teaspoon cinnamon
1 cup diced cooked turkey
1 (15-ounce) can garbanzo beans, drained
⅓ cup raisins
½ cup plain yogurt
⅛ teaspoon black pepper

1. In a medium saucepan, cook the couscous according to package directions, adding the cinnamon at the start of cooking.

2. When done, stir in the turkey, garbanzos, raisins, yogurt, and pepper.

3. Cook over low heat, stirring constantly, until hot, about 4–5 minutes. Serve immediately.

PER SERVING Calories: 610 | Fat: 5g | Sodium: 490mg | Carbohydrates: 107g | Fiber: 11g | Protein: 33g

Turkey Chili

Turkey plus beans make this chili a protein powerhouse!

INGREDIENTS | SERVES 6

1 pound ground turkey
1 cup onions, chopped
½ cup green pepper, chopped
2 teaspoons garlic, finely chopped
2 (28-ounce) cans crushed canned tomatoes
1 cup canned black beans, drained
1 cup canned red kidney beans, drained
3 tablespoons chili powder
1 tablespoon ground cumin
1 teaspoon crushed red pepper
Dash Tabasco

1. Brown ground turkey in large nonstick pot over medium-high heat. Drain any fat.

2. Add chopped onion, green pepper, and garlic. Continue cooking until onion is translucent, about 5 minutes.

3. Add remaining ingredients; bring to a slow boil.

4. Reduce heat, cover, and let simmer at least 2–3 hours before serving.

PER SERVING | Calories: 281 | Fat: 4g | Sodium: 347mg | Carbohydrates: 38g | Fiber: 11g | Protein: 26g

Indian Turkey Pilaf

A pilaf is a spicy combination of rice and other ingredients. Yogurt is added for a cooling contrast.

INGREDIENTS | SERVES 6

2 cups water

1 tablespoon curry powder

½ teaspoon ground turmeric

1 onion, chopped

3 cloves garlic, minced

½ teaspoon cinnamon

1 cup long-grain brown rice

1 (9-ounce) package frozen green beans, thawed

2 peaches, peeled and chopped

3 cups diced cooked turkey breast

½ cup plain yogurt

1. In a medium saucepan, combine water, curry powder, turmeric, onion, garlic, and cinnamon. Bring to a boil.

2. Add the rice, cover, reduce the heat to low, and cook until the liquid is absorbed and the rice is tender, about 35–45 minutes.

3. Preheat oven to 375°F.

4. Drain beans thoroughly. When the rice is tender, spoon half into a 2½-quart baking dish. Top with beans, peaches, and turkey, then remaining rice mixture. Cover with foil.

5. Bake for 30 minutes, then uncover and top with yogurt.

6. Bake for 10–15 minutes longer until food is hot. Serve immediately.

PER SERVING Calories: 280 | Fat: 4g | Sodium: 60mg | Carbohydrates: 35g | Fiber: 4g | Protein: 26g

Fiesta Turkey

The combination of flavors and textures in this recipe is really good. If your family likes spicy food, triple the chili powder and double the amount of cayenne pepper.

INGREDIENTS | SERVES 6

1 (8-ounce) can tomato sauce

½ cup fresh orange juice

1 minced onion

¼ cup dried currants

2 tablespoons chopped pimiento

½ teaspoon dried oregano leaves

1 teaspoon chili powder

1 clove garlic, minced

¼ teaspoon salt

⅛ teaspoon cayenne pepper

1½ pounds turkey tenderloin, cubed

1 tablespoon arrowroot

2 tablespoons water

¼ cup chopped fresh flat-leaf parsley

3 cups hot cooked rice

1. In a large skillet, combine tomato sauce, orange juice, onion, currants, pimiento, oregano, chili powder, garlic, salt, and pepper. Bring to a boil, cover, reduce the heat to low, and simmer for 5 minutes.

2. Add turkey to skillet and return to a simmer. Cover and simmer until internal temperature reaches 165°F, about 6–9 minutes.

3. Meanwhile, in small bowl, combine arrowroot and water. Stir into skillet; cook and stir until thickened and bubbly, about 3–4 minutes.

4. Toss parsley into hot rice and spoon onto a platter or individual plates. Serve turkey mixture over rice.

PER SERVING Calories: 300 | Fat: 2g | Sodium: 400mg | Carbohydrates: 40g | Fiber: 2g | Protein: 31g

Cayenne Pepper

The heat from cayenne peppers, or any hot peppers, comes from capsaicin, a molecule concentrated in the seeds and membranes of the peppers. It is a good source of vitamin A, a powerful antioxidant. Cayenne peppers also trigger release of a natural pain-relieving and anti-inflammatory agent called substance P.

CHAPTER 9

Sandwiches, Wraps, and Savory Snacks

Roasted Vegetable Sandwich

The variety of vegetables in this sandwich provide a lot of fiber with a lot of flavor. If you leave the skin on the eggplant, you'll have even more fiber. If grilling, add extra vegetables and use them the next day. Try to find whole-grain focaccia; it's got loads more nutrition and fiber than white bread.

INGREDIENTS | YIELDS 1 SANDWICH

1 (½" thick) slice eggplant

2 (½" thick) slices zucchini

2 (½" thick) slices yellow summer squash

1 (½" thick) slice red onion

1 (½" thick) slice fennel bulb

2 teaspoons olive oil

½ teaspoon salt

¼ teaspoon black pepper

1 teaspoon mayonnaise

1 teaspoon basil pesto

1 square focaccia bread, split horizontally

1 large piece roasted red bell pepper

¼ cup alfalfa sprouts

Carrot sticks

1. Preheat the oven to 375°F.

2. Brush the eggplant, zucchini, summer squash, red onion, and fennel slices with the olive oil and sprinkle them with salt and pepper.

3. Place on a baking pan lined with nonstick foil and roast in oven for about 35 minutes. Let cool.

4. Mix the mayonnaise and pesto and spread onto the inside of both the top and bottom pieces of foccacia.

5. Layer the roasted vegetables, including the red bell pepper, on the bottom half of the focaccia, and then top with alfalfa sprouts. Place top half of focaccia on and cut the sandwich in half diagonally. Serve with carrot sticks.

PER SERVING Calories: 340 | Fat: 14g | Sodium: 1570mg | Carbohydrates: 48g | Fiber: 6g | Protein: 7g

Grilled Vegetables

From sandwich fillings to salads to side dishes, grilled vegetables are incredibly versatile. They are beautiful when dressed with a bit of sesame oil for an Asian flavor and served over brown rice. Add Mediterranean herbs, such as basil, oregano, and rosemary and toss them over an arugula salad. This makes a colorful and healthy meal full of cancer-fighting nutrients.

Waldorf Salad Sandwiches

This delicious sandwich has the best texture and flavor combinations. Serve it for a special luncheon.

INGREDIENTS | SERVES 4–6

½ cup plain yogurt

2 tablespoons Dijon mustard

⅛ teaspoon white pepper

2 Granny Smith apples, chopped

½ cup chopped walnuts

1 cup diced celery

½ cup golden raisins

½ cup dried blueberries

8 slices Cinnamon-Swirl Raisin Bread (Chapter 13)

3 tablespoons honey

4 leaves red lettuce

1. In large bowl, combine yogurt, mustard, and pepper; mix well.

2. Stir in apples, walnuts, celery, raisins, and blueberries and mix to coat.

3. Toast the bread until light golden brown.

4. Spread one side of each bread slice with honey. Top half of slices with a lettuce leaf, then divide fruit mixture on lettuce. Top with remaining bread slices, honey-side down. Cut in half diagonally, and serve.

PER SERVING Calories: 500 | Fat: 15g | Sodium: 440mg | Carbohydrates: 87g | Fiber: 8g | Protein: 11g

Health Benefits of Walnuts

Walnuts are excellent sources of B vitamins, magnesium, and antioxidants like vitamin E. Studies also show that a diet rich in walnuts helps reduce the risk of heart disease by improving blood vessel elasticity, plaque accumulation, and lowering LDL cholesterol. Walnuts are high in calories, though, so eat them in moderation or use them as replacements for higher fat items in your diet.

Open-Faced Tomato Basil Sandwiches

The combination of hot bread and melted cheese with cold
seasoned tomatoes and basil is simply spectacular.

INGREDIENTS | SERVES 8

3 tablespoons olive oil, divided

4 tomatoes, chopped

¼ cup chopped fresh basil

1 teaspoon fresh oregano leaves

2 cloves garlic, minced

Pinch salt

⅛ teaspoon white pepper

12 slices Hearty-Grain French Bread
(Chapter 13)

1 cup shredded Havarti cheese

Basil

Basil is an easy-to-grow herb that adds lots of flavor to foods, especially Italian recipes. For best flavor, make sure that you harvest the leaves before the plant bolts, or forms flowers. Rinse off the leaves, shake off excess water, and freeze the leaves in heavy-duty freezer bags. When you want to use some, just break off a small amount.

1. In small bowl, combine 1 tablespoon olive oil, tomatoes, basil, oregano, and garlic and mix well. Sprinkle with salt and pepper, stir, and set aside.

2. Preheat broiler.

3. Brush bread slices on one side with remaining olive oil. Place oil-side up on broiler pan.

4. Broil 6" from heat for 2–5 minutes or until bread is lightly toasted. Turn bread.

5. Sprinkle cheese on untoasted side of bread slices.

6. Return to broiler and broil for 3–4 minutes or until cheese is melted and bubbling. Remove from broiler and immediately top each open-faced sandwich with a spoonful of the tomato mixture. Serve immediately.

PER SERVING Calories: 250 | Fat: 13g | Sodium: 170mg | Carbohydrates: 27g | Fiber: 3g | Protein: 8g

Cranberry Chicken Sandwiches

You can make this recipe using leftover Thanksgiving turkey as well as poached chicken. It's both delicious and colorful.

INGREDIENTS | SERVES 4

2 cups poached chicken, cubed

⅓ cup mayonnaise

¼ cup Cranberry Chutney (Chapter 12)

½ cup dried cranberries

½ cup chopped red onion

½ cup chopped celery

½ teaspoon salt

⅛ teaspoon white pepper

4 wedges focaccia bread, split

1. In medium bowl, combine all ingredients except focaccia; mix well. Cover and refrigerate 2–3 hours to blend flavors.

2. Construct sandwiches using focaccia bread.

3. Grill until bread is toasted and filling is hot, turning once.

PER SERVING Calories: 500 | Fat: 25g | Sodium: 780mg | Carbohydrates: 43g | Fiber: 2g | Protein: 26g

Dried Cranberries

Dried cranberries are a delicious snack. They usually contain sugar, as plain cranberries are very tart. Dried cranberries contain 300 calories per cup, so they aren't a diet food, but they have a good amount of fiber, so may be helpful in regulating your bowels. Stir them into homemade snack mixes, add to muffins, and use in salads.

Avocado Reuben Sandwiches

Commercial Thousand Island dressing can be used, but for a taste treat make your own by combining 1 cup of mayonnaise with ½ cup of your favorite salsa. This recipe works well as a topping for turkey or veggie burgers as well.

INGREDIENTS | SERVES 4

1 (10-ounce) package soy tempeh

8 slices Hearty-Grain French Bread (Chapter 13)

2 tablespoons olive oil

8 tablespoons Thousand Island dressing, divided

1½ cups sauerkraut

1 ripe avocado, sliced

4 slices Monterey jack cheese

What Is Tempeh?

Tempeh is an Indonesian protein food made from cultured grains or soy. It is pressed into a block, packaged, and sold in natural foods stores. Soy tempeh can be very low in carbohydrates, especially when you subtract the substantial amounts of fiber it provides. It is a very versatile food and a great vegetarian substitute for animal protein. Tempeh, like other soy foods, contains phytoestrogens, which some people have to avoid if they have been diagnosed with estrogen receptor-positive types of cancers.

1. Cut block of tempeh in half, then cut in half crosswise, making 4 thin slabs.

2. Lightly toast bread.

3. Heat oil in a heavy skillet; brown tempeh slabs on both sides.

4. Arrange 4 pieces of bread on separate plates; spread each with 1 tablespoon dressing. Top each slice with a slab of tempeh, spoonful of sauerkraut, a few slices of avocado, and a slice of cheese.

5. Place sandwich half under broiler to melt the cheese.

6. Spread another tablespoon of dressing on second piece of bread; lay it on top of cheese.

7. Slice each sandwich on the diagonal and serve immediately.

PER SERVING Calories: 640 | Fat: 38g | Sodium: 1110mg | Carbohydrates: 51g | Fiber: 11g | Protein: 30g

Lentil Burritos

Lentils are a super source of iron. They're also a plentiful source of vitamin B1, folate, and dietary fiber.

INGREDIENTS | SERVES 6

1 cup lentils, rinsed

2 cups Chicken Stock (Chapter 3) or vegetable stock

1 cup water

1 teaspoon olive oil

½ cup white onions, diced

1 clove garlic, minced

1 cup zucchini, chopped

1 cup red bell pepper, chopped

½ teaspoon ground cumin

¼ teaspoon hot pepper sauce

1 cup mild taco sauce

Salt, to taste

4 ounces shredded Cheddar jack cheese

12 whole-wheat tortillas

1. Wash and drain lentils. Bring lentils, stock, and water to a boil. Cover saucepan and simmer until lentils are tender yet holding their shape, 25–40 minutes.

2. Sauté olive oil, onions, garlic, zucchini, and bell peppers over medium heat.

3. When veggies are tender, stir in lentils, cumin, hot sauce, and taco sauce; add salt to taste.

4. Stir in cheese until melted.

5. Spoon ½ cup mixture into the center of each tortilla. Roll and serve.

PER SERVING Calories: 450 | Fat: 14g | Sodium: 860mg | Carbohydrates: 60g | Fiber: 8g | Protein: 18g

Curried Turkey Pockets

Curry powder adds great flavor to this complex sandwich. Vary the amount to suit your taste buds.

INGREDIENTS | SERVES 4

¾ cup plain yogurt

2 teaspoons curry powder

⅛ teaspoon ground mace

2 cups cubed cooked turkey

½ cup Vinaigrette (Chapter 12)

1 green apple, cubed

½ cup sliced celery

¼ cup sliced almonds, toasted

¼ cup raisins

4 pita bread

8 curly lettuce leaves

Toasting Nuts

Toasting nuts helps bring out their flavors and keeps them crunchy even when cooked in moist mixtures. To toast nuts, spread on a cookie sheet and bake at 350°F for 8–10 minutes, shaking the pan occasionally, until fragrant. If you're running short on time, you can microwave the nuts on high for 1–2 minutes, stirring once, until fragrant. Let cool before chopping.

1. In a small bowl, stir the yogurt with curry powder and mace and mix well. Cover and refrigerate for at least 4 hours or up to 24 hours to blend the flavors.

2. Meanwhile, in a medium bowl, combine turkey and Vinaigrette. Cover and marinate in the refrigerator for at least 4 hours or up to 8 hours.

3. Add the apple, celery, almonds, and raisins to the turkey.

4. Stir the curry-yogurt dressing into turkey mixture.

5. Cut the pita breads in half, forming 8 pockets. Line each pocket with 1 lettuce leaf, then spoon in the turkey mixture, dividing it evenly. Serve immediately.

PER SERVING Calories: 510 | Fat: 28g | Sodium: 380mg | Carbohydrates: 52g | Fiber: 5g | Protein: 15g

Sprout Sandwich with Avocado

This simple bagel treat works well at any time of day. It's easy to double or triple this recipe for others in the family.

INGREDIENTS | **SERVES 1**

1 whole-wheat bagel
½ ripe avocado, diced
4 tablespoons mixed sprouts
2 tablespoons mayonnaise, or more as desired
2 tablespoons toasted pumpkin seeds
1 teaspoon Dijon mustard
Salt and black pepper, to taste

1. Slice the bagel in half and toast it.

2. Mix the remaining ingredients together and spread on both halves of the bagel. Serve.

PER SERVING Calories: 700 | Fat: 40g | Sodium: 880mg | Carbohydrates: 76g | Fiber: 18g | Protein: 16g

Avocados

It's next to impossible to find ripe avocados in the grocery store. To ripen, buy avocados that are firm but not rock hard. Place them in a paper bag with a red apple, close the bag, and let stand on the counter for 1–3 days. Check the avocados every day. When they yield to gentle pressure, they're ready to use.

Quinoa and Hummus Sandwich Wrap

Lunch is the perfect time to fill up on whole grains.

INGREDIENTS | **SERVES 1**

1 tortilla or flavored wrap, warmed
3 tablespoons hummus
⅓ cup cooked quinoa
½ teaspoon fresh lemon juice
2 teaspoons Vinaigrette (Chapter 12)
1 roasted red pepper, sliced into strips
¼ cup sprouts
Salt and black pepper, to taste

1. Spread a warmed tortilla or wrap with a layer of hummus, then quinoa, and drizzle with lemon juice and Vinaigrette.

2. Layer red pepper and sprouts on top; season to taste. Wrap, and serve.

PER SERVING Calories: 690 | Fat: 35g | Sodium: 650mg | Carbohydrates: 82g | Fiber: 11g | Protein: 17g

Salmon Salad Wrap

Vary the amounts of mayonnaise and mustard to suit your taste, or substitute roasted pine nuts for the peanuts. Feel free to improvise to ensure you get the flavors you love.

INGREDIENTS | SERVES 2

1 (6-ounce) can salmon

¼ cup minced sweet onion

¼ cup minced celery

2 tablespoons roasted peanuts

1 tablespoon mayonnaise

1 teaspoon Dijon mustard

Salt and black pepper, to taste

2 tortilla wraps

2 large leaves of lettuce

Canned Salmon

Always keep a few cans of wild Alaskan or red sockeye salmon on hand for quick meals. In the off-season, when fresh wild salmon is not available, you can use the canned salmon to add to soups, stir-fries, pasta dishes, or as a pâté on crackers.

1. Open salmon and remove and discard any pieces of skin.

2. In a medium-size bowl, combine salmon, onion, celery, peanuts, mayonnaise, mustard, salt, and pepper; mix well.

3. Heat a skillet; warm 1 tortilla at a time. Remove to individual plates.

4. Divide salmon mixture; spread along one side of a tortilla.

5. Lay lettuce along length of mixture; roll up tortilla.

6. Slice wrap in half along the diagonal and serve.

PER SERVING Calories: 390 | Fat: 19g | Sodium: 560mg | Carbohydrates: 30g | Fiber: 3g | Protein: 24g

Fiesta Chicken Wrap

Instead of using sour cream and salsa for this recipe, you could try a little sauce made by mixing 1 cup fat-free ranch and 1 teaspoon chili powder.

INGREDIENTS | **SERVES 1**

1 small whole-wheat tortilla
1 grilled chicken breast
1 tablespoon shredded Cheddar cheese
½ tablespoon plum tomatoes, diced
½ tablespoon red onion, diced
1 tablespoon black beans
½ tablespoon sour cream
½ tablespoon Super Spicy Salsa (Chapter 12)

1. Lay tortilla flat on a plate.

2. Slice chicken.

3. Place all ingredients in the center of the tortilla. Roll tortilla into a wrap.

PER SERVING Calories: 270 | Fat: 8g | Sodium: 370mg | Carbohydrates: 24g | Fiber: 3g | Protein: 32g

Fast Food

Many people use limited time as an excuse to eat poorly. Healthy food can be quick, and fast-food joints are starting to appease the health-conscious consumer. So go ahead and zoom through that drive-thru; just order lean meat and fresh or raw veggies, and ignore everything fried and ask them to hold the mayo!

Turkey Wraps

These flavorful wrap sandwiches are really delicious. If you like
your food spicy, add another jalapeño or two.

INGREDIENTS | SERVES 6

1 tablespoon olive oil

½ cup chopped red onion

1 red bell pepper, chopped

1 jalapeño pepper, minced

2 cups cubed cooked turkey

1 tablespoon fresh lemon juice

2 tablespoons chopped fresh flat-leaf parsley

6 (8") corn tortillas

2 (3-ounce) packages cream cheese, softened

1 cup baby spinach leaves

Leftover Turkey

When you roast a turkey for Thanksgiving or other holiday, remove the meat within 2 days. Chop or dice, then package into hard-sided freezer containers. Label, seal, and freeze up to 3 months. To use, let stand in refrigerator overnight, then use in recipes from casseroles to sandwich spreads. Use the bones to make stock.

1. In medium saucepan, heat olive oil over medium heat. Add red onion; cook and stir 2 minutes.

2. Add bell pepper and jalapeño pepper; cook and stir 3–4 minutes longer.

3. Remove from heat and stir in turkey, lemon juice, and parsley.

4. Soften tortillas as directed on package. Arrange on work surface. Spread each with 1 ounce of cream cheese. Layer spinach leaves on top of the cream cheese, and divide turkey mixture over.

5. Roll up the tortillas, enclosing filling. Cut in half. Serve immediately.

PER SERVING Calories: 270 | Fat: 14g | Sodium: 120mg | Carbohydrates: 19g | Fiber: 3g | Protein: 18g

Asian Veggie Wraps

You could add cooked pork or chicken to this simple wrap recipe if you'd like.

INGREDIENTS | SERVES 6

1 tablespoon olive oil
1 onion, chopped
1 shallot, minced
2 tablespoons minced ginger root
2 cups shredded cabbage
½ cup shredded carrot
2 tablespoons soy sauce
2 tablespoons Chicken Stock (Chapter 3) or vegetable stock
3 tablespoons Plum Sauce (Chapter 12)
⅛ teaspoon white pepper
2 cups cooked rice
6–8 romaine lettuce leaves

1. In large skillet, heat olive oil over medium heat. Add onion, shallot, and ginger; stir-fry 4 minutes.

2. Add cabbage and carrot; stir-fry 4–5 minutes longer, until crisp-tender.

3. In small bowl, combine soy sauce, stock, plum sauce, and pepper; mix well. Add to skillet along with rice; stir-fry until hot.

4. Divide rice mixture among lettuce leaves; roll up. Serve immediately.

PER SERVING Calories: 160 | Fat: 2.5g | Sodium: 350mg | Carbohydrates: 31g | Fiber: 1g | Protein: 4g

Edamame

Edamame are fresh soybeans. They are the base of soy sauce, tofu, and soymilk. You can eat them as a snack before sushi or as part of a crudités platter. Edamame are also an excellent addition to salads, soups, and rice dishes.

INGREDIENTS | SERVES 6

6 cups of water
½ teaspoon salt
1 pound frozen edamame in pods

1. Bring the water and the salt to a boil in a saucepan.

2. Add the edamame and let the water come back to a boil.

3. Cook on medium-high for 5 minutes.

4. Drain the edamame and rinse with cold water.

5. Drain again, and serve either warm or cool.

PER 1/6 POUND Calories: 100 | Fat: 3g | Sodium: 220mg | Carbohydrates: 9g | Fiber: 4g | Protein: 8g

Spinach Artichoke Pizza

This pizza is just full of vegetables, nutrition, fiber, and flavor!

INGREDIENTS | SERVES 8

1 (10-ounce) package frozen chopped spinach, thawed and drained

1 (9-ounce) package frozen artichoke hearts, thawed and drained

1 tablespoon olive oil

1 onion, chopped

3 cloves garlic, minced

1 red bell pepper, chopped

1 (8-ounce) package sliced mushrooms

1 cup ricotta cheese

¼ cup grated Parmesan cheese

1 Whole-Grain Pizza Crust (Chapter 13)

1 cup shredded mozzarella cheese

½ cup shredded extra-sharp Cheddar cheese

1. Preheat oven to 400°F.

2. Press spinach between paper towels to remove all excess moisture. Cut artichoke hearts into small pieces.

3. In large saucepan, heat olive oil. Cook onion, garlic, and red pepper until crisp-tender, about 4 minutes.

4. Add spinach; cook and stir until liquid evaporates, about 5 minutes longer.

5. Add mushrooms; cook and stir for 2–3 minutes longer.

6. Drain vegetable mixture if necessary. Place in medium bowl and let cool for 20 minutes. Blend in ricotta and Parmesan cheeses.

7. Spread on pizza crust. Top with mozzarella and Cheddar cheeses.

8. Bake for 20–25 minutes or until pizza is hot and cheese is melted and begins to brown. Serve immediately.

PER SERVING Calories: 380 | Fat: 17g | Sodium: 630mg | Carbohydrates: 38g | Fiber: 6g | Protein: 20g

Potato Pizza

Thinly sliced potatoes make an unusual and delicious topping on this special pizza.
Serve it with a nice green salad for a simple late-night dinner.

INGREDIENTS | SERVES 6–8

1 tablespoon olive oil
1 tablespoon butter
1 onion, finely chopped
5 cloves garlic, minced
3 Yukon Gold potatoes, thinly sliced
2 teaspoons fresh thyme leaves
⅛ teaspoon salt
⅛ teaspoon cayenne pepper
1 Whole-Grain Pizza Crust (Chapter 13)
1 cup shredded Havarti cheese
2 tablespoons grated Romano cheese

1. Preheat oven to 400°F.

2. In large saucepan, combine olive oil and butter over medium heat. When butter melts, add onion and garlic; cook and stir until crisp-tender, about 4 minutes.

3. Add potatoes. Cook, stirring occasionally, until potatoes are slightly softened. Add thyme, salt, and cayenne pepper and remove from heat.

4. Spread potato mixture on the pizza crust. Top with cheeses.

5. Bake for 20–25 minutes or until potatoes are tender, pizza is hot, and cheeses are melted and starting to brown. Serve immediately.

PER SERVING Calories: 390 | Fat: 15g | Sodium: 290mg | Carbohydrates: 53g | Fiber: 5g | Protein: 12g

Popcorn Snack Mix

This party mix with popcorn is perfect for movie night at home. Just serve it in a big bowl with individual plastic cups for each person.

INGREDIENTS | SERVES 12

4 cups popped popcorn
2 cups toasted oat-rings cereal
3 cups wheat cereal squares
1 cup peanuts
1 cup cashews
1 cup mini pretzel twists
6 tablespoons butter, melted
2 tablespoons Worcestershire sauce
1 teaspoon garlic powder
½ teaspoon onion powder
1 teaspoon seasoning salt
1 cup chocolate-covered raisins

1. Preheat oven to 250°F.

2. Combine popcorn, cereals, peanuts, cashews, and pretzels in a large roasting pan.

3. Combine melted butter, Worcestershire sauce, garlic powder, onion powder, and seasoning salt in a small bowl. Drizzle over the popcorn mixture and toss to distribute.

4. Bake in the oven for 15 minutes, stir; repeat 4 more times.

5. Remove from oven. Spread mix on baking sheets and let cool. Toss in chocolate-covered raisins in and mix to distribute evenly. Store in an airtight container.

PER 1 CUP Calories: 430 | Fat: 22g | Sodium: 240mg | Carbohydrates: 54g | Fiber: 6g | Protein: 10g

Peanut Bananas

Try this recipe with almond or cashew butter for variation;
honey may be substituted for the brown rice syrup.

INGREDIENTS	SERVES 4

3 bananas
1 cup crunchy peanut butter
¼ cup brown rice syrup
1 cup granola

Nature's Flatware

You may serve these banana snacks with bamboo skewers or toothpicks, but fingers are just fine. Bananas are loaded with fiber and potassium; they really fill you up. They are especially wonderful for the lonely traveler, sitting in the airport, waiting for a plane that's late.

1. Peel the bananas and cut them into quarters crosswise.

2. Stand the banana pieces cut-side up on a platter. (Cut the pointed tips off the end pieces so they can stand up.)

3. Mix the peanut butter with the brown rice syrup in a glass bowl and microwave on high for 15–20 seconds. Stir well.

4. Spoon the peanut butter mixture onto the banana pieces.

5. Sprinkle granola over the peanut butter and serve.

PER 3 PIECES Calories: 700 | Fat: 38g | Sodium: 390mg | Carbohydrates: 77g | Fiber: 9g | Protein: 22g

Trail Mix

Pack individual servings of this mix to take in the car when you don't have time to stop for a meal. If your digestive system is sensitive, perhaps due to chemotherapy or radiation treatment, then you may want to stay away from whole nuts and have nut butters instead.

INGREDIENTS	SERVES 8; SERVING SIZE: 1 CUP

2 cups dried cherries
2 cups roasted pecans
1 cup M&Ms
2 cups granola
1 cup shelled sunflower seeds
1 cup Pretzel Goldfish

1. Combine all ingredients in a large bowl.

2. Divide into individual portions.

3. Store in resealable plastic bags or serve in individual paper cups.

PER SERVING Calories: 810 | Fat: 45g | Sodium: 490mg | Carbohydrates: 92g | Fiber: 10g | Protein: 16g

Asian Gingered Almonds

Almonds and many other tree nuts fall within the good fats category because they contain healthy oils, including omega-9 in almonds and omega-3 in macadamia, walnuts, and pecans. Pistachios may be especially healthful for those watching their weight.

INGREDIENTS	YIELDS 1 CUP; SERVING SIZE: 1 TABLESPOON

2 teaspoons butter
1 tablespoon soy sauce
1 teaspoon ground ginger
1 cup slivered almonds

1. Preheat oven to 350°F.

2. In microwave-safe bowl, mix butter, soy sauce, and ginger. Microwave on high 30 seconds, or until butter is melted; blend well.

3. Spread almonds on baking sheet treated with nonstick spray. Bake for 12–15 minutes, stirring occasionally.

4. Pour seasoned butter over almonds; stir to mix. Bake for an additional 5 minutes. Store in airtight containers in cool place.

PER SERVING Calories: 45 | Fat: 4g | Sodium: 65mg | Carbohydrates: 1g | Fiber: <1g | Protein: 2g

Homemade Tahini

If you're serving this as a Middle Eastern dip or spread, use the paprika for extra flavor, but leave it out if your tahini will be the basis for a salad dressing or a noodle dish.

INGREDIENTS | **YIELDS 1 CUP**

2 cups sesame seeds

½ cup olive oil

½ teaspoon paprika (optional)

1. Heat oven to 350°F. Once oven is hot, spread sesame seeds in a thin layer on a baking sheet and toast for 5 minutes in oven, shaking the sheet once to mix.

2. Allow sesame seeds to cool, then process with oil in a food processor or blender until thick and creamy. You may need a little more or less than ½ cup oil.

3. Garnish with paprika, if desired. Tahini will keep for up to 1 month in the refrigerator in a tightly sealed container, or store in the freezer and thaw before using.

PER 1 TABLESPOON Calories: 163 | Fat: 16g | Sodium: 2mg | Fiber: 2g | Protein: 3g

Baked Tortilla Chips

Instead of stocking up with bags of oily chips and crackers, keep corn tortillas in the fridge and bake up an exact amount of chips whenever you want.

INGREDIENTS | **SERVES 10**

10 corn tortillas

Salt, to taste

1. Preheat oven to 400°F.

2. Cover 2 cookie sheets with nonstick spray.

3. Cut each tortilla into 6 wedges. Scatter wedges onto cookie sheets.

4. Spray wedges with nonstick cooking spray and sprinkle with salt. Bake for 12 minutes.

PER SERVING Calories: 60 | Fat: 0.5g | Sodium: 10mg | Carbohydrates: 12g | Fiber: 2g | Protein: 1g

Tropical Cashew Nut Butter

You can make a homemade cashew nut butter with any kind of oil, so feel free to substitute using whatever you have on hand, but you're in for a real treat when you use coconut oil in this recipe! These are great ways to add calories when appetite is poor.

INGREDIENTS | **YIELDS ¾ CUP**

2 cups roasted cashews

½ teaspoon sugar (optional)

¼ teaspoon salt (optional)

3–4 tablespoons canola oil

Making Nut Butters

Nut butters can be very expensive to purchase, but are so easy to make at home! Try making almond, walnut, or macadamia nut butter for a delicious alternative to store-bought peanut butter. Roasted nuts work best, so heat them in the oven at 400°F for 6–8 minutes, or toast them on the stove top in a dry skillet for a few minutes.

1. Process the cashews, sugar, and salt in a food processor on high speed until finely ground. Continue processing until cashews form a thick paste.

2. Slowly add coconut oil until smooth and creamy, scraping down sides and adding more oil as needed.

PER 2 TABLESPOONS Calories: 280 | Fat: 24g | Sodium: 5mg | Fiber: 1g | Protein: 6g

CHAPTER 10

Vegetable Side Dishes and Vegetarian Entrées

Lemon Asparagus and Carrots

Steaming is one of the best ways to cook vegetables; it retains nutrients and keeps the bright color you want.

INGREDIENTS | **SERVES 6**

1 pound baby carrots

1 pound fresh asparagus

2 tablespoons fresh lemon juice

1 tablespoon olive oil

1 tablespoon mustard

½ teaspoon lemon pepper

½ teaspoon salt

Steaming Vegetables

To steam vegetables, place water in a large saucepan and bring to a simmer. Cover with a steamer insert or a metal colander, making sure the insert or colander sits above the water. Add the vegetables to the insert, cover, and simmer for 10–15 minutes or until tender. Stir the vegetables occasionally for even steaming.

1. Steam the carrots until crisp tender, about 15 minutes, then plunge them into cold water to cool. Drain and place in a bowl. Steam asparagus until tender.

2. In a small bowl, combine lemon juice, oil, mustard, lemon pepper, and salt and mix well.

3. To serve, arrange the carrots and asparagus on a platter; drizzle with lemon mixture.

PER SERVING Calories: 70 | Fat: 2.5g | Sodium: 320mg | Carbohydrates: 11g | Fiber: 4g | Protein: 2g

Cheese and Veggie-Stuffed Artichokes

This is a delicious main dish for a hot summer day. Serve with
iced green tea and some fruit sorbet for dessert.

INGREDIENTS | **SERVES 4**

1 cup shredded Havarti cheese

2 tablespoons grated Parmesan cheese

¼ cup plain yogurt

¼ cup mayonnaise

1 tablespoon fresh lemon juice

2 scallions, chopped

1 tablespoon capers

1 cup grated carrots

1 cup grape tomatoes

⅛ teaspoon salt

4 globe artichokes

1 lemon, cut into wedges

Artichoke Health Benefits

Artichokes contain a phytochemical called cynarin, which studies show may help the liver regenerate. Since the liver is essential to processing and removing cholesterol from the body, it's critical to your health. Artichokes are nutrient-dense, providing potassium, fiber, vitamin C, and folate. They are also low in fat and contain no cholesterol.

1. In medium bowl, combine Havarti, Parmesan, yogurt, mayonnaise, lemon juice, scallions, and capers and mix well. Stir in carrots, tomatoes, and salt, and set aside.

2. Cut off the top inch of the artichokes. Cut off the sharp tip of each leaf. Pull off the tough outer leaves and discard. Rub cut edges with lemon wedges. Cut artichokes in half lengthwise.

3. Bring a large pot of salted water to a boil and add lemon wedges. Add artichokes and simmer for 20–25 minutes or until a leaf pulls easily from the artichoke. Cool, then carefully remove choke with spoon.

4. Stuff artichokes with the cheese mixture. Place on serving plate; cover and chill for 2–4 hours before serving.

PER SERVING | Calories: 320 | Fat: 22g | Sodium: 540mg | Carbohydrates: 21g | Fiber: 8g | Protein: 11g

Beets with Beet Greens

This recipe takes the whole beet and transforms it into a combination vegetable side dish. It's full of soluble and insoluble fiber; the greens provide roughage and the beets themselves are loaded with soluble fiber and vitamins.

INGREDIENTS | **SERVES 4; SERVING SIZE 4 BEETS**

16 baby beets, greens attached
2 tablespoons butter
1 tablespoon fresh lemon juice
½ teaspoon salt

1. Wash beets but don't peel them.

2. Bring about 3" of water to a boil and then put the beets, root down, into the boiling water. Beet roots will be in the water and the greens will cook in the steam above the water.

3. Cover and cook for 12 minutes. Drain and cut the greens off the roots.

4. Chop the greens and peel the roots. (The skin will slip off easily.)

5. Put the beets, greens, and roots in a saucepan and add butter, lemon juice, and salt. Warm over low heat, and serve hot.

PER SERVING Calories: 210 | Fat: 6g | Sodium: 760mg | Carbohydrates: 35g | Fiber: 12g | Protein: 7g

Gingered Bok Choy and Tofu Stir-Fry

Dark leafy bok choy is a highly nutritious cruciferous vegetable that can be found in well-stocked groceries. Keep an eye out for light-green baby bok choy, which are a bit more tender but carry a similar flavor. Choy means "cabbage" in Chinese.

INGREDIENTS | SERVES 3

3 tablespoons soy sauce

2 tablespoons fresh lemon or lime juice

1 tablespoon ginger root, minced

1 (14-ounce block) firm or extra-firm tofu, well pressed

2 tablespoons olive oil

1 head bok choy or 3–4 small baby bok choy

½ teaspoon sugar

½ teaspoon sesame oil

1. In shallow pan, whisk together soy sauce, lemon or lime juice, and ginger. Cut tofu into cubes and marinate for at least 1 hour. Drain, reserving marinade.

2. In a large skillet or wok, sauté tofu in olive oil for 3–4 minutes.

3. Carefully add reserved marinade, bok choy, and sugar, stirring well to combine.

4. Cook, stirring, for 3–4 more minutes, or until bok choy is done.

5. Drizzle with sesame oil, and serve over rice.

PER SERVING Calories: 270 | Fat: 18g | Sodium: 1190mg | Carbohydrates: 11g | Fiber: 5g | Protein: 22g

It's Easy Being Green!

Learn to love your leafy greens! Pound for pound and calorie for calorie, dark, leafy green vegetables are the most nutritious food on the planet! Try a variety of greens: bok choy, collard greens, spinach, kale, mustard greens, Swiss chard, and watercress. When you find one or two that you like, sneak it in as many meals as you can!

Broccoli and Tomatoes in Anchovy Sauce

The broccoli and tomatoes can be tossed with the sauce and served as a side dish, or the whole thing can be combined with cooked angel-hair pasta and served with a fresh green salad and a hunk of country whole-grain bread.

INGREDIENTS | SERVES 4

⅓ cup olive oil

3 cloves garlic

6 anchovy fillets or 2 tablespoons anchovy paste

½ cup fresh parsley, stems removed

1 pound broccoli florets

2 large, ripe tomatoes

½ cup grated Romano cheese

Salt, to taste

What Does Water Sauté Mean?

When you want a quick, fat free way to cook vegetables while still retaining flavor and nutrients, a water sauté is the way to go. Simply pour 1"–2" of water into a skillet, add the chopped vegetables, cover, and bring to a low simmer. Cook until the vegetables are just tender, then cool under running water and set aside until ready to use.

1. In a mortar and pestle or food processor, combine the oil, garlic, anchovies, and parsley; process to a loose paste. Add more oil as needed for consistency.

2. Steam or water sauté the broccoli until just tender. Remove from the heat; place in a medium-size bowl.

3. Quarter and chop tomatoes; add to the broccoli.

4. Spoon anchovy sauce into the broccoli and tomatoes; toss gently to coat.

5. Sprinkle with Romano cheese, add salt as desired, and serve.

PER SERVING Calories: 260 | Fat: 21g | Sodium: 1220mg | Carbohydrates: 12g | Fiber: 5g | Protein: 8g

Broccoli Raab with Pine Nuts

Make sure to blanch the broccoli before beginning the recipe.

INGREDIENTS | **SERVES 4**

¾ pound broccoli raab, cooked

1 tablespoon olive oil

4 cloves garlic, chopped

¼ cup sundried tomatoes, chopped

2 tablespoons pine nuts

¼ teaspoon salt

¼ teaspoon crushed red pepper

Preventing Bitter Broccoli Raab

Broccoli raab and other leafy greens (mustard or collard greens) can have a bitter taste once cooked. Rather than add extra salt to offset bitterness, this recipe calls for blanching 2 minutes, which helps reduce bitterness. Blanching should be done as quickly as possible by starting with water at full rolling boil, then removing after 2 minutes of boiling. If allowed to cook too long, boiling process will reduce amount of water-soluble nutrients found in vegetables.

1. Rinse broccoli raab well and trim stems. Loosely chop leafy parts, then blanch in 2 quarts boiling water 2 minutes. Drain well.

2. Heat olive oil in large skillet; add garlic. Sauté garlic 1–2 minutes.

3. Add cooked broccoli. Toss garlic and broccoli together well, so that oil and garlic are mixed evenly.

4. Add remaining ingredients; cook additional 2–3 minutes, until broccoli is tender.

PER SERVING Calories: 110 | Fat: 8g | Sodium: 229mg | Carbohydrates: 6g | Fiber: 4g | Protein: 5g

Southwestern Sprouts

*Brussels sprouts are like little cabbages, but with more flavor
and packed with cancer-fighting phytonutrients.*

INGREDIENTS | SERVES 4

1 pound Brussels sprouts, trimmed and halved

1 tablespoon olive oil

1 tablespoon taco seasoning, or to taste

½ cup crushed spicy taco chips

½ cup Super Spicy Salsa (Chapter 12)

½ cup shredded Cheddar cheese

½ cup sunflower seeds (optional)

1. Preheat the oven to 350°F.

2. Toss the sprouts with the oil and taco seasoning and put in a roasting pan.

3. Cook for about 30 minutes, or until the sprouts become tender.

4. Put them in a serving bowl and toss with the taco chips, salsa, cheese, and sunflower seeds, if using. Serve hot.

PER SERVING Calories: 390 | Fat: 24g | Sodium: 510mg | Carbohydrates: 35g | Fiber: 8g | Protein: 14g

Sautéed Fennel with Lemon

Fennel has a licorice taste and, like most root vegetables, gets sweeter the longer it's cooked.

INGREDIENTS | SERVES 4

2 fennel bulbs

2 tablespoons olive oil

1 lemon, sliced

⅛ teaspoon salt

⅛ teaspoon black pepper

2 tablespoons water

2 tablespoons fresh lemon juice

1. Trim fronds and ends from fennel bulbs and remove outer layer. Cut the bulb into quarters lengthwise.

2. Heat olive oil in large pan over medium heat. Add fennel and sauté, stirring occasionally, for 5 minutes.

3. Add lemon, salt, pepper, water, and lemon juice. Bring to a simmer, then cover, and simmer over low heat for 10 minutes until fennel is tender. Serve immediately.

PER SERVING Calories: 110 | Fat: 7g | Sodium: 135mg | Carbohydrates: 10g | Fiber: 4g | Protein: 1g

Curried Cauliflower

Cauliflower is mild and nutty and adapts well to almost any spice or herb. Roasted with curry, it becomes tender and spicy. Cauliflower is another cruciferous vegetable, and provides cancer-fighting benefits.

INGREDIENTS | SERVES 4

1 cauliflower, cut into florets
1 onion, chopped
2 cloves garlic, minced
1 tablespoon olive oil
1 tablespoon butter
2–3 teaspoons curry powder
¼ teaspoon salt
⅛ teaspoon white pepper
1 tablespoon apple cider vinegar

1. Preheat oven to 400°F.

2. Place cauliflower, onion, and garlic in roasting pan and toss to mix.

3. In a small saucepan, combine remaining ingredients; heat over low heat until butter melts.

4. Drizzle butter mixture over vegetables and toss to coat. Roast for 25–35 minutes or until cauliflower is tender when pierced with a knife. Serve immediately.

PER SERVING Calories: 130 | Fat: 7g | Sodium: 230mg | Carbohydrates: 18g | Fiber: 6g | Protein: 5g

Cauliflower's Health Benefits

Phenethyl isothiocyanate is the compound in cauliflower that helps lower your risk of cancer. It is released when food is chopped, chewed, or otherwise exposed to the enzymes that release it.

Eggplant with Romesco Sauce

This dish gets its Catalonian flavor from grilled eggplant slices, puréed roasted red bell peppers, and ground almonds. To add protein, you can sprinkle some grated Manchego cheese on top or add more fiber with snipped fresh herbs, such as parsley or oregano.

INGREDIENTS | SERVES 4; SERVING SIZE 3 SLICES

1 eggplant
3 tablespoons kosher salt
¾ cup roasted red bell pepper
¼ cup toasted sliced almonds
1 clove peeled garlic
1½ teaspoons red wine vinegar
1½ teaspoons paprika
¼ teaspoon cayenne pepper
½ teaspoon salt
½ cup olive oil, divided

Eggplant Facts

Any big eggplant will do for frying or baking. Most cooks today find the tiny eggplants and their wonderful range of colors easier to deal with because they don't need soaking to reduce the bitterness like large eggplants. Smaller versions don't need peeling, and you get added fiber by eating the tender skins.

1. Slice the eggplant into ½"-thick rounds and place them in a colander over a bowl or in the sink. Sprinkle kosher salt over the eggplant and let sit for 30 minutes.

2. Meanwhile, make the romesco sauce by putting the roasted red bell peppers in a food processor with the almonds, garlic, vinegar, paprika, cayenne, and salt. Purée. Add ¼ cup olive oil while the motor is running.

3. Rinse the eggplant and drain on paper towels. Blot dry and brush with remaining olive oil.

4. Grill the eggplant on a preheated grill or grill pan for about 5 minutes per side.

5. Place half of the grilled eggplant on a platter and spoon half of the sauce over it. Top with the remaining eggplant rounds and spoon the remaining sauce over the top.

PER SERVING Calories: 330 | Fat: 31g | Sodium: 5530mg | Carbohydrates: 11g | Fiber: 6g | Protein: 3g

Green Bean Almondine

Fresh green beans are so much tastier than the frozen or canned varieties! Try preparing them with almonds and mushrooms with this easy, rhyming green bean almondine. Almondine is an Americanization of the French word amandine; *sometimes you find dishes made with almonds spelled amandine.*

INGREDIENTS | SERVES 4

1 pound fresh green beans, trimmed and chopped

2 tablespoons olive oil

⅓ cup sliced almonds

¾ cup sliced mushrooms

½ yellow onion, chopped

½ teaspoon fresh lemon juice

Green Beans

Green beans are a wonderful source of vitamins A and C, both antioxidants. They stop cholesterol from oxidizing, which can slow plaque formation in your arteries. They're also a good source of fiber, potassium, and magnesium. Don't overcook the beans; they're best cooked until crisp-tender. They'll also retain more color cooked that way.

1. Boil green beans in water for just 3–4 minutes; do not overcook. Alternately, you can steam them for 4–5 minutes. Drain and rinse under cold water.

2. In pan, heat olive oil over medium heat. Add almonds, mushrooms, and onion; heat 3–4 minutes, stirring frequently.

3. Add green beans and lemon juice and heat for another 1–2 minutes.

PER SERVING Calories: 150 | Fat: 11g | Sodium: 0mg | Carbohydrates: 11g | Fiber: 5g | Protein: 4g

Stir-Fried Green Beans with
Asian Eggplant, Garlic, and Fried Tofu

This stir-fry works well as a topping over steamed brown rice.

INGREDIENTS | SERVES 4

2 tablespoons soy sauce, or more to taste

1 tablespoon arrowroot

1 tablespoon agave syrup

2 teaspoons toasted sesame oil

1 cup water

3 tablespoons canola oil

1 tablespoon minced garlic

1 tablespoon minced ginger

1 pound green beans, trimmed

1 Chinese or Japanese eggplant, cut into 2" long pieces

3 Thai eggplants, quartered

1 (9-ounce) package fried tofu, cut into small pieces

1 bunch scallions, trimmed

1. Mix the soy sauce, arrowroot, agave, sesame oil, and water together and set aside.

2. Heat canola oil in a large wok or skillet over medium-high heat. Add the garlic and ginger and stir-fry for 30 seconds.

3. Add the beans, eggplants, tofu, and scallions and stir-fry for 2–3 minutes. If the mixture seems too dry, add a little water.

4. Stir in the soy sauce mixture and stir to coat vegetables. Keep stirring for about 2 more minutes, or until vegetables are crisp-tender. Remove from the heat and serve.

PER SERVING Calories: 420 | Fat: 26g | Sodium: 520mg | Carbohydrates: 38g | Fiber: 13g | Protein: 17g

About Asian Eggplants

The general eggplant category known as Asian eggplant includes the long, slender, pale purple variety used in Chinese cooking and the slightly plumper and darker purple ones favored in Japan. Thais also favor a small, round, green or white eggplant that resembles plump golf balls or very small green ones that resemble peas. Look for these eggplants in well-stocked supermarkets or in Asian groceries.

Mango and Bell Pepper Stir-Fry

Add some marinated tofu to make it a main dish, or enjoy just the mango and veggies for a light lunch. Use thawed frozen cubed mango if you can't find fresh.

INGREDIENTS | SERVES 4

2 tablespoons lime juice

2 tablespoons orange juice

1 tablespoon hot chili sauce

3 tablespoons soy sauce

2 cloves garlic, minced

2 tablespoons canola oil

1 red bell pepper

1 yellow or orange bell pepper

1 bunch broccoli, chopped

1 mango, cubed

3 scallions, chopped

1. Whisk together the lime juice, orange juice, hot sauce, and soy sauce.

2. Heat garlic in oil for just 1–2 minutes. Add bell peppers and broccoli and cook, stirring frequently, for another 2–3 minutes. Add juice and soy sauce mixture, reduce heat, and cook for another 2–3 minutes until broccoli and bell peppers are almost soft.

3. Reduce heat to low, and add mango and scallions, gently stirring to combine. Heat for just another 1–2 minutes, until mango is warmed.

PER SERVING Calories: 190 | Fat: 8g | Sodium: 820mg | Carbohydrates: 27g | Fiber: 7g | Protein: 7g

Mustard Greens and Lemon Sauté

Pungent mustard greens nourish lung function. These health-promoting greens are another example of vegetables from the cruciferous family. They have also been shown to protect against rheumatoid arthritis, cancer, memory loss, osteoporosis, and cardiovascular disorders.

INGREDIENTS | SERVES 4

1 bunch mustard greens, chopped

2 teaspoons sesame oil

2 tablespoons spring water

Fresh lemon juice, to taste

¼ cup walnuts, toasted and chopped

1. In a skillet, sauté greens in oil for 2 minutes. Add water. Bring to boil, lower heat, and simmer, covered, 2 minutes.

2. Season with lemon juice; garnish with walnuts.

PER SERVING Calories: 82 | Fat: 7g | Sodium: 14mg | Carbohydrate: 4g | Fiber: 2g | Protein: 3g

Roasted Kale

You can slice up some collard greens or Swiss chard as a substitute for kale, or mix them all together for a tasty medley. Both vegetables are part of the cruciferous family and are packed full of cancer-fighting phytonutrients.

INGREDIENTS | **SERVES 2**

6 cups kale
1 tablespoon olive oil
1 teaspoon garlic powder
1 teaspoon sea salt

1. Preheat oven to 375°F.

2. Wash and trim kale by pulling leaves off the tough stems or running a sharp knife down the length of the stem.

3. Place leaves in a medium-size bowl; toss with olive oil and garlic powder.

4. Roast for 5 minutes; turn kale over and roast another 7–10 minutes, until kale turns brown and becomes paper thin and brittle.

5. Remove from oven and sprinkle with salt. Serve immediately.

PER SERVING Calories: 170 | Fat: 8g | Sodium: 1250mg | Carbohydrates: 21g | Fiber: 4g | Protein: 7g

Parsnip Curry

Related to carrots, parsnips are even more fibrous and have a stronger flavor. They are a winter vegetable that contains a huge amount of vitamin A.

INGREDIENTS	SERVES 4; SERVING SIZE 2½ CUPS

3 tablespoons canola oil

2 minced cloves garlic

1 tablespoon grated ginger root

1 teaspoon minced fresh red chili pepper

6" lemongrass stalk, thinly sliced

1 cup diced onion

⅓ cup tomato paste

1½ cups coconut milk

½ cup Chicken Stock (Chapter 3)

2 pounds parsnips, peeled and cubed

3 tablespoons light soy sauce

1 teaspoon grated lime zest

3 tablespoons fresh lime juice

2 tablespoons chopped cilantro

4 cups steamed jasmine rice

1. In large pot, heat the oil on medium. Add the garlic, ginger, red chili pepper, lemongrass, and onion and sauté for 10 minutes.

2. Add the tomato paste; stir well.

3. Add the coconut milk, chicken stock, and parsnips. Bring to a boil, then reduce and simmer for about 15 minutes, until the parsnips are tender.

4. Add soy sauce, lime zest, lime juice, and cilantro. Stir and remove from heat.

5. Pour curry into soup tureen or large serving bowl. Put the steamed jasmine rice on a serving platter and serve it with the curry.

PER SERVING Calories: 650 | Fat: 30g | Sodium: 920mg | Carbohydrates: 92g | Fiber: 15g | Protein: 10g

Winter Vegetables

Winter vegetables got their name because they could keep in a root cellar or cold pantry over the winter. They include parsnips, carrots, cabbages, Brussels sprouts, and onions. Apples keep well in a cool place, too, and were dried for use as long as 300 years ago. People tended to use milk only for cheese and butter, so the juice of winter fruit slaked thirsts instead.

Snow Peas with Shallots

Snow peas are completely edible, pod and all. You can usually find them fully prepped in the produce aisle.

INGREDIENTS | SERVES 4

1 pound snow peas
2 tablespoons olive oil
4 shallots, minced
½ pound cremini mushrooms, sliced
2 tablespoons sherry vinegar
1 teaspoon fresh lemon juice

Cleaning Mushrooms

Use a soft, slightly dampened cloth to wipe off the mushrooms; do not rinse them or soak to clean because they'll soak up the water. You may want to trim off the bottoms of the stems because they can be slightly tough.

1. Trim off ends of snow peas and pull strings, if necessary.

2. In large saucepan, heat olive oil over medium heat. Add shallots, snow peas, and mushrooms; stir-fry for 3–5 minutes or until vegetables are crisp-tender.

3. Stir in vinegar and lemon juice, then remove from heat and serve immediately.

PER SERVING Calories: 210 | Fat: 7g | Sodium: 25mg | Carbohydrates: 24g | Fiber: 4g | Protein: 6g

Ginger and Orange Garden Veggies

When you cook snow peas in their pod, you preserve a truckload of fiber and the peas' natural flavor!

INGREDIENTS | SERVES 6

1 teaspoon ground ginger
½ teaspoon sugar
½ teaspoon all-purpose seasoning
1 clove garlic, minced
1 tablespoon soy sauce
1 tablespoon olive oil
1 teaspoon arrowroot
½ cup fresh orange juice
1 cup red onions, chopped
3 cups broccoli chunks
2 cups cauliflower chunks
2 cups carrot chunks
2 cups snow peas in pod

1. Mix ginger, sugar, all-purpose seasoning, garlic, soy sauce, olive oil, arrowroot, and orange juice in a large bowl.

2. Add all vegetables and mix well to coat veggies.

3. Place vegetables in a steamer and cook for 8–12 minutes, or until tender.

PER SERVING Calories: 110 | Fat: 3g | Sodium: 270mg | Carbohydrates: 20g | Fiber: 5g | Protein: 5g

Chili Fries

This recipe can be doubled; bake it on 2 cookie sheets, rotating the sheets in the oven halfway through the cooking time.

INGREDIENTS | SERVES 4–6

4 russet potatoes

2 tablespoons olive oil

2 tablespoons chili powder

1 tablespoon grill seasoning such as McCormick Mesquite Grill Seasoning

1 teaspoon ground cumin

1 teaspoon paprika

¼ teaspoon pepper

Grill Seasoning

Grill seasoning mixes usually contain pepper, garlic, salt, and a bit of sugar, along with spices like oregano and rosemary. There are quite a few different varieties, from Cajun spice to chili lime to chipotle. Read labels carefully, and choose a seasoning mix that has a low salt content.

1. Preheat oven to 425°F. Scrub potatoes and pat dry; cut into ½" strips, leaving skin on. A few strips won't have any skin. Toss with olive oil and arrange in single layer on a large cookie sheet.

2. In small bowl, combine remaining ingredients and mix well. Sprinkle over potatoes and toss to coat. Arrange in single layer.

3. Bake for 35–45 minutes, turning once during baking time, until potatoes are deep golden brown and crisp. Serve immediately.

PER SERVING Calories: 250 | Fat: 8g | Sodium: 55mg | Carbohydrates: 40g | Fiber: 6g | Protein: 5g

Scalloped Potatoes with Aromatic Vegetables

Layered casseroles are a great choice to serve at potlucks or with simple meats like baked chicken or pork chops.

INGREDIENTS | SERVES 8

2 carrots, peeled and sliced

2 parsnips, peeled and sliced

3 russet potatoes, sliced

¼ cup olive oil

⅛ teaspoon salt

⅛ teaspoon white pepper

1 onion, finely chopped

4 cloves garlic, minced

⅓ cup grated Parmesan cheese

¾ cup dry breadcrumbs

1 cup milk

Aromatic Vegetables

Aromatic vegetables are so called because they give off a rich aroma when cooked. They include onions, garlic, celery, and carrots. They are used in most ethnic cuisines. The French mirepoix uses mostly onion, with celery and carrot. The Italian soffritto uses onion, garlic, and fennel. And the Cajun "holy trinity" includes celery, onion, and carrots.

1. Preheat oven to 375°F. Spray a 9" × 13" baking dish with nonstick cooking spray and set aside.

2. In large bowl, combine carrots, parsnips, and potatoes; drizzle with olive oil, sprinkle with salt and pepper, and toss to coat.

3. Layer vegetables in prepared baking dish, sprinkling each layer with onion, garlic, Parmesan, and finishing with breadcrumbs. Pour milk into casserole.

4. Cover tightly with foil. Bake for 45 minutes, then uncover. Bake for 15–25 minutes longer, or until vegetables are tender and top is browned. Serve immediately.

PER SERVING Calories: 250 | Fat: 10g | Sodium: 290mg | Carbohydrates: 38g | Fiber: 5g | Protein: 7g

Summer Swiss Chard

Both stalks and leaves are edible parts of the chard plant, and the stems can be separated and cooked separately for a different dish. Chard is rich in cancer fighting nutrients as it is a cruciferous vegetable. Chard adds a bit of spice to any dish.

INGREDIENTS | SERVES 4; SERVING SIZE: ½ CUP

1 pound Swiss chard
3 tablespoons olive oil
1 cup diced onion
Pinch of salt
½ teaspoon oregano
3 tablespoons red wine vinegar
Salt and pepper, to taste

1. Chop the chard and set aside.

2. Heat the olive oil in a skillet over medium heat. Add onion, salt, and oregano and cook until the onions are tender.

3. Add the chopped chard and sauté for a few minutes and then remove from heat.

4. Stir in the vinegar and season with salt and pepper to taste.

PER SERVING Calories: 130 | Fat: 11g | Sodium: 240mg | Carbohydrates: 8g | Fiber: 2g | Protein: 2g

Zucchini Stir-Fry

If you have a garden, you know August and September can mean bumper crops of zucchini and tomatoes. Use the proceeds in this easy side dish recipe.

INGREDIENTS | SERVES 4

2 tablespoons olive oil
2 cups sliced zucchini
2 shallots, minced
2 cups grape tomatoes, halved
½ teaspoon salt
⅛ teaspoon black pepper
½ teaspoon dried thyme leaves

1. In wok or large skillet, heat olive oil over medium-high heat. Add zucchini and shallots; stir-fry until crisp-tender, about 5–7 minutes.

2. Add tomatoes, salt, pepper, and thyme; stir-fry until hot and all vegetables are tender, about 3–5 minutes longer. Serve immediately.

PER SERVING Calories: 100 | Fat: 7g | Sodium: 300mg | Carbohydrates: 8g | Fiber: 2g | Protein: 2g

Mama's Ratatouille with Tofu

Ratatouille is a French vegetable stew. It's a combination of garden vegetables and root vegetables that originated with French peasants. By adding tofu, you increase the amount of protein while still maintaining the vegetarian aspect of the dish.

INGREDIENTS | SERVES 6

1 clove fresh garlic, minced
1 cup carrots, sliced
1 cup sweet potatoes, cubed
2 tablespoons dried basil
½ cup bell peppers, diced
1 cup tomatoes, diced
1 teaspoon all-purpose seasoning
1 teaspoon ground cumin
2 cups zucchini, sliced
2 cups squash, sliced
2 cups kale, chopped
2 cups tomato sauce
1 tablespoon dried thyme leaves
½ teaspoon black pepper
1 (16-ounce) package firm tofu, cubed

1. Add all ingredients to a large saucepan. Cook over medium-high heat until it boils.

2. Simmer for 20 minutes, or until sweet potatoes are tender.

PER SERVING Calories: 162 | Fat: 4g | Sodium: 548mg | Carbohydrates: 26g | Fiber: 6g | Protein: 11g

Veggie Enchiladas

Cooking vegetables until they brown caramelizes the sugars, creating rich and complex flavors. These enchiladas are different and delicious.

INGREDIENTS | SERVES 8

1 tablespoon olive oil
1 onion, chopped
1 (8-ounce) package sliced mushrooms
2 yellow summer squash, chopped
1 green bell pepper, chopped
1 red bell pepper, chopped
1 (17-ounce) can sweet potatoes, drained
1 teaspoon dried basil leaves
1 teaspoon dried thyme leaves
½ teaspoon salt
⅛ teaspoon black pepper
½ cup Chicken Stock (Chapter 3) or vegetable stock
3 cups tomato sauce
2 tablespoons taco seasoning
12 (6") corn tortillas
2 cups shredded Cheddar cheese

Enchiladas and Burritos

Enchiladas and burritos are similar, but differ in preparation. The fillings can be the same, but enchiladas are usually baked in a sauce and covered with cheese, while burritos are just filled and rolled corn or flour tortillas, baked or deep fried until crisp. They can be made with just about any filling—vegetarian, beef, chicken, or fish.

1. Preheat oven to 375°F.

2. In a large skillet, heat olive oil over medium heat. Add the onion; cook and stir until the onion starts to brown, about 8–10 minutes.

3. Add the mushrooms; cook and stir until tender, about 8 minutes longer.

4. Add the squash and bell peppers. Cook and stir until the liquid evaporates and vegetables begin to brown, about 7–9 minutes longer.

5. Place the sweet potatoes in medium bowl; add basil, thyme, salt, pepper, and stock. Mash using a potato masher until smooth.

6. In a medium bowl, combine tomato sauce and taco seasoning; stir until blended. Place ½ cup of the sauce mixture in bottom of a 13" × 9" baking dish.

7. Arrange the tortillas on a work surface. Spread with potato mixture, then divide the vegetable mixture on top. Roll up and place seam-side down in the sauce in a baking dish. Top with cheese.

8. Bake 30–40 minutes, or until casserole is bubbling.

PER SERVING Calories: 350 | Fat: 13g | Sodium: 840mg | Carbohydrates: 47g | Fiber: 7g | Protein: 14g

Italian Vegetable Bake

Basil and oregano are the classic Italian herbs that give unmistakable flavor to this healthy and colorful dish.

INGREDIENTS | SERVES 6

2 (14-ounce) cans diced tomatoes, undrained
1 onion, chopped
½ pound green beans, sliced
½ pound okra, cut into ½" lengths
1 chopped green bell pepper
2 tablespoons fresh lemon juice
1 tablespoon chopped fresh basil
1½ teaspoons fresh oregano leaves
3 medium zucchini, cut into 1" chunks
1 eggplant, peeled and cut into 1" cubes
2 tablespoons grated Parmesan cheese

1. Preheat oven to 325°F.

2. In a large baking dish, combine tomatoes and their liquid, onion, green beans, okra, bell pepper, lemon juice, basil, and oregano.

3. Cover with foil or lid; bake for 15 minutes.

4. Add zucchini and eggplant to baking dish, cover, and continue to bake, stirring occasionally, until vegetables are tender, about 1 hour.

5. Sprinkle with Parmesan cheese and bake, uncovered, for 10 minutes longer, or until cheese melts and casserole is bubbly. Serve immediately.

PER SERVING Calories: 110 | Fat: 1g | Sodium: 95mg | Carbohydrates: 23g | Fiber: 9g | Protein: 6g

CHAPTER 11

Salads

Avocado Grapefruit Salad

This pretty pink and green salad is studded with jewels of ruby pomegranate seeds. Pomegranates are loaded with protective phytochemicals, which include antioxidants. Try to incorporate them into different salads and desserts.

INGREDIENTS | SERVES 4

2 avocados

1 ruby red grapefruit

¼ cup pomegranate seeds

1 tablespoon minced shallot

¼ cup olive oil

1 tablespoon pomegranate juice

Salt and black pepper, to taste

Grenadine

The pomegranate used in this salad recipe is a source of ruby red juice. Grenadine is a tart-sweet syrup that is made from pomegranate juice and sugar. It is used to make mixed drinks, including the nonalcoholic Shirley Temple and Roy Rogers. Try mixing a little grenadine in your lemonade.

1. Cut the avocados in half and remove the pits. Cut the avocado halves, still in the skin, into long thin strips. Scoop the meat out of the skins with a large spoon. Fan the strips out on a serving plate.

2. Peel the grapefruit. Cut sections off the grapefruit with a sharp knife.

3. Squeeze the juice from some of the grapefruit sections onto the avocados. Scatter the remaining grapefruit sections over the avocados. Sprinkle pomegranate seeds over top.

4. Whisk the shallot, olive oil, pomegranate juice, salt, and pepper together in a bowl.

5. Drizzle the mixture over the salad, and serve at room temperature.

PER SERVING Calories: 340 | Fat: 29g | Sodium: 10mg | Carbohydrates: 21g | Fiber: 8g | Protein: 3g

Kale Fennel Salad

Toasted pumpkin seeds add a nice touch of fall to this deliciously nutritious salad.

INGREDIENTS | **SERVES 4**

1 bunch kale

1 bulb fennel

1 teaspoon anchovy paste or 3 anchovy fillets

1 shallot

¼ cup olive oil

2 tablespoons balsamic vinegar

½ teaspoon garlic powder

1 teaspoon agave syrup

2 tablespoons mayonnaise

¼ cup toasted pumpkin seeds

1. Wash and drain the kale. Run a sharp knife down the length of the stem to remove the leaf and set aside.

2. Cover the bottom of a large skillet with ½" of water; set kale into the pan. Cover, bring to a boil, reduce heat, and simmer until kale is tender but still bright green.

3. While kale is cooking, slice the fennel into narrow strips and set aside.

4. In a blender or using a mortar and pestle, combine anchovy, shallot, oil, vinegar, garlic, agave, and mayonnaise; mix to a dressing consistency.

5. Rinse cooked kale under cool water, drain, and press out water. Chop kale well; place in a medium-size salad bowl along with the fennel.

6. Spoon dressing over salad; toss well, or serve dressing on the side and serve salad on individual plates.

7. Top with toasted pumpkin seeds before eating.

PER SERVING Calories: 280 | Fat: 21g | Sodium: 540mg | Carbohydrates: 22g | Fiber: 3g | Protein: 5g

Lentil Rice Salad

This hearty salad is popular in France and is appearing in gourmet stores and delis in the United States. Curry not only gives the dish a delicious flavor, but is also full of cancer-fighting spices and herbs.

INGREDIENTS | SERVES 8–10

3 tablespoons fresh lemon juice

1 tablespoon white-wine vinegar

1 tablespoon sesame oil

¼ cup olive oil

⅓ cup mayonnaise

1–2 tablespoons curry powder

⅓ teaspoon black pepper

4 green onions, sliced

¼ cup chopped flat-leaf parsley

1 (16-ounce) package lentils

1 cup brown rice

2 red bell peppers, chopped

½ cup red onion, chopped

1. In large bowl, combine lemon juice, vinegar, sesame oil, olive oil, mayonnaise, curry powder, pepper, onions, and parsley; mix well. Cover and refrigerate.

2. Pick over lentils and rinse; cover with cold water and cook according to package directions.

3. Meanwhile, cook rice according to package directions.

4. As soon as lentils and rice are cooked, add to mayonnaise mixture along with bell peppers and onion.

5. Stir the salad to coat all ingredients. Cover and refrigerate for 2–4 hours before serving.

PER SERVING Calories: 230 | Fat: 17g | Sodium: 120mg | Carbohydrates: 18g | Fiber: 6g | Protein: 5g

Grilled Steak Salad

*Any fresh vegetable adds flavor, nutrition, and color to this pretty salad;
use sliced mushrooms or sugar snap peas if you'd like.*

INGREDIENTS | SERVES 4

2 Savory Grilled Steaks (Chapter 7)
1 red bell pepper, chopped
1 cucumber, peeled and sliced
4 cups baby spinach leaves
2 cups watercress
½ cup Vinaigrette (Chapter 12)

Cucumbers

Cucumbers belong to the watermelon family. They are about 95 percent water and are very refreshing to eat. They contain vitamin C, as well as potassium and magnesium. They are usually sold with a wax coating, which is why they are peeled before use. Look for English cucumbers, which are not waxed, to use the peel for more fiber. Some people find cucumber a little difficult to digest; adding a little salt to the slices draws the fluid out and makes them more digestible.

1. If the steaks are cold, let stand at room temperature for 30 minutes, no longer. Slice thinly against grain.

2. Combine in a serving bowl with the bell pepper, cucumber, spinach, and watercress.

3. Drizzle half of the Vinaigrette over the salad and toss to coat. Serve with remaining dressing on the side.

PER SERVING Calories: 370 | Fat: 29g | Sodium: 190mg | Carbohydrates: 9g | Fiber: 3g | Protein: 17g

Couscous Fruit and Nut Salad

Don't be alarmed by the long list of ingredients. This salad comes together in minutes, and bursts with so much flavor and texture you will want to serve it often.

INGREDIENTS | **SERVES 4–6**

1 (10-ounce) box quick-cooking couscous

1 cup chopped fresh flat-leaf parsley

1 cup cashews

½ cup raisins

½ cup cubed dried papaya

½ cup chopped dates

½ cup diced dried figs

½ cup chopped dried apricots

3 kiwifruit, peeled and sliced

½ red onion, diced

1 (6-ounce) container lime yogurt

2 tablespoons balsamic vinegar

1 tablespoon olive oil

Creole seasoning salt, to taste

Fresh mint leaves, for garnish

1. Cook the couscous according to package directions and when it is cool add to the salad bowl.

2. Meanwhile, add the parsley, cashews, raisins, papaya, dates, figs, apricots, kiwifruit, and red onion to the bowl and stir to combine.

3. Whisk together the yogurt, vinegar, and olive oil and toss with the salad ingredients.

4. Season with the Creole seasoning salt, garnish with mint leaves, and serve.

PER SERVING Calories: 560 | Fat: 14g | Sodium: 40mg | Carbohydrates: 102g | Fiber: 9g | Protein: 13g

What Is Kiwifruit?

A fuzzy, small, oval fruit, the kiwifruit is a native of New Zealand, and was apparently named after the country's national pride, the kiwi bird. Its inner green flesh contains little black seeds and offers a bright, slightly tart flavor. It's commonly called just kiwi outside of New Zealand.

Minted Lentil and Tomato Salad

This recipe needs to be refrigerated for several hours before serving to allow the flavors to mingle.

INGREDIENTS | SERVES 6

1 cup dry lentils

2 cups water

½ cup onion, chopped

2 teaspoons garlic, minced

¼ cup celery, chopped

½ cup green pepper, chopped

½ cup parsley, finely chopped

2 tablespoons fresh mint, finely chopped, or 2 teaspoons dried

¼ cup fresh lemon juice

¼ cup olive oil

½ teaspoon salt

1 cup fresh tomato, diced

1. Place lentils and water in medium-size saucepan; bring to quick boil. Reduce heat; cover and cook on low 15–20 minutes, or until tender. Drain and transfer to medium bowl.

2. Add onion, garlic, celery, green pepper, parsley and mint; mix well.

3. In small bowl, whisk together lemon juice, olive oil, and salt. Pour into lentils; mix well. Cover and refrigerate several hours. Before serving, mix in diced tomatoes.

PER SERVING Calories: 136 | Fat: 9g | Sodium: 211mg | Carbohydrates: 11g | Fiber: 4g | Protein: 4g

Tomatoes Stuffed with Quinoa Salad

The flavors of the Mediterranean are not only delicious, but also good for you! Many consider the Mediterranean diet to be one of the healthiest due to the focus on plant-based foods.

INGREDIENTS | SERVES 6

½ cup quinoa

1 cup water

6 large (3 pounds) tomatoes

1½ cups cucumber, peeled and finely diced

⅓ cup fresh parsley, chopped

¼ cup fresh mint, chopped

½ cup red onion, finely chopped

3 tablespoons feta cheese, crumbled

2 tablespoons fresh lemon juice

3 tablespoons olive oil

1. Rinse quinoa in fine mesh strainer before cooking. To cook, place quinoa and water in small saucepan; bring to a boil. Reduce heat; cover and cook until all water is absorbed, about 15 minutes. Cool.

2. To prepare tomatoes, remove caps and hollow out, leaving shell about ½" thick. In mixing bowl, combine quinoa, cucumbers, parsley, mint, onion, and feta.

3. Mix lemon juice and olive oil together; pour over quinoa and vegetables. Stuff tomatoes with mixture, and serve.

PER SERVING Calories: 180 | Fat: 9g | Sodium: 78mg | Carbohydrates: 24g | Fiber: 4g | Protein: 5g

Marinated Roasted Peppers and Eggplant

You can use zucchini or yellow squash in place of eggplant. Other herb choices for the marinade include basil, thyme, or savory. Use marinated vegetables on top of tossed salads or with grilled London broil.

INGREDIENTS | **SERVES 4**

1 pound sweet red peppers

1 large eggplant, sliced into ¼" thick rounds

4 tablespoons olive oil, divided

1 tablespoon balsamic vinegar

1 tablespoon onion, finely chopped

1 teaspoon dried oregano

Black pepper, to taste

Roasting Red Peppers

The traditional method of roasting a red pepper is to use a long-handled fork to hold the pepper over the open flame of a gas burner until it is charred. Of course, there are a variety of other methods as well. You can place the pepper on a rack set over an electric burner and turn it occasionally, until the skin is blackened. This should take about 4 to 6 minutes. You can also put the pepper over direct heat on a preheated grill. Use tongs to turn the pepper occasionally. Another method is to broil the pepper on a broiler rack about 2 inches from the heat, turning the pepper every 5 minutes. Total broiling time will be about 15 to 20 minutes, or until the skins are blistered and charred. The key to peeling the peppers is letting them sit in their steam in a closed container until they are cool. Once the peppers are cool, the skin will rub or peel off easily.

1. Follow procedure for roasting red peppers in sidebar. Set aside. Brush eggplant slices with 2 tablespoons olive oil; place on grill. Grill on both sides for about 5 minutes each, until softened.

2. Remove from grill and place in container. Add roasted peppers to container.

3. Prepare marinade by whisking together balsamic vinegar, 2 tablespoons olive oil, chopped onion, oregano, and pepper; pour over vegetables. Cover and refrigerate.

PER SERVING Calories: 179 | Fat: 14g | Sodium: 5mg | Carbohydrates: 14g | Fiber: 6g | Protein: 2g

Spinach Salad with Pomegranate

Tired of getting messy with pomegranates? Try opening in a bowl of water; the seeds should rise to the top, and if any burst, the mess will get dumped out with the water rather than on your shirt!

INGREDIENTS | SERVES 6

1 pound fresh spinach
½ cup red onion, very thinly sliced
8 ounces fresh tomatoes, cut into ½"
wedges
⅓ cup walnuts, chopped
½ teaspoon salt
¼ cup fresh lemon juice
1½ tablespoons olive oil
¼ cup pomegranate seeds

For a Different Twist: Toasted Almond Seasoning

Add an extra flavor dimension to salads, rice dishes, or vegetables by sprinkling toasted almonds over the top. Toast ½ cup ground raw almonds in a nonstick skillet over low heat, stirring frequently, until they are a light brown color. Store the cooled almonds in an airtight container in a cool, dry place.

1. Wash spinach thoroughly and drain well; loosely chop.

2. Add onions, tomato, and walnuts; toss lightly.

3. In small bowl, whisk together salt, lemon juice, and olive oil. Drizzle over salad; toss lightly.

4. Garnish salad with pomegranate seeds.

PER SERVING Calories: 107 | Fat: 8g | Sodium: 259mg | Carbohydrates: 8g | Fiber: 3g | Protein: 4g

Red Lettuce Jicama Salad

Jicama is a tropical tuber, the root of a legume. It is slightly sweet and very crisp, and almost always eaten raw.

INGREDIENTS | SERVES 4

½ pound jicama
1 head red lettuce, shredded
1 head radicchio, thinly sliced
½ red onion, thinly sliced
½ cup Balsamic Vinaigrette (Chapter 12)

1. In a large salad bowl, combine jicama with lettuce, radicchio, and onion and toss gently.

2. Drizzle with vinaigrette, and serve immediately.

PER SERVING Calories: 240 | Fat: 21g | Sodium: 150mg | Carbohydrates: 10g | Fiber: 4g | Protein: 2g

Taming Onions

Onion tastes very sharp and can overwhelm a recipe. By simmering an onion in water with a bit of sugar, the sulfur compounds escape into the air, making it very mild, almost sweet. You can do this with any onion, but it works especially well with sliced onions used in sandwiches.

Mandarin Snap Pea Salad

Asked to bring a salad to a potluck? This is a fresh take on the boring side dish. People will love it!

INGREDIENTS | SERVES 8

¾ pound snap peas, cut into ½" pieces
1 cup canned mandarin oranges, drained
1½ cups canned kidney beans, rinsed and drained
1 cup red onion, thinly sliced
½ cup fresh parsley, chopped
2 cups cabbage, chopped
⅓ cup poppy and chia seed dressing (recipe in sidebar)

1. In medium bowl, combine peas, oranges, kidney beans, onions, parsley, and cabbage.

2. Mix in poppy seed dressing; refrigerate several hours before serving.

PER SERVING Calories: 76 | Fat: 0g | Sodium: 344mg | Carbohydrates: 16g | Fiber: 4g | Protein: 4g

Poppy and Chia Seed Dressing

Combine ½ cup red wine vinegar, ¼ cup orange juice, 3 tablespoons lemon juice, ½ cup canola oil, 1 teaspoon sugar, 1 teaspoon dry mustard, 1 teaspoon salt, 1 tablespoon soaked chia seeds, and 1 tablespoon poppy seeds; mix well in covered jar. Store in refrigerator. Nutritional Analysis 1 ounce serving (1½ tablespoons): 100 Calories; Protein: 0g; Carbohydrates: 2g; Fat: 10g; Sodium: 190mg; Fiber: 0g.

Avocado and Peach Salad

When it comes to new herbs and spices, err on the side of caution. Not sure whether or not you like a seasoning? Mix all other ingredients together and test a bite of salad with pinch of herb or spice before adding it to entire recipe.

INGREDIENTS | SERVES 4

⅛ cup water

⅛ cup frozen orange juice concentrate

1 clove garlic, crushed

1 teaspoon rice wine vinegar

1 tablespoon chia seeds, soaked

1 tablespoon olive oil

½ teaspoon vanilla

1½ cups tightly packed baby arugula

2 tablespoons fresh tarragon leaves

1 avocado, peeled and diced

1 peach, peeled and diced

½ cup thinly sliced Vidalia onion

Salt and black pepper, to taste (optional)

1. In measuring cup, whisk water, orange juice concentrate, garlic, vinegar, chia seeds, oil, and vanilla together until well mixed.

2. Prepare salad by arranging layers of arugula and tarragon, then avocado, peach, and onions; drizzle with vinaigrette.

3. Season with salt and pepper, if desired, and serve.

PER SERVING Calories: 160 | Fat: 12g | Sodium: 5mg | Carbohydrates: 14g | Fiber: 5g | Protein: 2g

Preparing Avocados

It's not difficult to prepare an avocado; it just takes some practice. Cut the avocado in half lengthwise around the pit. Twist the halves to pull apart, then hit the pit with a chef's knife, twist, and pull out. Scoop the flesh out of the skin with a large spoon, then slice or dice as recipe directs.

Greek Pasta Salad

This is a nutritious and delicious salad for all year round.

INGREDIENTS | SERVES 4

1 tablespoon lemon juice

3 tablespoons olive oil

1 teaspoon dried oregano

1 teaspoon Dijon mustard

1 clove garlic, minced

2 cups cooked pasta

1 cup slivered almonds

1 cup sliced cucumber

1 cup diced tomato

½ cup chopped red onion

½ cup Greek olives

2 ounces crumbled feta cheese

1½ cups romaine lettuce leaves

1. In large salad bowl, whisk lemon juice with olive oil, oregano, mustard, and garlic. Cover and refrigerate 1 hour or up to 12 hours.

2. Immediately before serving, toss pasta with almonds, cucumbers, tomatoes, onions, olives, and feta cheese, and prepared dressing. Serve over lettuce.

PER SERVING Calories: 420 | Fat: 29g | Sodium: 312mg | Carbohydrates: 31g | Fiber: 6g | Protein: 12g

Taco Salad

You can have the toppings on hand so that each person can build their own taco salad to their liking.

INGREDIENTS | SERVES 8

1 recipe Turkey Chili with Veggies (Chapter 8)

8 cups tightly packed salad greens

8 ounces Cheddar cheese, shredded (to yield 2 cups)

8 ounces Baked Tortilla Chips (Chapter 9)

Vegetables of your choice, such as chopped celery, onion, or banana or jalapeño peppers (optional)

1. Prepare Turkey Chili with Veggies.

2. Divide salad greens between 8 large bowls.

3. Top with chili, Cheddar cheese, tortilla chips, and vegetables or peppers, if using.

PER SERVING Calories: 390 | Fat: 15g | Sodium: 1240mg | Carbohydrates: 50g | Fiber: 11g | Protein: 17g

Ultimate Garden Salad

Garden salads often get a bad rap because they are usually made with iceberg lettuce. It's certainly not bad for you, but it's not very nutritious, either. Stick with dark-leaf lettuce and pile on the veggies for a fabulous garden salad.

INGREDIENTS | SERVES 1

1 cup romaine lettuce

1 cup spinach

2 tablespoons diced bell peppers

2 tablespoons diced red onions

½ cup plum tomatoes

2 tablespoons diced cucumbers

1 tablespoon dried cranberries

½ cup broccoli florets

1 tablespoon peas

2 tablespoons carrots, shredded

1 tablespoon shredded Cheddar cheese

1 tablespoon balsamic vinegar

1. Combine all ingredients in a bowl.

2. Drizzle with balsamic vinegar.

PER SERVING Calories: 140 | Fat: 3g | Sodium: 150mg | Carbohydrates: 26g | Fiber: 6g | Protein: 6g

Red and White Bean Salad

Arugula has several other names such as rocket, rugula, roquette, and rucola. It is sometimes found in baby greens or mesclun mixes. It has nutty and peppery flavor, which can add interest to a salad or sandwich. Give arugula a try!

INGREDIENTS | SERVES 8

2 cups navy beans, cooked

2 cups red beans, cooked

1 cup arugula, chopped

¼ cup fresh lemon juice

3 tablespoons olive oil

¼ teaspoon pepper

1 cup red onion, thinly sliced

8 ounces cherry tomatoes, cut in half

1. Combine beans together in medium bowl.

2. Whisk together arugula, lemon juice, olive oil, and pepper; pour over beans.

3. Add onions; toss lightly to mix. Let mixture refrigerate at least 3 hours.

4. Just before serving, toss in cherry tomatoes; mix lightly.

PER SERVING Calories: 86 | Fat: 6g | Sodium: 7mg | Carbohydrates: 27g | Fiber: 7g | Protein: 8g

Tomato Arranged Salad

Tomatoes are so good for you, and delicious with this delicately flavored salad dressing. Serve this recipe in late summer when the fruit is at its peak.

INGREDIENTS | **SERVES 4**

2 red tomatoes

2 yellow tomatoes

3 plum tomatoes

1 cup grape tomatoes

¼ cup olive oil

2 tablespoons lemon juice

1 tablespoon honey

1 teaspoon curry powder

⅛ teaspoon pepper

¼ teaspoon salt

1. Core red, yellow, and plum tomatoes and slice ½" thick. Arrange on a serving plate; top with grape tomatoes.

2. In small bowl, combine remaining ingredients and mix with wire whisk until blended.

3. Drizzle over tomatoes and let stand 20 minutes, then serve.

PER SERVING Calories: 190 | Fat: 15g | Sodium: 180mg | Carbohydrates: 15g | Fiber: 2g | Protein: 2g

Tomatoes

If you aren't picking tomatoes out of your backyard or from a farmer's market, you can still get good tomatoes from the grocery store. Feel the tomatoes while you're sorting through them. The best tomatoes have thin, delicate skin and give slightly when pressed with a finger. Store tomatoes at room temperature for best flavor and texture.

Fruit Sparkle Salad

Any canned, frozen, or fresh fruits (except fresh pineapple) can be used in this quick and easy salad. It's great for breakfast as well as dinner.

INGREDIENTS | **SERVES 9**

2 (.25-ounce) packages unflavored gelatin

⅓ cup sugar

1 (13-ounce) can pineapple tidbits in light syrup

1 cup canned pineapple juice

1 cup sparkling water

1 cup sliced canned peaches, drained

1 cup red grapes, cut in half

1. In large bowl, combine gelatin with sugar; mix well.

2. Drain pineapple, reserving syrup.

3. In glass measuring cup, combine reserved pineapple syrup with enough pineapple juice and sparkling water to measure 2 cups. Pour ¾ cup of this mixture over gelatin mixture.

4. Microwave remaining liquid on 100 percent power 2–3 minutes, until it just comes to a boil. Pour over gelatin mixture; stir until gelatin and sugar dissolve completely.

5. Stir in sparkling water along with drained pineapple, peaches, and grapes.

6. Pour into a 2-quart, shallow glass casserole dish; refrigerate until firm. Cut into squares to serve.

PER SERVING Calories: 100 | Fat: 0g | Sodium: 10mg | Carbohydrates: 23g | Fiber: <1g | Protein: 2g

Roasted Vegetables with Walnut Parsley Sauce

Make extra sauce and toss with your favorite pasta or roasted potatoes.

INGREDIENTS | **SERVES 8**

1 onion
1 large zucchini
2 cups broccoli florets
2 cups cauliflower florets
7 small red skin potatoes
1 pound green beans
½ cup olive oil
1 cup raw walnuts
3 cloves garlic
1 cup fresh parsley
Sea salt, to taste

What's a Mortar and Pestle?

A mortar is a heavy, round bowl that, when used with a grinding tool or pestle, can mash food or grind it to a paste. When not available, use a food processor, but with a gentle pulsing-action effect for chopping, rather than a smooth purée.

1. Preheat oven to 400°F.

2. Chop onion, zucchini, broccoli, cauliflower, and potatoes into medium-size pieces. Trim green beans, but leave long.

3. Place vegetables in a large bowl; toss with ¼ cup olive oil to lightly coat.

4. Spread vegetables on a baking sheet; roast uncovered 20 minutes, or until potatoes are tender.

5. Meanwhile, grind walnuts in a mortar and pestle; add garlic, parsley, and sea salt and continue to grind.

6. Add remaining olive oil a bit at a time to moisten ingredients. (You can use a food processor, but use the pulsing action.) Sauce should be thick with walnuts, but wet with oil. To use on pasta, thin sauce with warm water before adding.

7. Spoon sauce into a serving bowl.

8. When vegetables are done, move them to a platter and top each serving with a dollop of sauce.

PER SERVING Calories: 360 | Fat: 23g | Sodium: 30mg | Carbohydrates: 34g | Fiber: 7g | Protein: 7g

Summer Salmon Salad

This salad is reminiscent of a Tuscan bread salad and needs a little time to marinate before serving. Allow the bread to soak up some of the dressing but not get too soggy.

INGREDIENTS | **SERVES 4**

1 large beefsteak tomato
½ cup fresh parsley
⅓ cup fresh basil
1 shallot
12 walnut halves
2 slices thick sour dough bread
1 (10-ounce) can salmon
Juice of ½ a lemon
2 tablespoons olive oil
½ cup fresh orange juice
1 teaspoon orange zest
½ teaspoon honey
2 tablespoons white wine vinegar
½ teaspoon balsamic vinegar
1 clove minced garlic
½ cup grated Romano cheese

Salmon Choices

As a substitute for canned salmon, poach some fresh salmon in vegetable broth and serve chilled on top of the tomato salad. If there is no salmon to be found, seared tuna fish will do, or try a piece of halibut or sea bass. The beauty of this salad is that it works no matter what protein you use.

1. Slice tomato into bite-size pieces; place in a medium-size ceramic bowl.

2. Mince parsley and basil until very fine; add to tomatoes.

3. Slice shallot into thin half moons; add to tomatoes.

4. Break walnuts into pieces with your hands; add to tomatoes.

5. Lightly toast bread; slice into bite-size cubes; add to tomatoes.

6. Open can of salmon and separate out skin and visible bones if needed; place in a bowl and squeeze some lemon over salmon. Set aside.

7. In a small bowl, whisk together oil, orange juice, zest, honey, vinegars, and garlic. Pour dressing over salad ingredients; toss well to cover. Set aside to marinate for 15 minutes.

8. Serve the salad on individual plates topped first with the salmon and then with the grated Romano cheese.

PER SERVING Calories: 420 | Fat: 18g | Sodium: 440mg | Carbohydrates: 40g | Fiber: 3g | Protein: 24g

Quinoa Black Bean Salad

For grain salads, the longer it marinates the better the flavors are absorbed by the ingredients. Make it the night before and take some to work for lunch the next day. Bring this salad along for a potluck meal, and watch how your friends enjoy something new and delicious.

INGREDIENTS | SERVES 8

1 cup quinoa

2 cups water

½ teaspoon sea salt

1 carrot

2 green onions

⅓ cup pumpkin seeds

½ cup parsley leaves

1 (14-ounce) can black beans

Juice of 1 lemon

1 clove minced garlic

2 tablespoons apple cider vinegar

3 tablespoons olive oil

½ teaspoon salt

Toasting Pumpkin Seeds

Raw pumpkin seeds can be toasted in a dry skillet over medium-low heat. Keep them moving around by shaking the pan from time to time or stirring them with a wooden spoon. You'll know they are done when they've stopped popping or turned a golden brown.

1. In a medium saucepan, combine quinoa, water, and ½ teaspoon sea salt. Cover, bring to a boil, reduce heat to low, and simmer until all water is absorbed, about 20 minutes.

2. When done, spoon into a large bowl and allow to cool.

3. Meanwhile, grate carrots, slice onions, toast pumpkin seeds, mince parsley, and rinse canned beans.

4. When quinoa is cool, add carrots, green onions, pumpkin seeds, black beans, and parsley; mix well.

5. In a small bowl, whisk together lemon, garlic, vinegar, oil, and salt.

6. Add vinaigrette; mix completely and allow to marinate a few minutes before serving.

PER SERVING Calories: 190 | Fat: 7g | Sodium: 340mg | Carbohydrates: 26g | Fiber: 5g | Protein: 6g

Spinach Fruit Salad

This sweet and tangy salad dressing is good on any mixed greens. Try it on coleslaw, too.

INGREDIENTS | SERVES 6

½ cup sliced strawberries

1 tablespoon lemon juice

1 tablespoon agave syrup

1 tablespoon chia seeds, soaked

¼ teaspoon salt

1 tablespoon mustard

1 tablespoon minced onion

¼ cup apple juice

¼ cup olive oil

6 cups baby spinach

2 cups watercress

2 cups sliced strawberries

1 cup raspberries

1. In food processor or blender, combine ½ cup strawberries, lemon juice, agave syrup, chia seeds, salt, mustard, minced onion, apple juice, and olive oil; process or blend until smooth. Cover and refrigerate up to 3 days.

2. In serving bowl, toss together spinach, watercress, 2 cups strawberries, and raspberries.

3. Drizzle with half of the dressing; toss again. Serve immediately with remaining dressing on the side.

PER SERVING Calories: 150 | Fat: 10g | Sodium: 170mg | Carbohydrates: 14g | Fiber: 5g | Protein: 2g

Wheat Berry Salad

Wheat berries are actually the whole grain. You can find them in the bulk section of health food stores and co-ops.

INGREDIENTS | SERVES 6

1 cup wheat berries

3 cups water

2 cups broccoli florets

¼ cup olive oil

3 tablespoons mustard

½ cup plain yogurt

2 tablespoons fresh lemon juice

⅛ teaspoon pepper

½ cup dried cranberries

4 green onions, chopped

1. Rinse wheat berries and drain. Combine in large saucepan with water over high heat. Bring to a boil, cover, reduce heat, and simmer for about 55–65 minutes.

2. Add broccoli florets to pan, cover, and simmer for another 5 minutes to steam the broccoli. Drain well.

3. In large bowl, combine olive oil, mustard, yogurt, lemon juice, and pepper and mix well. Add wheat berries, broccoli, cranberries, and onions; mix gently.

4. Cover and refrigerate for 3–4 hours before serving.

PER SERVING Calories: 260 | Fat: 14g | Sodium: 110mg | Carbohydrates: 39g | Fiber: 6g | Protein: 5g

Potato Barley Salad

Can't find the agave syrup in your grocery store? Try looking in the natural foods aisle.
If you're still stumped, you can order it through an online retailer.

INGREDIENTS | SERVES 12

1 (5-pound) bag potatoes, cut into 1"cubes
2 tablespoons olive oil
1 onion, chopped
5 cloves garlic, minced
1 cup pearl barley
3 cups water
1 cup plain yogurt
½ cup mayonnaise
1 tablespoon agave syrup
¼ cup mustard
¼ cup skim milk
1 teaspoon dried basil
⅛ teaspoon pepper
1 green bell pepper, chopped
1 red bell pepper, chopped
1 yellow bell pepper, chopped
1 yellow summer squash, chopped

1. Preheat oven to 400°F.

2. In a large roasting pan, combine potatoes, olive oil, onion, and garlic.

3. Roast for 30 minutes, turn vegetables with a spatula, then roast for 30–40 minutes longer, until potatoes are tender and browning on the edges.

4. Meanwhile, combine barley and water in large saucepan. Bring to a boil, then reduce heat to low, cover, and simmer for 40–50 minutes or until barley is tender. Drain if necessary.

5. Meanwhile, in large bowl combine yogurt, mayonnaise, agave syrup, mustard, milk, basil, and pepper and mix well.

6. Add warm potatoes and warm barley to yogurt mixture and stir to coat.

7. Add remaining vegetables and stir to coat. Cover and refrigerate for 4–6 hours before serving.

PER SERVING Calories: 310 | Fat: 11g | Sodium: 125mg | Carbohydrates: 52g | Fiber: 7g | Protein: 8g

Red Bean Salad with Taco Chips

Any type of bean or legume can be substituted for another. You could use kidney beans, black beans, Great Northern beans, navy beans, black-eyed peas, pink beans, or chickpeas in this delicious salad.

INGREDIENTS | SERVES 6

¼ cup fresh lime juice

½ cup sour cream

½ cup plain yogurt

½ teaspoon crushed red pepper flakes

1 red onion, chopped

2 jalapeño peppers, minced

1 green bell pepper, chopped

3 stalks celery, chopped

4 cups beans, dried, cooked or canned

6 cups shredded lettuce

½ cup pumpkin seeds

2 cups crushed Baked Tortilla Chips (Chapter 9)

1. In large bowl combine lime juice, sour cream, yogurt, pepper flakes, onion, and jalapeño peppers; mix well.

2. Add bell pepper, celery, and beans and mix well. This can be chilled, well covered, until ready to eat.

3. When ready to serve, arrange lettuce on a serving platter and spoon the bean mixture over all. Sprinkle with pumpkin seeds and crushed taco chips and serve immediately.

PER SERVING Calories: 640 | Fat: 13g | Sodium: 300mg | Carbohydrates: 94g | Fiber: 32g | Protein: 36g

Black-Eyed Pea Salad

Black-eyed peas contain pectin, another soluble fiber that helps reduce cholesterol levels and regulate bowel function. And they're delicious!

INGREDIENTS | SERVES 6–8

1 (16-ounce) package dried black-eyed peas

8 cups cold water

1 cup plain yogurt

¼ cup olive oil

¼ cup Dijon mustard

1 teaspoon dried thyme leaves

¼ teaspoon salt

⅛ teaspoon black pepper

2 green bell peppers, chopped

1 red bell pepper, chopped

1 red onion, finely chopped

½ cup crumbled goat cheese

1. Pick over the peas and rinse; drain well. Place in a large pot with cold water, cover, and let stand overnight. In the morning, drain and rinse the peas and cover with cold water. Bring to a boil, then reduce heat and simmer peas for 75–85 minutes until tender.

2. Meanwhile, in large bowl combine yogurt, olive oil, mustard, thyme, salt, and pepper and mix well.

3. Drain peas well and add to yogurt mixture along with peppers and red onion. Toss to coat, then sprinkle with goat cheese. Cover and refrigerate for 4–6 hours.

PER SERVING Calories: 330 | Fat: 12g | Sodium: 310mg | Carbohydrates: 40g | Fiber: 7g | Protein: 18g

Summer Pineapple Fruit Salad

*This fresh salad can even be served as dessert. For a special treat,
toast some angel food cake and top it with this salad.*

INGREDIENTS | SERVES 8

1 cup lemon yogurt

¼ cup plain yogurt

1 teaspoon lemon zest

1 tablespoon chia seeds, soaked

2 tablespoons honey

1 teaspoon chopped fresh thyme

1 fresh pineapple

1 cantaloupe

1 honeydew melon

2 cups sliced strawberries

1 pint blueberries

1 cup raspberries

Fresh Fruit

Soft fruits like berries are sold perfectly ripe,
so should be eaten within 1–2 days. Melons
are usually unripe, and can sit on the kitchen
counter for a couple of days until they give
when gently pressed. All fruit is very fragile,
so toss it gently in the dressing. Fruit salads
can be varied according to the season; use
apples and pears in the fall.

1. In large bowl, combine yogurts, lemon zest, chia
   seeds, and honey, and mix well. Stir in thyme and set
   aside.

2. Twist top off pineapple and discard. Slice pineapple in
   half, then cut off rind. Cut into quarters, then cut out
   center core. Slice pineapple and add to yogurt
   mixture.

3. Cut cantaloupe and melon in half. Scoop out seeds
   and discard, and peel. Cut into cubes.

4. Add to yogurt mixture along with strawberries and
   blueberries. Toss gently and top with raspberries.

5. Serve immediately, or cover and refrigerate up to 4
   hours.

PER SERVING Calories: 210 | Fat: 1.5g | Sodium: 80mg |
Carbohydrates: 49g | fiber: 6g | Protein: 5g

CHAPTER 12

Salad Dressings, Chutneys, and Sauces

Tangy Lemon Garlic Tomato Dressing

In addition to providing fiber, ground flaxseeds are rich sources of omega-3 and -6 essential fatty acids. Flaxseed goes rancid easily, so grind the seeds freshly and store tightly sealed in the refrigerator.

INGREDIENTS | YIELDS ABOUT ¾ CUP; SERVING SIZE: 1 TABLESPOON

1 tablespoon ground flaxseeds
2 cloves garlic
⅛ cup cider vinegar
⅛ teaspoon black pepper
1 small tomato, chopped
¼ teaspoon celery seed
1 tablespoon fresh lemon juice
¼ cup water

Place all ingredients in blender; blend until smooth.

PER SERVING Calories: 7 | Fat: 1g | Sodium: 1mg | Carbohydrates: 1g | Fiber: 1g | Protein: 0g

Lemon Almond Dressing

Make a quick salad without dressing by mixing chopped celery, onion, and other vegetables such as cucumbers or zucchini. Add low-salt seasoning or toss vegetables with low-sodium soy sauce and serve over salad greens.

INGREDIENTS | YIELDS ABOUT ⅔ CUP; SERVING SIZE: 1 TABLESPOON

¼ cup raw almonds
1 tablespoon fresh lemon juice
¼ cup water
1½ teaspoons honey
¼ teaspoon lemon pepper
½ slice (1" diameter) peeled ginger
¼ clove garlic
1½ teaspoons chopped fresh chives, or ½ teaspoon dried chives
1½ teaspoons chopped fresh sweet basil, or ½ teaspoon dried basil

Place all ingredients in blender; blend until smooth.

PER SERVING Calories: 25 | Fat: 2g | Sodium: 0mg | Carbohydrates: 2g | Fiber: 1g | Protein: 1g

Vinaigrette

This is a versatile, basic oil and vinegar dressing.

INGREDIENTS | SERVES 8

½ teaspoon Dijon mustard

1 tablespoon minced shallots

¼ cup red wine vinegar

2 tablespoons chia seeds, soaked

1 cup olive oil

Salt and black pepper, to taste

1. Combine mustard, shallots, vinegar and chia seeds in a bowl with a whisk.

2. Drizzle in olive oil while whisking, and season with salt and pepper.

3. Store in a jar and shake to combine before using.

PER SERVING Calories: 270 | Fat: 29g | Sodium: 10mg | Carbohydrates: 1g | Fiber: <1g | Protein: 0g

Vinegars

Some varieties of vinegars include champagne vinegar, red wine vinegar, white wine vinegar, rice vinegar, cider vinegar, tarragon vinegar, blueberry vinegar, raspberry vinegar, sherry vinegar, and balsamic vinegar.

Sesame Dressing

This can be used for dressing a chicken and cabbage salad, cooked and chilled vegetables, or basic salad greens. It is also a great marinade for grilling.

INGREDIENTS | SERVES 8

1 cup canola oil

½ cup sesame oil

1 tablespoon peeled, chopped fresh ginger root

1 tablespoon minced whole green onions

1 teaspoon minced garlic

½ cup rice vinegar

1 tablespoon honey

1 tablespoon soy sauce

2 tablespoons sesame seeds

Salt and black pepper, to taste

Combine ingredients in a blender or a bowl with a whisk. Adjust seasoning with salt and pepper.

PER SERVING Calories: 390 | Fat: 43g | Sodium: 125mg | Carbohydrates: 3g | Fiber: 0g | Protein: 1g

Caesar Dressing

This creamy and flavorful dressing is usually made with raw eggs. Using low-fat mayonnaise instead is a better choice for food safety reasons.

INGREDIENTS | YIELDS 1 CUP; SERVING SIZE: 2 TABLESPOONS

1 garlic clove, minced

1 anchovy fillet

½ cup mayonnaise

¼ cup plain yogurt

2 tablespoons fresh lemon juice

¼ cup olive oil

¼ teaspoon black pepper

⅓ cup grated Parmesan cheese

1. Combine garlic, anchovy, mayonnaise, yogurt, and lemon juice in blender or food processor. Blend or process until smooth.

2. Stream in olive oil while blending or processing, until smooth.

3. Add pepper and Parmesan and mix well. Cover and refrigerate for up to 4 days.

PER SERVING Calories: 190 | Fat: 19g | Sodium: 530mg | Carbohydrates: 1g | Fiber: 0g | Protein: 2g

Caesar Salad Dressing

Caesar dressing is traditionally served over romaine lettuce with croutons. You can add cooked chicken, cubed ham, or salmon fillets to the salad to turn it into a main dish. The anchovy adds a salty touch and depth of flavor. It can be omitted, but the flavor of the dressing will be very mild.

Honey Mustard Dressing

This dressing is lower in fat than others because part of the oil is replaced by chicken broth. You may also simply add water in place of broth to reduce calories. Store in refrigerator if not using immediately.

INGREDIENTS | **SERVES 8**

½ cup Chicken Stock (Chapter 3)

½ cup olive oil

2 tablespoons Dijon mustard

1 tablespoon honey

2 tablespoons white wine vinegar

1 teaspoon minced onion

Salt and black pepper, to taste

1. Combine ingredients in a blender until smooth.

2. Adjust seasoning to taste with salt and pepper.

PER SERVING Calories: 140 | Fat: 15g | Sodium: 115mg | Carbohydrates: 3g | Fiber: 0g | Protein: 1g

Oils

Try using different oils in vinaigrette to vary the flavor and weight of the dressing. Extra-virgin olive oil is more flavorful than pure olive oil, which is lighter in taste. Oils to experiment with include canola, sunflower, peanut, safflower, grape seed, corn, and vegetable. Accent oils include sesame, walnut, hazelnut, and chili.

Balsamic Vinaigrette

There are many different kinds of balsamic vinegar, and they vary in price. The oldest and most expensive ones are thick and sweet from aging in oak barrels. For this dressing use a moderately aged (and priced) one.

INGREDIENTS | SERVES 8

1 clove garlic, crushed
½ teaspoon kosher salt
1 teaspoon Dijon mustard
2 tablespoons balsamic vinegar
1 tablespoon red wine vinegar
1 cup olive oil
Black pepper, to taste

1. Combine garlic and salt in a wooden bowl and smash to a paste with a wooden spoon, or combine in blender.

2. Add mustard and vinegars and whisk together.

3. Drizzle in the oil while whisking.

4. Season with pepper.

PER SERVING Calories: 260 | Fat: 28g | Sodium: 160mg | Carbohydrates: 1g | Fiber: 0g | Protein: 0g

Raspberry Chia Vinaigrette

This is a tangy, tart, and slightly sweet dressing that adds a touch of fruit to salad greens.

INGREDIENTS | SERVES 8

¼ cup fresh raspberries, puréed and strained
1 cup olive oil
2 tablespoons raspberry vinegar
1 tablespoon minced shallots
1 teaspoon agave syrup
1 teaspoon Dijon mustard
2 tablespoons chia seeds, ground
Salt and black pepper, to taste

1. Combine ingredients in a blender until smooth.

2. Adjust seasoning with salt and pepper.

PER SERVING Calories: 270 | Fat: 29g | Sodium: 15mg | Carbohydrates: 2g | Fiber: 1g | Protein: 0g

Sun-Dried Tomato Vinaigrette

This dressing can be puréed in a blender or left chunky. It also makes a good dip for artichokes.

INGREDIENTS | **SERVES 8**

1 teaspoon minced garlic
3 tablespoons red wine vinegar
1 tablespoon balsamic vinegar
1 cup olive oil
¼ cup minced sun-dried tomatoes
1 tablespoon chopped fresh basil
Salt and black pepper, to taste

1. Combine garlic and vinegars in a bowl with a whisk.

2. Drizzle in the oil while whisking, until all of it has been incorporated.

3. Stir in tomatoes and basil. Season with salt and pepper.

PER SERVING Calories: 260 | Fat: 28g | Sodium: 35mg | Carbohydrates: 1g | Fiber: 0g | Protein: 0g

Cranberry Chutney

Cranberry Chutney is very different in taste from traditional sweet cranberry sauce. It can be used as a topping or filling for desserts. Optional additional ingredients would be dried cherries and apricots, raisins, and apples.

INGREDIENTS | **SERVES 6**

2 cups raw cranberries
2 cups apple or orange juice
1 slice ginger
½ teaspoon ground cloves
½ teaspoon ground cardamom
½ teaspoon cinnamon
1 tablespoon vanilla extract
1 tablespoon orange zest

1. Combine all ingredients in a sauce pan.

2. Cook over low heat for 1 hour.

PER SERVING Calories: 60 | Fat: 0g | Sodium: 0mg | Carbohydrate: 14g | Fiber: 2g | Protein: 0g

Mango Chutney

You can store this chutney in the refrigerator for up to 9 days, or process it in a hot-water bath for longer storage. The chutney can be frozen up to 3 months.

INGREDIENTS	YIELDS 2 PINTS; SERVING SIZE: ¼ CUP

5 mangoes, peeled and chopped

⅓ cup white vinegar

¼ cup fresh lemon juice

⅔ cup brown sugar

1 onion, finely chopped

3 cloves garlic, minced

½ cup golden raisins

¼ cup dried currants

3 tablespoons minced fresh ginger root

½ teaspoon salt

1 teaspoon cinnamon

1 tablespoon curry powder

⅛ teaspoon white pepper

1. Combine all ingredients in a large, heavy saucepan and bring to a boil over medium-high heat. Reduce heat to medium-low; simmer, stirring frequently, until mixture thickens and becomes syrupy, about 15–25 minutes.

2. While chutney is simmering on stove, place ½ pint jars or freezer containers in dishwasher and wash. Leave the containers in the dishwasher until ready to fill.

3. Ladle chutney into clean hot containers, leaving about ½" of headspace. Cover and chill in refrigerator until cold; store in refrigerator or freezer.

PER SERVING Calories: 210 | Fat: 0g | Sodium: 160mg | Carbohydrates: 55g | Fiber: 4g | Protein: 2g

Preparing Mangoes

Mangoes can be tricky to peel and slice. First, be sure you have ripe mangoes that yield slightly to gentle pressure. Remove the peel with a swivel-bladed vegetable peeler or sharp knife. Then stand the mango on end and slice down, curving around the pit. If you want chopped mango, just keep paring off flesh until you reach the pit.

Spaghetti Sauce

*Grated carrots add nutrition and fiber to this rich sauce, and
help reduce the problem of sauce separation.*

INGREDIENTS	YIELDS 6 CUPS; SERVING SIZE: 1 CUP

2 tablespoons olive oil

1 onion, chopped

4 cloves garlic, minced

1 cup chopped celery

1 (8-ounce) package sliced mushrooms

1 (6-ounce) can tomato paste

2 (14-ounce) cans diced tomatoes, undrained

1 tablespoon dried Italian seasoning

½ cup grated carrots

⅛ teaspoon white pepper

½ cup dry red wine

½ cup water

1. In large saucepan, heat olive oil over medium heat. Add onion and garlic; cook and stir until crisp-tender, about 4 minutes.

2. Add celery and mushrooms; cook and stir for 2–3 minutes longer.

3. Add tomato paste; let paste brown a bit without stirring (this adds flavor to the sauce).

4. Add remaining ingredients and stir gently but thoroughly.

5. Bring sauce to a simmer, then reduce heat to low and partially cover. Simmer for 60–70 minutes, stirring occasionally, until sauce is blended and thickened. Serve over hot cooked pasta, couscous, or rice.

PER SERVING Calories: 140 | Fat: 5g | Sodium: 330mg | Carbohydrates: 18g | Fiber: 5g | Protein: 4g

Freezing Spaghetti Sauce

Spaghetti sauce freezes beautifully, and it can be used in all sorts of casseroles and soups in addition to just serving over spaghetti. To freeze, portion 4 cups into a hard-sided freezer container, leaving about 1" of head space for expansion. Seal, label, and freeze for up to 3 months. To thaw, let stand in fridge overnight, then heat in saucepan.

Tuna Tomato Sauce

Tuna is a nice change from beef or pork in this flavorful pasta dish. Serve it with a green salad and some fresh fruit for dessert.

INGREDIENTS | SERVES 4

1 tablespoon olive oil
2 cloves garlic, minced
1 teaspoon anchovy paste
½ teaspoon red pepper flakes
1 (28-ounce) can tomato purée
½ teaspoon black pepper
1 (12-ounce) package spaghetti pasta
1 (7-ounce) can tuna in water, drained
⅓ cup minced fresh parsley

Tuna

You can buy processed tuna in several forms—canned in water, canned in oil, and in pouches. The one you use is up to you. Tuna in oil doesn't have many more calories than tuna packed in water if it's well drained, and it is more flavorful. The pouch type, which is aseptic packaging, is packed in less liquid and has more flavor.

1. Bring a large pot of water to a boil.

2. Meanwhile, in large saucepan, heat olive oil over medium heat. Add garlic; cook and stir for 2 minutes.

3. Add anchovy paste and red pepper flakes; cook for 1 minute.

4. Add tomato purée and pepper; bring to a boil over medium-high heat. Reduce heat to low and simmer for 15 minutes.

5. Cook pasta according to package directions until al dente. Drain well.

6. Stir tuna and parsley into tomato sauce. Add pasta; toss over medium heat for 2 minutes. Serve immediately.

PER SERVING Calories: 200 | Fat: 6g | Sodium: 1450mg | Carbohydrates: 25g | Fiber: 5g | Protein: 17g

Putanesca

This traditional Italian pasta sauce is a spicy and pungent tomato-based sauce made with capers, black olives, and anchovies. Serve it over cooked pasta such as spaghetti, linguini, or fettuccine, along with a green salad and crusty bread.

INGREDIENTS | **SERVES 4**

2 cloves garlic, minced

¼ cup olive oil

1 (28-ounce) can crushed tomatoes

1 teaspoon dried crushed red pepper

½ teaspoon dried oregano

2 tablespoons drained capers

1 cup oil-cured black olives, chopped coarse

5 anchovies, chopped

Salt and black pepper, to taste

2 tablespoons chopped fresh parsley

1. In a 6-quart soup pot, sauté garlic in oil for a few minutes.

2. Add tomatoes, red pepper, and oregano, and cook over medium heat for 10 minutes. Add capers, olives, and anchovies and cook for another 5 minutes.

3. Season sauce with salt (if necessary) and pepper.

4. Toss cooked pasta in the sauce, and top with chopped fresh parsley.

PER SERVING (DOES NOT INCLUDE PASTA) Calories: 240 | Fat: 19g | Sodium: 870mg | Carbohydrates: 18g | Fiber: 5g | Protein: 5g

Plum Sauce

This recipe can be used as a meat seasoning or a dip for eggrolls.

INGREDIENTS | **YIELDS 1¼ CUPS; SERVING SIZE: 1 TABLESPOON**

1 cup plum jam

2 teaspoons grated lemon zest

1 tablespoon fresh lemon juice

1 tablespoon rice wine vinegar

½ teaspoon ground ginger

½ teaspoon crushed anise seeds

¼ teaspoon dry mustard

¼ teaspoon ground cinnamon

⅛ teaspoon ground cloves

⅛ teaspoon hot pepper sauce

1. Heat plum jam in small saucepan over medium heat until melted.

2. Stir in remaining ingredients.

3. Bring the mixture to a boil; lower heat and simmer for 1 minute, stirring constantly.

4. Remove sauce, and cool before serving.

PER SERVING Calories: 40 | Fat: 0g | Sodium: 0mg | Carbohydrates: 11g | Fiber: 0g | Protein: 0g

Roasted Garlic Aioli Mayonnaise

To save time or when you don't have a blender, you can use 1 cup of a good-quality store-bought mayonnaise in place of making it from scratch. Add dried herbs of your choice for extra flavor. Serve aioli mayonnaise over vegetables, grilled meats, fish, or swirled into a thick purée of hot lentil soup.

INGREDIENTS | MAKES 1 CUP

1 head garlic
¾ cup olive oil
1 egg
1 tablespoon fresh lemon juice
1 tablespoon apple cider vinegar
Pinch salt

For Serious Garlic Lovers

The more garlic cloves you add to the mayonnaise the more pungent the flavor, resulting in an almost chili-pepper-like fire. If you prefer a heavier garlic flavor, try roasting 2 heads of garlic and mixing them both into the mayonnaise.

1. Preheat oven to 375°F.

2. Wrap garlic in aluminum foil; bake for 20 minutes.

3. Allow to cool. Remove foil, and slice across flat end of head. Squeeze softened cloves out the end into a small bowl; set aside.

4. Pour ¼ cup of oil into a blender with egg, lemon juice, vinegar, and salt.

5. Turn on blender; pour remaining oil into mixture in a slow stream. The mayonnaise will thicken as you pour the oil.

6. Add roasted garlic to mayonnaise; pulse to combine.

7. Run blender additional 30 seconds after garlic has been added.

8. Keep mixture refrigerated in a glass container 5–7 days.

PER SERVING Calories: 1680 | Fat: 173g | Sodium: 370mg | Carbohydrates: 22g | Fiber: 1g | Protein: 10g

Parsley Pesto Sauce

Simple, easy, and surprisingly quick to make using a mortar and pestle. Spread this pesto on salmon fillets and allow to marinate 30 minutes before grilling; nothing else is needed. Serve over cooked pasta, on bread, as a pizza topping, with cooked vegetables, or even mixed into cooked brown rice.

INGREDIENTS | MAKES ¾ CUP

⅓ cup fresh walnuts

3 cloves garlic

2 cups curly leaf parsley (no stems)

2 cups fresh basil leaf

½ cup olive oil

½ teaspoon salt

What Parsley to Use

The Italian flat-leaf parsley will give a stronger, sweeter taste, while the curly leaf will complement flavors. Always look to complement the main entrée with your sauce, rather than overpowering it with an herb's aroma.

1. Add the walnuts to the grinding bowl or processor; grind to a pulp.

2. Add garlic; continue to grind.

3. Add parsley and basil in batches, along with 1 tablespoon of oil; continue to grind.

4. As ingredients break down, continue to add oil and salt to mixture until you have a thick paste.

5. Adjust consistency by adding more oil to make a sauce that is not too thick yet not loose and runny.

PER SERVING Calories: 1350 | Fat: 140g | Sodium: 1240mg | Carbohydrates: 20g | Fiber: 10g | Protein: 12g

Caribbean Kiwi Salsa

This zippy salad is a great kick start for the summer.

INGREDIENTS | SERVES 6

1 cup kiwi, peeled and chopped
1 cup pineapple, chopped
1 cup mango, peeled and chopped
2 tablespoons chia seeds, ground
⅓ cup red onion, chopped
1 cup red bell pepper, chopped
⅓ cup black beans, cooked
3 tablespoons fresh cilantro, chopped
2 tablespoons fresh lime juice
½ teaspoon chili powder
Dash cayenne

1. Mix all ingredients together in medium bowl.

2. Chill at least 2 hours before serving

PER SERVING Calories: 90 | Fat: 1.5g | Sodium: 5mg | Carbohydrates: 19g | Fiber: 4g | Protein: 2g

Avocado Corn Salsa

Radishes give this salsa a delicious crunch and zesty flavor.

INGREDIENTS | SERVES 4

1 cup corn kernels, blanched fresh or thawed frozen
1 small banana pepper, seeded and chopped
¼ cup diced red radishes
⅛ cup thinly sliced green onion
1 avocado, diced
1 tablespoon fresh lime juice
½ teaspoon white wine vinegar
1 teaspoon olive oil
¼ teaspoon dried oregano
Dash of ground cumin
Dash of Tabasco sauce
Black pepper (optional)

1. Combine corn, banana pepper, radishes, and onion in a medium bowl.

2. In another bowl, combine half of the diced avocado and lime juice; stir to thoroughly coat.

3. In a blender, combine the other ½ of avocado, vinegar, oil, oregano, cumin, and Tabasco (and pepper if using), and process until smooth. Pour over corn mixture and stir.

4. Add avocado mixture. Serve immediately.

PER SERVING Calories: 133 | Fat: 9g | Sodium: 10mg | Carbohydrates: 14g | Fiber: 4g | Protein: 2g

Zesty Black Bean Salsa

Canned beans are very convenient and can save you time, but keep in mind that the sodium content of recipes will be higher with canned beans. Reduce sodium content in canned beans by draining and thoroughly rinsing with cold water before using.

INGREDIENTS | SERVES 10

1 cup red onion
¼ cup fresh cilantro
¼ cup fresh parsley
1 small jalapeño pepper
1½ cups black beans, cooked
4 cups tomatoes, chopped
3 tablespoons fresh lime juice
2 tablespoons olive oil
Black pepper, to taste

1. Place onion, cilantro, parsley, and jalapeño in food processor; finely chop.

2. In medium bowl, combine onion mixture, black beans, and tomatoes.

3. In separate small bowl, whisk together lime juice, olive oil, and black pepper. Pour over beans; mix well. Chill before serving.

PER SERVING Calories: 86 | Fat: 3g | Sodium: 125mg | Carbohydrates: 12g | Fiber: 4g | Protein: 3g

Fresh Peach Mango Salsa

This salsa can be eaten with chips or served atop grilled or baked fish.

INGREDIENTS | SERVES 6

1 cup mango, peeled and cut into ¼" pieces
1 peach, peeled and cut into ¼" pieces
1 cup red onion, finely chopped
1 cup cucumber, peeled and cut into ¼" pieces
2 tablespoons chia seeds, ground
1 tablespoon balsamic vinegar
1 tablespoon fresh lime juice
1 teaspoon chili powder
½ teaspoon ground cumin
1 tablespoon fresh cilantro, chopped
1 tablespoon fresh parsley, chopped
¼ teaspoon salt

1. Mix all ingredients together in medium bowl.

2. Chill at least 4 hours before serving.

PER SERVING Calories: 60 | Fat: 1g | Sodium: 105mg | Carbohydrates: 13g | Fiber: 3g | Protein: 1g

Super Spicy Salsa

Salsa can be used in so many ways, including as a fabulous garnish for chili or grilled chicken.

INGREDIENTS | YIELDS 3 CUPS;
SERVING SIZE: ¼ CUP

2 jalapeño peppers, minced

1 habanero pepper, minced

1 green bell pepper, minced

4 cloves garlic, minced

1 red onion, chopped

5 ripe tomatoes, chopped

3 tablespoons fresh lemon juice

¼ teaspoon salt

⅛ teaspoon white pepper

¼ cup chopped fresh cilantro

1. In a large bowl, combine jalapeños, habanero pepper, bell pepper, garlic, onion, and tomatoes.

2. In a small bowl, combine lemon juice, salt, and pepper and stir to dissolve the salt. Add to the tomato mixture along with cilantro.

3. Cover and refrigerate for 3–4 hours before serving.

PER SERVING Calories: 25 | Fat: 0g | Sodium: 50mg | Carbohydrates: 6g | Fiber: <1g | Protein: 1g

Pepper Heat

The heat in a pepper is concentrated in its seeds and inner membranes. If you prefer a milder taste, just remove and discard the seeds and membranes before mincing. Remember, the smaller the pepper, the hotter. Habaneros and Scotch bonnet peppers are the hottest, while pepperoncini and Poblano peppers are milder.

CHAPTER 13

Breads and Muffins

Whole-Wheat Bread

*This is a basic loaf of bread that can be used for sandwiches
or toast or used to make stuffing and croutons.*

INGREDIENTS | SERVES 8; SERVING
SIZE: 1 SLICE

1 (¼-ounce) packet yeast

3 tablespoons sugar

1⅓ cups warm water

3 tablespoons soft butter

1 teaspoon salt

¼ teaspoon baking powder

1¾ cups all-purpose flour

1¾ cups whole-wheat flour

Whole-Wheat to Whole-Grain Bread

You can add all kinds of grains to your whole-wheat bread. Mix in some ground corn, millet, wheat bran flakes, ground soy or soy flour, or malt. You can sweeten the bread with honey, maple syrup, or red bean paste. The flavors expand geometrically, and the grainy texture makes fabulous toast, French toast, and sandwiches. Giving your body what it needs is not that hard; it simply takes a little time and thought.

1. Combine yeast, ½ teaspoon sugar, and ⅓ cup water in a bowl. Let sit for 5 minutes.

2. In a mixing bowl, combine remaining water, butter, remaining sugar, salt, and baking powder.

3. Mix in the all-purpose flour, followed by the yeast mixture, with an electric mixer.

4. Add the whole-wheat flour and knead with dough hook for 10 minutes.

5. Turn dough into an oiled bowl. Cover and set in a warm place. Let rise for 1–2 hours, until doubled in bulk.

6. Punch down dough, then shape into a cylinder and place in an oiled loaf pan. Cover and let rise in a warm place for 90 minutes, until doubled in size.

7. Preheat oven to 350°F. Uncover and bake for 40 minutes.

PER SERVING Calories: 250 | Fat: 5g | Sodium: 310mg | Carbohydrates: 45g | Fiber: 4g | Protein: 7g

Whole-Grain Oatmeal Bread

This hearty bread is delicious toasted and spread with whipped honey or jam.

INGREDIENTS | **YIELDS 2 LOAVES; 32 SERVINGS**

1 cup warm water
2 (¼-ounce) packages active dry yeast
¼ cup honey
1 cup skim milk
1 cup oatmeal
1 teaspoon salt
3 tablespoons canola oil
1 egg
1½ cups whole-wheat flour
½ cup medium rye flour
¼ cup ground flax seeds
3–4 cups bread flour
2 tablespoons butter

Rolls or Bread?

Any yeast bread mixture can be made into rolls. Just divide the dough into 2" balls and roll between your hands to smooth. Place on greased cookie sheets about 4" apart. Cover and let rise for 30–40 minutes. Then bake at 375°F for 15–25 minutes, until deep golden brown. Let cool on wire racks. Freeze if not using within 1 day.

1. In small bowl, combine water and yeast; let stand until bubbly, about 5 minutes.

2. Meanwhile, in medium saucepan, combine honey, milk, oatmeal, salt, and canola oil. Heat just until very warm (about 120°F). Remove from heat and beat in egg.

3. Combine in large bowl with whole-wheat flour, rye flour, flax seeds, and 1 cup bread flour. Add yeast mixture and beat for 1 minute. Cover and let rise for 30 minutes.

4. Gradually stir in enough remaining bread flour to make a firm dough. Turn onto floured surface and knead until dough is elastic, about 10 minutes. Place in greased bowl, turning to grease top. Cover and let rise for 1 hour.

5. Punch down dough, divide in half, and form into loaves. Place in greased 9" × 5" loaf pans, cover, and let rise for 30 minutes.

6. Bake in preheated 350°F oven for 25–30 minutes, or until golden brown. Brush with butter, then remove to wire racks to cool.

PER SERVING Calories: 120 | Fat: 3g | Sodium: 80mg | Carbohydrates: 20g | Fiber: 2g | Protein: 4g

Honey Wheat Sesame Bread

Sesame seeds add not only flavor and crunch to these delicious loaves but fiber and healthy monounsaturated fat as well.

INGREDIENTS | **YIELDS 2 LOAVES; 32 SERVINGS**

1 cup milk
1 cup water
½ cup honey
3 tablespoons butter
¼ teaspoon salt
1 egg
2 cups whole-wheat flour
2 (¼-ounce) packages instant-blend dry yeast
½ cup sesame seeds
3–4 cups all-purpose flour
1 egg white
2 tablespoons sesame seeds

1. In medium saucepan, combine milk, water, honey, butter, and salt. Heat over medium heat until butter melts. Remove from heat and let stand for 30 minutes, or until just lukewarm. Beat in egg.

2. Meanwhile, in large bowl combine whole-wheat flour, yeast, and ½ cup sesame seeds. Add milk mixture and beat for 1 minute.

3. Gradually stir in enough all-purpose flour to make a firm dough.

4. Turn out onto floured surface and knead, adding additional flour if necessary, until dough is elastic. Place in greased bowl, turning to grease top; cover and let rise until double, about 1 hour.

5. Grease two 9" × 5" loaf pans with unsalted butter and set aside.

6. Punch down dough and divide into 2 parts. On floured surface, roll or pat to 7" × 12" rectangle. Roll up tightly, starting with 7" side.

7. Place in prepared pans. Brush with egg white and sprinkle each with 1 tablespoon sesame seeds.

8. Cover with towel, and let rise until double, about 30 minutes.

9. Preheat oven to 350°F. Bake loaves for 35–45 minutes, or until golden brown. Turn onto wire rack to cool completely.

PER SERVING Calories: 120 | Fat: 3g | Sodium: 25mg | Carbohydrates: 20g | Fiber: 2g | Protein: 3g

Hearty-Grain French Bread

Cottage cheese, sour cream, and orange juice add a nice tang to this hearty French bread.

INGREDIENTS | **YIELDS 2 LOAVES; 32 SERVINGS**

1 cup quick-cooking oats

1 cup water

½ cup cottage cheese

½ cup sour cream

2 tablespoons fresh orange juice

½ teaspoon salt

2 cups bread flour

2 (¼-ounce) packages instant-blend dry yeast

¼ cup oat bran

2–3 cups whole-wheat flour

2 tablespoons cornmeal

1. In small microwave-safe bowl, combine oats and 1 cup water; microwave on high for 3–4 minutes until creamy. Let cool for 10 minutes.

2. Combine oatmeal mixture and cottage cheese in a blender or food processor; blend or process until creamy.

3. Place oatmeal mixture in large bowl. Stir in sour cream, orange juice, and salt; mix well.

4. Add bread flour, yeast, and oat bran and beat for 1 minute. Stir in enough whole-wheat flour to form a firm dough.

5. Knead dough on lightly floured surface until smooth and elastic, about 8 minutes. Place dough in greased bowl, turning to grease top. Cover and let rise until doubled, about 1 hour.

6. Punch down dough and place on counter. Cover with bowl and let stand for 10 minutes.

7. Grease two 12" long rectangles on a cookie sheet and sprinkle with cornmeal.

8. Divide dough into 2 balls. Roll each ball into a 12" cylinder and place on prepared cookie sheet. Cover and let rise until doubled, about 30 minutes.

9. Preheat oven to 375°F. Spray loaves with some cold water and bake for 30–40 minutes, or until loaves are deep golden brown and sound hollow when tapped with fingers. Cool on wire rack.

PER SERVING Calories: 80 | Fat: 1.5g | Sodium: 55mg | Carbohydrates: 15g | Fiber: 2g | Protein: 3g

Spicy Corn Bread

Corn bread is the perfect accompaniment to chili or any hot soup or stew. Serve this one with salsa.

INGREDIENTS | SERVES 9

1¼ cups flour
1¼ cups cornmeal
⅓ cup sugar
2 teaspoons baking powder
1 teaspoon baking soda
½ teaspoon salt
1 tablespoon chili powder
⅛ teaspoon Tabasco sauce
1 jalapeño pepper, minced
¼ cup canola oil
1 egg
2 egg whites
1 cup buttermilk, divided
½ cup frozen corn, thawed

1. Preheat oven to 400°F. Spray a 9" square pan with nonstick baking spray containing flour and set aside.

2. In a large bowl, combine flour, cornmeal, sugar, baking powder, baking soda, salt, and chili powder.

3. In a small bowl, combine Tabasco, jalapeño pepper, oil, egg, egg whites, and ¾ cup buttermilk and mix well.

4. In a food processor or blender, place corn and ¼ cup buttermilk. Process or blend until smooth; add to oil mixture.

5. Pour oil mixture into dry ingredients and mix until a batter forms. Spoon and spread into prepared pan.

6. Bake for 20–25 minutes, or until deep golden brown. Let cool for 10 minutes, then cut into squares to serve.

PER SERVING Calories: 250 | Fat: 8g | Sodium: 440mg | Carbohydrates: 40g | Fiber: 2g | Protein: 6g

Whole-Grain Cornbread

Cornbread should be eaten hot from the oven. Instead of slathering it with butter, spread with whipped honey or top with Super Spicy Salsa (Chapter 12).

INGREDIENTS | SERVES 9

¾ cup all-purpose flour
½ cup whole-wheat flour
¼ cup brown sugar
2 teaspoons baking powder
1 teaspoon baking soda
1 cup cornmeal
⅓ cup oat bran
1 egg
2 egg whites
¼ cup honey
1 cup buttermilk
¼ cup canola oil

1. Preheat oven to 400°F. Spray a 9" square pan with nonstick cooking spray containing flour, and set aside.

2. In large mixing bowl, combine flour, whole-wheat flour, brown sugar, baking powder, baking soda, cornmeal, and oat bran and mix well.

3. In small bowl, combine egg, egg whites, honey, buttermilk, and oil and beat to combine. Add to dry ingredients and stir just until mixed.

4. Spoon into prepared pan and smooth top.

5. Bake for 25–35 minutes, or until golden brown.

PER SERVING Calories: 260 | Fat: 8g | Sodium: 300mg | Carbohydrates: 42g | Fiber: 3g | Protein: 6g

Multigrain Bread

Whole-wheat flour, rolled oats, sunflower seeds, and millet are the grains in this hearty loaf. The fiber comes from whole wheat, millet, oats, and sunflower seeds. They all add some protein, too.

INGREDIENTS	SERVES 8; SERVING SIZE: 1 SLICE

1 (¼-ounce) packet yeast

3 tablespoons sugar

1⅓ cups warm water

3 tablespoons soft butter

1 teaspoon salt

¼ teaspoon baking powder

1½ cups all-purpose flour

1½ cups whole-wheat flour

½ cup rolled oats

¼ cup sunflower seeds

2 tablespoons uncooked millet

1. Combine yeast, ½ teaspoon sugar, and ⅓ cup water in a bowl. Let sit for 5 minutes.

2. In a mixing bowl, combine remaining water, butter, remaining sugar, salt, and baking powder.

3. Mix in the all-purpose flour, followed by the yeast mixture, with an electric mixer.

4. Add the whole-wheat flour, rolled oats, sunflower seeds, and millet. Knead with a dough hook for 10 minutes.

5. Turn dough into an oiled bowl and put in a warm place. Cover and let rise for 1–2 hours, until doubled in bulk.

6. Punch down dough, then shape it into a cylinder, and place it in an oiled loaf pan. Cover and let rise in a warm place for 90 minutes, until doubled in size.

7. Preheat oven to 350°F. Uncover bread, and bake for 40 minutes.

PER SERVING Calories: 280 | Fat: 8g | Sodium: 310mg | Carbohydrates: 47g | Fiber: 5g | Protein: 8g

Olive Bread

Serve this bread dressed with olive oil and softened cheese for a cocktail snack.
The fiber comes with the delicious olives and whole-wheat flour.

INGREDIENTS | SERVES 8; SERVING SIZE: 1 SLICE

1 (¼-ounce) packet yeast

3 tablespoons honey

1⅓ cups warm water

3 tablespoons olive oil

1 teaspoon salt

¼ teaspoon baking powder

1¾ cups all-purpose flour

1¾ cups whole-wheat flour

1 cup pitted niçoise olives

2 tablespoons minced fresh thyme

Mediterranean Breads

Olive oil, olives, nuts, dried fruits, herbs, and nuts make Mediterranean breads more than just bread. Adding corn, barley, brown rice flour, and other goodies adds to the nutritional value and fiber in these breads. You can take any recipe and adapt it with your favorite flavors and ingredients. Try adding chestnut flour for a very Italian experience.

1. Combine yeast, ½ teaspoon honey, and ⅓ cup water in a bowl. Let sit for 5 minutes.

2. In a mixing bowl combine remaining water, olive oil, remaining honey, salt, and baking powder.

3. Mix in the all-purpose flour, then the yeast mixture with an electric mixer.

4. Add the whole-wheat flour, olives, and thyme. Knead with a dough hook for 10 minutes.

5. Turn dough into an oiled bowl. Cover and let rise in a warm place for 1–2 hours, until doubled in bulk.

6. Punch down dough, then shape into a cylinder and place in an oiled loaf pan. Cover and let rise in a warm place for 90 minutes, until doubled in size.

7. Preheat oven to 350°F. Uncover bread and bake for 40 minutes.

PER SERVING Calories: 280 | Fat: 8g | Sodium: 460mg | Carbohydrates: 48g | Fiber: 5g | Protein: 7g

Cinnamon Swirl Raisin Bread

Toast this bread for breakfast for a healthy start to a long workday or spread blue cheese and drizzle honey on toast points with poached pears. The whole-wheat flour gives you both protein and fiber, and the raisins add flavor and fiber.

INGREDIENTS	SERVES 8; SERVING SIZE: 1 SLICE

1 (¼-ounce) packet yeast

3 tablespoons sugar

1⅓ cups warm water

3 tablespoons soft butter

1 teaspoon salt

¼ teaspoon baking powder

1¾ cups all-purpose flour

1¾ cups whole-wheat flour

1 cup raisins

3 tablespoons cinnamon

1. Combine yeast, ½ teaspoon sugar, and ⅓ cup water in a bowl. Let sit for 5 minutes.

2. In a mixing bowl combine remaining water, butter, remaining sugar, salt, and baking powder.

3. Mix in the all-purpose flour and then the yeast mixture with an electric mixer.

4. Add the whole-wheat flour and raisins. Knead with dough hook for 10 minutes.

5. Turn dough into an oiled bowl, cover and let rise in a warm place for 1–2 hours until doubled in bulk.

6. Punch down dough, then roll into a rectangle.

7. Sprinkle the cinnamon over the dough, roll it into a cylinder, and place in an oiled loaf pan. Cover and let rise in a warm place for 90 minutes, until doubled in size.

8. Preheat oven to 350°F. Uncover bread and bake for 40 minutes.

PER SERVING Calories: 320 | Fat: 5g | Sodium: 310mg | Carbohydrates: 63g | Fiber: 6g | Protein: 8g

Apple Bread

Moist and full of apples, this bread is a great snack with a piece of Cheddar cheese. You give your family fiber with great flavor from the whole-wheat flour and apples.

INGREDIENTS | **SERVES 8; SERVING SIZE: 1 SLICE**

1 (¼-ounce) packet yeast
3 tablespoons sugar
1⅓ cups warm water
3 tablespoons soft butter
1 teaspoon salt
¼ teaspoon baking powder
1¾ cups all-purpose flour
1¾ cups whole-wheat flour
1 cup peeled, chopped apples
1 tablespoon cinnamon mixed with 1 tablespoon sugar

1. Combine yeast, ½ teaspoon sugar, and ⅓ cup water in a bowl. Let sit for 5 minutes.

2. In a mixing bowl combine remaining water, butter, remaining sugar, salt, and baking powder.

3. Mix in the all-purpose flour and then the yeast mixture, with an electric mixer.

4. Add the whole-wheat flour. Knead with a dough hook for 10 minutes.

5. Turn dough into an oiled bowl. Cover and let rise in a warm place for 1–2 hours, until doubled in bulk.

6. Punch down dough, then roll it into a rectangle.

7. Scatter the apples over the dough and sprinkle them with the cinnamon sugar. Roll into a cylinder and place in an oiled loaf pan. Cover and let it rise in a warm place for 90 minutes, until doubled in size.

8. Preheat oven to 350°F. Uncover bread and bake for 50 minutes.

PER SERVING Calories: 260 | Fat: 5g | Sodium: 310mg | Carbohydrates: 49g | Fiber: 5g | Protein: 7g

Pecan Bread

Chicken, tuna, or egg salad sandwiches made with this bread are great for a brown bag lunch or picnic. You can also slice it thinly for tea sandwiches filled with cream cheese and cucumber. Pecans add omega-3 benefits.

INGREDIENTS | SERVES 8; SERVING SIZE: 1 SLICE

1 (¼-ounce) packet yeast
3 tablespoons sugar
1⅓ cups warm water
3 tablespoons soft butter
1 teaspoon salt
¼ teaspoon baking powder
1¾ cups all-purpose flour
1¾ cups whole-wheat flour
1½ cups chopped pecans

1. Combine yeast, ½ teaspoon sugar, and ⅓ cup water in a bowl. Let sit for 5 minutes.

2. In a mixing bowl combine remaining water, butter, remaining sugar, salt, and baking powder.

3. Mix in the all-purpose flour and then the yeast mixture with an electric mixer.

4. Add the whole-wheat flour and pecans. Knead with a dough hook for 10 minutes.

5. Turn dough into an oiled bowl. Cover and let rise in a warm place for 1–2 hours, until doubled in bulk.

6. Punch down dough, then shape into a cylinder and place in an oiled loaf pan.

7. Cover and let rise in a warm place for 90 minutes, until doubled in size.

8. Preheat oven to 350°F. Uncover bread and bake for 40 minutes.

PER SERVING Calories: 340 | Fat: 16g | Sodium: 310mg | Carbohydrates: 45g | Fiber: 6g | Protein: 8g

Herbed Buttermilk Quick Bread

Choose this recipe for a quick and easy bread recipe to serve with dinner.
Serve it warm from the oven with olive oil for dipping.

INGREDIENTS | YIELDS 1 LOAF;
SERVES 12

1¼ cups whole-wheat flour

¾ cup flour

½ teaspoon baking powder

½ teaspoon baking soda

¼ teaspoon salt

½ teaspoon dried thyme leaves

½ teaspoon dried dill weed

2 tablespoons canola oil

1 cup buttermilk

Buttermilk in Baking

Buttermilk adds tang and rich flavor to baked goods. But you don't have to keep it on hand; you can make your own. Just put 1–2 tablespoons vinegar or lemon juice in a measuring cup and add enough regular milk to make 1 cup. Stir and let stand for 10 minutes, then use as directed in recipes.

1. Preheat oven to 425°F. Spray a nonstick baking sheet with nonstick baking spray containing flour and set aside.

2. In a medium bowl, combine whole-wheat flour, flour, baking powder, baking soda, salt, thyme, and dill and mix well.

3. Add oil and buttermilk and mix just until a dough forms.

4. Turn dough out onto floured work surface and knead 10 times. Shape into a flat, round loaf on prepared baking sheet.

5. Bake for 40–45 minutes, or until bread is deep golden brown. Cool on wire rack for 15 minutes before serving.

PER SERVING Calories: 100 | Fat: 3g | Sodium: 140mg | Carbohydrates: 16g | Fiber: 2g | Protein: 3g

Dark Dinner Rolls

Before serving, place these rolls in a 350°F oven for 5–6 minutes to warm and refresh.

INGREDIENTS	YIELDS 24 ROLLS; SERVING SIZE: 1 ROLL

2 cups milk

2 (¼-ounce) packages active dry yeast

¼ cup honey

½ teaspoon salt

3 tablespoons canola oil

1 egg

2 egg whites

2½ cups whole-wheat flour

1½ cups medium rye flour

2½–3 cups all-purpose flour

3 tablespoons butter, melted

Flour Substitutions

You can usually substitute most flours for others, measure for measure. Rye flour, corn flour (masa harina), whole-wheat flour, and buckwheat flour can be used instead of all-purpose flour and bread flour. If you are substituting a lot of whole-grain flours for regular flour, consider using bread flour to help add enough gluten.

1. In large saucepan, heat milk over medium heat until warm.

2. Pour ½ cup into a large mixer bowl. Combine with yeast; let stand for 10 minutes.

3. Add remaining milk, honey, salt, canola oil, egg, and egg whites and beat well.

4. Add whole-wheat flour and rye flour and beat well.

5. Gradually add enough all-purpose flour to form a soft dough.

6. Turn dough onto floured surface and knead until smooth, about 5–7 minutes.

7. Place dough in greased bowl, turning to grease top. Cover and let rise for 1 hour, or until doubled.

8. Turn dough out onto lightly floured surface. Divide dough into fourths, then divide each fourth into 6 pieces. Roll pieces between your hands to form a smooth ball. Place on cookie sheets about 3" apart. Let rise for 30–40 minutes, or until doubled.

9. Preheat oven to 400°F. Bake rolls for 15–25 minutes, or until golden brown and set. Remove to wire racks and brush with melted butter. Let cool.

PER SERVING Calories: 170 | Fat: 4.5g | Sodium: 65mg | Carbohydrates: 28g | Fiber: 3g | Protein: 5g

Multigrain Dinner Rolls

Whole-wheat flour, rolled oats, and sunflower seeds make up the multiple grains in these fiber-rich dinner rolls. They are delicious with butter, herbed olive oil, or cream cheese.

INGREDIENTS | SERVES 12; SERVING SIZE: 1 ROLL

1 (¼-ounce) packet yeast
3 tablespoons warm water
1 cup warm milk
2½ ounces melted butter
1 teaspoon salt
1 egg, beaten
3 tablespoons sugar
2 cups all-purpose flour
1¾ cups whole-wheat flour
¼ cup rolled oats
1 egg, beaten
½ cup sunflower seeds

1. Combine yeast and water and let sit for 5 minutes to proof.

2. Add milk, butter, salt, egg, and sugar to the yeast mixture. Mix well.

3. Stir in the all-purpose flour with a wooden spoon or the paddle attachment to an electric stand mixer.

4. Gradually add whole-wheat flour and rolled oats. Knead with a dough hook for 10 minutes.

5. Put dough in an oiled bowl, cover and let rise in a warm place for 90 minutes.

6. Punch down dough, divide into 12 pieces and roll each piece in a ball.

7. Place balls on a greased baking sheet. Cover and let rise until doubled, about 60 minutes.

8. Preheat oven to 350°F. Uncover rolls, brush with egg, and sprinkle with sunflower seeds. Bake for 15 minutes.

PER SERVING Calories: 260 | Fat: 10g | Sodium: 220mg | Carbohydrates: 36g | Fiber: 4g | Protein: 8g

Oat Bran Dinner Rolls

These excellent rolls are light yet hearty, with a wonderful flavor and a bit of crunch.

INGREDIENTS	YIELDS 30 ROLLS; SERVING SIZE: 1 ROLL

1½ cups water
¾ cup quick-cooking oats
½ cup oat bran
¼ cup brown sugar
2 tablespoons butter
1 cup buttermilk
2 (¼-ounce) packages active dry yeast
2–3 cups all-purpose flour, divided
1½ cups whole-wheat flour
½ teaspoon salt
2 tablespoons honey
1 egg white, beaten
2 tablespoons oat bran

1. In medium saucepan, bring water to a boil over high heat. Add oats, oat bran, brown sugar, and butter and stir until butter melts. Remove from heat and let cool to lukewarm.

2. Meanwhile, in microwave-safe glass cup, microwave buttermilk on medium for 1 minute, or until lukewarm (about 110°F). Sprinkle yeast over milk; stir and let stand for 10 minutes.

3. In large mixing bowl, combine 1 cup all-purpose flour, whole-wheat flour, and salt. Add honey, cooled oatmeal mixture, and softened yeast mixture and beat until smooth.

5. Gradually add enough remaining all-purpose flour to form a soft dough.

6. Turn onto lightly floured board and knead until smooth and elastic, about 5–7 minutes. Place in greased bowl, turning to grease top. Cover and let rise for 1 hour, or until dough doubles.

7. Punch down dough and divide into thirds. Divide each third into 10 pieces. Roll balls between your hands to smooth.

8. Place balls into two 9" round cake pans. Brush with egg white and sprinkle with 2 tablespoons oat bran. Cover and let rise until doubled, about 45 minutes.

9. Preheat oven to 375°F. Bake rolls for 15–25 minutes, or until firm to the touch and golden brown. Remove from pans and cool on wire racks.

PER SERVING Calories: 90 | Fat: 1.5g | Sodium: 50mg | Carbohydrates: 17g | Fiber: 2g | Protein: 3g

Whole-Wheat Hamburger Buns

These buns are a good way to add more fiber to a burger. They also make good sandwich rolls for mixed deli meats. The ginger adds a lot of flavor and may help aid with digestion.

INGREDIENTS | **SERVES 6; SERVING SIZE: 1 BUN**

1 (¼-ounce) packet yeast

3 tablespoons sugar

Pinch of dried ginger

1⅓ cups warm water

3 tablespoons soft butter

1 teaspoon salt

¼ teaspoon baking powder

1¾ cups all-purpose flour

1¾ cups whole-wheat flour

1 egg, beaten

Yeast Breads

Yeast has its own special flavor and aroma. It will stand up to fruits, nuts, and olives better than baking powder quick breads.

1. Combine yeast, ½ teaspoon sugar, ginger, and ⅓ cup water in a bowl. Let sit for 5 minutes.

2. In a mixing bowl combine remaining water, butter, remaining sugar, salt, and baking powder.

3. Mix in the all-purpose flour and then the yeast mixture with an electric mixer.

4. Add whole-wheat flour. Knead with a dough hook for 10 minutes.

5. Turn dough into an oiled bowl. Cover and let rise in a warm place for 1–2 hours, until doubled in bulk.

6. Punch down dough, then divide into 6 pieces and shape into buns. Cover and let rise in a warm place for 1½ hours, until doubled in size.

7. Preheat oven to 350°F. Uncover buns, gently brush with egg. Bake for 20 minutes.

PER SERVING Calories: 340 | Fat: 8g | Sodium: 420mg | Carbohydrates: 60g | Fiber: 6g | Protein: 10g

Whole-Grain Pizza Crust

*Make a couple of batches of this crust, prebake, and store in the
freezer to make your own homemade pizzas in a flash.*

INGREDIENTS | **YIELDS 2 CRUSTS;
12 SERVINGS**

1 cup warm water
2 (¼-ounce) packages active dry yeast
½ cup milk
2 tablespoons honey
2 tablespoons olive oil
½ teaspoon salt
1½ cups whole-wheat flour
1 cup cornmeal
1½–2½ cups bread flour

Freezing Pizza Dough

To freeze pizza dough, bake it for 10 minutes, until the crust is set but not browned.
Let cool completely, then place in heavy-
duty food storage freezer bags. Seal, label,
and freeze for up to 3 months. To use, you
can top the crust right from the freezer and
bake as recipe directs, adding 5–10 minutes to the baking time.

1. In large bowl, combine water and yeast; let stand for
   10 minutes until bubbly.

2. Add milk, honey, olive oil, and salt and mix well.

3. Stir in whole-wheat flour, cornmeal, and ½ cup bread
   flour; beat for 1 minute.

4. Stir in enough bread flour to make a firm dough. Turn
   onto floured surface and knead for 10 minutes. Place
   dough in greased bowl, turning to grease top. Cover
   and let rise for 1 hour.

5. Turn dough onto floured work surface and let rest for
   10 minutes.

6. Spray two 12" round pizza pans with nonstick cooking
   spray and sprinkle with some cornmeal.

7. Divide dough in half and roll to 12" circles. Place on
   pizza pans; press to edges if necessary. Let stand for
   10 minutes.

8. Preheat oven to 400°F. Bake crusts for 10 minutes or
   until set. Remove from oven, add toppings. Return to
   oven, and bake as the pizza recipe directs.

PER SERVING Calories: 200 | Fat: 3.5g | Sodium: 105mg |
Carbohydrates: 36g | Fiber: 3g | Protein: 6g

Whole-Wheat Blueberry Muffins

Because these muffins have very little fat, they'll want to stick to the papers or the muffin tin. Letting them cool before removing them will help prevent this. Be sure to grease your muffin tin well.

INGREDIENTS | **YIELDS APPROX 1½ DOZEN MUFFINS; SERVING SIZE: 1 MUFFIN**

2 cups whole-wheat flour
1 cup all-purpose flour
1¼ cups sugar
1 tablespoon baking powder
1 teaspoon salt
1½ cups soy milk
½ cup applesauce
½ teaspoon vanilla
2 cups blueberries

1. Preheat oven to 400°F.

2. In a large bowl, combine the flours, sugar, baking powder, and salt. Set aside.

3. In a separate small bowl, whisk together the soy milk, applesauce, and vanilla until well mixed.

4. Combine the wet ingredients with the dry ingredients, stirring just until mixed. Gently fold in half of the blueberries.

5. Spoon batter into lined or greased muffin tins, filling each muffin about ⅔ full. Sprinkle remaining blueberries on top.

6. Bake for 20–25 minutes, or until lightly golden brown on top.

PER SERVING Calories: 150 | Fat: 1g | Sodium: 220mg | Carbohydrates: 33g | Fiber: 2g | Protein: 3g

Oat Bran Date Muffins

Dates contain lots of soluble fiber and are naturally sweet.
Keep some Medjool dates on hand for snacking.

INGREDIENTS | YIELDS 12 MUFFINS;
SERVING SIZE:
1 MUFFIN

1¼ cups all-purpose flour
½ cup rolled oats
¼ cup oat bran
1½ teaspoons baking powder
1 teaspoon baking soda
⅓ cup brown sugar
1 egg
¼ cup canola oil
⅓ cup applesauce
1 teaspoon grated orange zest
1 cup finely chopped dates
½ cup chopped hazelnuts

1. Preheat oven to 350°F. Line 12 muffin cups with paper liners and set aside.

2. In large bowl, combine flour, oats, oat bran, baking powder, baking soda, and brown sugar, and mix well.

3. In medium bowl, combine egg, canola oil, applesauce, and orange zest and beat to combine.

4. Add to dry ingredients and stir just until moistened. Fold in dates and hazelnuts.

5. Fill prepared muffin cups ⅔ full. Bake for 25–35 minutes, or until muffins are set and toothpick inserted in center comes out clean. Remove from muffin cups to wire racks to cool.

PER SERVING Calories: 210 | Fat: 9g | Sodium: 170mg | Carbohydrates: 33g | Fiber: 3g | Protein: 4g

Savory Zucchini Chia Muffins

Serve these flavorful muffins with grilled fish or chicken, along with a spinach salad, for a nice dinner.

INGREDIENTS | **YIELDS 12 MUFFINS; SERVING SIZE: 1 MUFFIN**

1 tablespoon olive oil
⅓ cup finely chopped onion
4 cloves garlic, minced
¼ cup canola oil
1 cup buttermilk
2 eggs, beaten
1 cup grated zucchini, drained
1¼ cups all-purpose flour
1 cup whole-wheat flour
1 teaspoon baking powder
½ teaspoon baking soda
¼ cup chia seeds, finely ground
1 tablespoon fresh chopped rosemary
¼ cup minced flat-leaf parsley
¼ cup grated Parmesan cheese
¼ teaspoon black pepper

1. Preheat oven to 375°F. Line 12 muffin cups with paper liners and set aside.

2. In small saucepan, combine olive oil, onion, and garlic; cook and stir until tender, about 6 minutes. Remove from heat and place in large mixing bowl. Let cool for 30 minutes.

3. Stir in canola oil, buttermilk, eggs, and zucchini and mix well.

4. Add flour, whole-wheat flour, baking powder, baking soda, chia seeds, rosemary, and parsley and mix until dry ingredients are moistened. Stir in cheese and pepper.

5. Fill prepared muffin cups ¾ full. Bake for 20–25 minutes, or until muffins are golden brown and set. Remove from cups and serve immediately.

PER SERVING Calories: 180 | Fat: 9g | Sodium: 160mg | Carbohydrates: 21g | Fiber: 3g | Protein: 6g

Vegetables in Breads

When using vegetables in breads, especially grated vegetables, be sure to drain them well before adding them to the batter. Some vegetables, especially zucchini and tomatoes, can add significant amounts of water to the batter and may throw off the proportion of flour to liquid. Follow the recipe carefully.

Rhubarb Muffins

Rhubarb is one of the first fruits or vegetables to appear in the spring. It is a great source of vitamin C and dietary fiber, and provides a gentle laxative affect.

INGREDIENTS | YIELDS 12 MUFFINS; SERVING SIZE: 1 MUFFIN

2 cups finely chopped rhubarb

¾ cup sugar, divided

1 teaspoon grated orange zest

¼ cup brown sugar

2 cups all-purpose flour

½ cup whole-wheat flour

1 teaspoon baking soda

½ teaspoon baking powder

½ teaspoon salt

2 eggs, beaten

½ cup buttermilk

¼ cup orange juice

1 teaspoon vanilla

3 tablespoons butter, melted

½ teaspoon cinnamon

1. Preheat oven to 375°F. Spray a 12-cup muffin tin with nonstick baking spray containing flour and set aside.

2. In a small bowl, combine rhubarb, ¼ cup sugar, and orange zest; let stand for 5 minutes.

3. In a large bowl, combine 6 tablespoons sugar, brown sugar, and all-purpose flour, whole wheat flour, baking soda, baking powder, and salt and mix well.

4. Make a well in the center of the dry ingredients and add rhubarb mixture, eggs, buttermilk, orange juice, vanilla, and melted butter. Mix just until combined.

5. Fill prepared muffin cups ¾ full.

6. In a small bowl, combine remaining 2 tablespoons sugar and ½ teaspoon cinnamon; sprinkle over each muffin.

7. Bake for 20–25 minutes, or until muffins are golden brown and firm. Remove from muffin tin and cool on wire rack for 15 minutes before serving.

PER SERVING Calories: 210 | Fat: 4g | Sodium: 250mg | Carbohydrates: 39g | Fiber: 2g | Protein: 5g

Desserts and Comfort Foods

Tangy Lime Pie

This signature dessert is equally tangy and sweet, with a smooth fluffy texture.
Serve it on chilled plates, garnished with more lime peel.

INGREDIENTS | SERVES 8

12 graham crackers, crushed

3 tablespoons butter, melted

⅓ cup frozen apple juice concentrate, thawed

1 (0.25-ounce) envelope unflavored gelatin

½ cup sugar

1 teaspoon grated lime zest

⅓ cup fresh lime juice

1 teaspoon vanilla

1 cup plain yogurt

½ cup lime- or lemon-flavored yogurt

Unflavored Gelatin

Don't confuse unflavored gelatin, which comes in small packets of about 1 tablespoon, with the preflavored kind containing sugar. Using unflavored gelatin lets you avoid artificial colors and flavors and lets you add the amount of sugar you want to your desserts. Follow the recipe instructions exactly for best results.

1. For crust, combine crushed graham crackers and melted butter in a small bowl. Press into bottom and up sides of a 9" pie plate; place in freezer.

2. For filling, in medium saucepan, combine juice concentrate with gelatin; let stand for 5 minutes. Stir in the sugar; place over low heat and cook, stirring frequently, until gelatin and sugar dissolve.

3. Pour into medium bowl and add lime zest, lime juice, and vanilla; stir well. Cover and chill until mixture is consistency of unbeaten egg whites, about 30 minutes.

4. Whip chilled mixture until fluffy. Add yogurts and beat again until smooth.

5. Pour into prepared pie crust, cover, and chill until firm, about 4–5 hours.

PER SERVING Calories: 190 | Fat: 7g | Sodium: 95mg | Carbohydrates: 30g | Fiber: <1g | Protein: 3g

Orange Chiffon Pie

*You must start this pie a day ahead of time so the yogurt has
a chance to thicken. It's tart, smooth, and creamy.*

INGREDIENTS | **SERVES 8**

2 cups vanilla yogurt

1 (3-ounce) package orange-flavored gelatin

¼ cup sugar

1 (15-ounce) can mandarin oranges

½ cup orange juice

1 cup frozen whipped topping, thawed

1 pie crust, baked and cooled

3 tablespoons toasted coconut

1. The day before, line a strainer with cheesecloth or a coffee filter. Place the strainer in a large bowl and add the yogurt. Cover and refrigerate overnight.

2. The next day, place the thickened yogurt in a large bowl. Discard the liquid, or whey.

3. In medium bowl, combine gelatin and sugar.

4. Drain oranges, reserving juice. In small pan, heat reserved juice over high heat until it boils. Pour over gelatin mixture; stir until gelatin and sugar are dissolved. Add orange juice and refrigerate for 30 minutes.

5. Beat the thickened yogurt and gradually add orange-juice mixture, beating until smooth.

6. Add the drained oranges and fold in the whipped topping.

7. Pour into pie crust and top with coconut. Cover and refrigerate for at least 4 hours before serving.

PER SERVING Calories: 260 | Fat: 9g | Sodium: 180mg | Carbohydrates: 41g | Fiber: <1g | Protein: 5g

Crème Brûlée

Crème brûlée is simply creamy custard with a crunchy, caramelized top. You can omit the caramelizing and serve this recipe as plain custard, topped with berries or grated chocolate.

INGREDIENTS | **SERVES 6**

1 cup half-and-half
2 cups heavy cream
½ cup sugar
1 teaspoon vanilla extract
6 egg yolks
Granulated sugar for caramelizing

Propane Torches and Caramelizing

Propane torches can be found in hardware stores, and special propane torches just for the purpose of caramelizing sugar can be found at cookware stores. Be careful not to touch or get splashed by molten sugar as you use the propane torch! Keep the flame close to the custard and move it around for an even color.

1. Preheat oven to 325°F. Put 6 ramekins (4-ounce porcelain cups used for baking custards and soufflés) in a 2" deep baking dish; set aside.

2. In a saucepan, heat the half-and-half, cream, and sugar to melt the sugar.

3. Stir in the vanilla. Remove from heat and slowly whisk the hot mixture into the egg yolks in a bowl. Strain the custard into a pitcher.

4. Pour the hot custard into the ramekins, dividing it evenly. Pour hot water into the baking dish around the ramekins to come halfway up the ramekins. Cover the baking dish tightly with foil.

5. Bake for 30 minutes, and then check to see if custard is set by carefully jiggling the pan. If the custard is not set, cover and bake for 10 more minutes. Check again; if necessary, cover pan again and bake another 10 minutes or so, until set. Remove from oven and uncover if necessary. When ramekins are cool enough to handle, remove them from the water to finish cooling. Refrigerate until completely chilled, about 4 hours.

6. To caramelize, sprinkle the top of each custard with about 1 tablespoon of sugar. Place ramekins on a baking sheet and use a propane torch to caramelize the sugar.

PER SERVING Calories: 450 | Fat: 38g | Sodium: 55mg | Carbohydrates: 21g | Fiber: 0g | Protein: 5g

Chocolate Mousse

Top this luxurious classic with raspberries, mint leaves, or chocolate shavings. For a fancier presentation, put chilled mousse in a pastry bag with a star tip and pipe into martini glasses. Substitute white chocolate for the semisweet, and you will have white chocolate mousse.

INGREDIENTS | **SERVES 6**

12 ounces semisweet chocolate chips
4 egg whites, room temperature
2 whole eggs
4 egg yolks
¾ cup heavy cream

Dark Chocolate

There is evidence that dark chocolate may be good for you! Chocolate contains compounds called flavonoids, which may help prevent cancer and heart disease. The saturated fat in chocolate is stearic acid, a fatty acid which does not raise blood cholesterol levels; in fact, it contains a monounsaturated fat, oleic acid, which actually helps lower blood cholesterol levels.

1. Melt the chocolate in a metal or glass bowl set over simmering (not boiling) water. When chocolate is melted, remove the bowl from heat and set aside.

2. Whip egg whites to stiff peaks with a wire whisk or electric mixer; set aside.

3. Crack the whole eggs into the egg yolks; beat well to combine. Stir the yolk mixture into the melted chocolate.

4. Fold the whipped egg whites into the chocolate/yolk mixture with a rubber spatula.

5. Whip the heavy cream in a chilled bowl. Whisk half of the whipped cream into the chocolate/egg mixture to lighten it. Gently fold the remaining whipped cream in, just to incorporate. Chill at least 2 hours before serving.

PER SERVING Calories: 450 | Fat: 33g | Sodium: 85mg | Carbohydrates: 37g | Fiber: 3g | Protein: 9g

Lemon Mousse

Pear nectar is very mild, and it adds a nice bit of sweetness to this tart mousse.

INGREDIENTS | SERVES 4

1 (0.25-ounce) envelope unflavored gelatin

¼ cup cold water

⅓ cup fresh lemon juice

⅔ cup pear nectar

¼ cup sugar, divided

1 teaspoon grated lemon zest

1 cup lemon yogurt

2 pasteurized egg whites

¼ teaspoon cream of tartar

Pasteurized Egg Whites

You can find pasteurized eggs in any grocery store. Be sure to carefully abide by the sell-by and use-by dates that are stamped on the package and usually on each egg. Pasteurized egg whites take longer to whip to peaks than ordinary eggs; just keep beating them until the peaks form. Cream of tartar helps stabilize the foam.

1. In microwave-safe glass measuring cup, combine gelatin and cold water; let stand for 5 minutes to soften gelatin.

2. Stir in lemon juice, pear nectar, and 2 tablespoons sugar. Microwave on high for 1–2 minutes, stirring twice during cooking time, until sugar and gelatin completely dissolve.

3. Stir in lemon zest. Let cool for 30 minutes.

4. When gelatin mixture is cool to the touch, blend in the lemon yogurt.

5. In a medium bowl, combine egg whites with cream of tartar; beat until soft peaks form. Gradually stir in remaining 2 tablespoons sugar, beating until stiff peaks form.

6. Fold gelatin mixture into egg whites until combined. Pour into serving glasses or goblets. Cover and chill until firm, about 4–6 hours.

PER SERVING Calories: 140 | Fat: 1g | Sodium: 530mg | Carbohydrates: 30g | Fiber: 0g | Protein: 5g

Sabayon with Fresh Berries

Sabayon is a light, foamy custard sauce. It is traditionally made with Marsala wine, but this recipe replaces it with orange juice. You may also add a dash of Marsala.. Sabayon can be served chilled or warm. It can also be enriched and stabilized by folding whipped cream into the chilled version.

INGREDIENTS | SERVES 8

6 egg yolks
½ cup sugar
1 cup fresh orange juice
1 cup sliced strawberries
1 cup raspberries
1 cup blueberries
1 cup blackberries
8 sprigs mint
8 shortbread cookie wedges

1. Whisk the egg yolks and sugar in a metal or glass bowl set over simmering water until the mixture is combined and warm.

2. Whip the orange juice into the yolk mixture ¼ cup at a time. It is important to keep beating so the yolks don't overcook and curdle.

3. When all of the juice has been incorporated, keep whisking until the mixture is very pale yellow and thick enough that if you run your finger through it the mark should remain. This is the ribbon stage. The mixture will have expanded a lot in volume. Remove from heat, and store the sabayon in the refrigerator until it cools completely.

4. Whisk occasionally while it is cooling to help retain the volume.

5. Divide berries evenly among 8 dessert cups and spoon the chilled sabayon on top. Garnish each serving with a sprig of mint and a shortbread cookie.

PER SERVING Calories: 210 | Fat: 8g | Sodium: 45mg | Carbohydrates: 32g | Fiber: 3g | Protein: 4g

Lemon Floating Island

Floating island refers to the poached egg-white mixture that "floats" on the lemon mousse. This is a low-fat version of lemon meringue pie. Yum!

INGREDIENTS | SERVES 4

2 cups milk

6 egg whites

2 tablespoons fresh lemon juice

½ cup sugar

Pinch salt

6 tablespoons crushed hard lemon candies, divided

1 recipe Lemon Mousse (Chapter 14)

1. Preheat oven to 275°F. In large skillet, bring milk to a simmer over medium heat. Reduce heat to low.

2. Meanwhile, in large bowl, combine egg whites and lemon juice; beat until foamy.

3. Gradually add sugar and salt, beating until very stiff peaks form. Fold in 3 tablespoons of the crushed candies.

4. With a large spoon, scoop out about ¼ cup of the egg-white mixture and gently place in the simmering milk.

5. Poach for 2 minutes, then carefully turn each meringue and poach for another 2 minutes. Remove from heat, drain briefly on kitchen towel, and place on Silpat-lined cookie sheets. Repeat with remaining egg-white mixture.

6. Bake 12–16 minutes, or until they puff slightly and start to turn light golden brown. Remove and refrigerate, uncovered, for 1–2 hours before serving.

7. Prepare the Lemon Mousse and spoon into individual custard cups; chill until firm. Top each with a poached meringue, sprinkle with remaining 3 tablespoons crushed candies, and serve immediately.

PER SERVING Calories: 380 | Fat: 5g | Sodium: 710mg | Carbohydrates: 70g | Fiber: 0g | Protein: 15g

Blueberry Cloud

This can be made with many other fruits. Chopped strawberries, raspberries (fresh or frozen), and peaches would all be delicious.

INGREDIENTS | SERVES 4

1 (0.25-ounce) envelope unflavored gelatin

¼ cup cold water

¾ cup orange juice

3 tablespoons sugar

1 cup blueberries

1 cup vanilla frozen yogurt

1 cup frozen whipped topping, thawed

Blueberry Heaven

The United States produces 95 percent of the world's supply of blueberries. Maine produces the bulk of U.S. blueberries, followed by other northeastern states and Oregon. Many farms in these regions allow you to pick your own berries when they're in season.

1. In microwave-safe glass measuring cup, combine gelatin with water; let stand for 5 minutes to let gelatin soften.

2. Add orange juice and sugar. Microwave on high for 1–2 minutes, stirring twice during cooking time, until gelatin and sugar dissolve. Pour into blender or food processor.

3. Add berries; blend or process until smooth. Let stand until cool, about 20 minutes.

4. Add yogurt; process until smooth. Pour into medium bowl and fold in whipped topping.

5. Spoon into serving dishes. Cover and freeze for at least 4 hours before serving.

PER SERVING Calories: 200 | Fat: 4g | Sodium: 35mg | Carbohydrates: 38g | Fiber: <1g | Protein: 5g

Peach Melba Parfait

This fresh and easy dessert can be made with many flavor combinations. Try sliced pears with orange yogurt and mandarin orange segments.

INGREDIENTS | SERVES 4

4 ripe peaches, peeled and sliced

1 tablespoon fresh lemon juice

2 tablespoons sugar

1 cup raspberry yogurt

1 pint fresh raspberries

4 sprigs fresh mint

Melba

Peach Melba is a dessert invented in the 1890s to honor the opera singer Nellie Melba. The chef Escoffier created Peach Melba by combining peaches and raspberries into a warm syrup served over ice cream.

1. In a medium bowl, combine the peaches, lemon juice, and sugar and let stand for 10 minutes. Stir to dissolve sugar.

2. In 4 parfait or wine glasses, place some of the peach mixture. Top with a spoonful of the yogurt, then some fresh raspberries. Repeat layers, ending with raspberries.

3. Cover and chill for 2–4 hours before serving. Garnish with mint sprig.

PER SERVING Calories: 140 | Fat: 1g | Sodium: 30mg | Carbohydrates: 33g | Fiber: 6g | Protein: 3g

Quinoa "Tapioca" Pudding

Instead of tapioca pudding or baked rice pudding, try this whole-grain version made with quinoa. Healthy enough to eat for breakfast, but sweet enough for dessert, too.

INGREDIENTS | SERVES 4

1 cup quinoa

2 cups water

2 cups milk or soy milk

2 tablespoons maple syrup or brown rice syrup

1 teaspoon arrowroot

2 bananas, sliced thin

½ teaspoon vanilla

⅓ cup raisins

Dash cinnamon or nutmeg (optional)

1. In a medium saucepan, cook quinoa in water over medium heat, stirring frequently, for 10–15 minutes, until done and water is absorbed.

2. Reduce heat to medium-low and stir in milk, syrup, arrowroot, and bananas, combining well. Heat, stirring constantly, for 6–8 minutes, until bananas are soft and pudding has thickened.

3. Stir in vanilla and raisins while still hot and sprinkle with a dash of cinnamon or nutmeg, to taste.

PER SERVING Calories: 360 | Fat: 7g | Sodium: 60mg | Carbohydrates: 67g | Fiber: 5g | Protein: 10g

No-Sugar Apricot Applesauce

You don't really need to peel the apples if you're short on time, but it only takes about 5 minutes and will give you a smoother sauce. Try adding a touch of nutmeg or pumpkin pie spice for extra flavor.

INGREDIENTS | **YIELDS 4 CUPS; SERVING SIZE: ½ CUP**

6 apples
⅓ cup water
½ cup dried apricots, chopped
4 dates, chopped
Cinnamon, to taste (optional)

1. Peel, core, and chop apples. Add apples and water to a large soup or stock pot and bring to a low boil. Simmer, covered for 15 minutes, stirring occasionally.

2. Add chopped apricots and dates and simmer for another 10–15 minutes.

3. Mash with a large fork until desired consistency is reached, or allow to cool slightly and purée in a blender until smooth.

4. Sprinkle with cinnamon to taste.

PER SERVING Calories: 190 | Fat: 0g | Sodium: 10mg | Carbohydrates: 50g | Fiber: 9g | Protein: 1g

Blueberry Hazelnut Crisp

Blueberries are so good for you! Enjoy them warm in this crisp with some vanilla frozen yogurt.

INGREDIENTS | **SERVES 8**

3 cups blueberries
¼ cup sugar
1 teaspoon cinnamon
½ teaspoon nutmeg
1½ cups quick-cooking oatmeal
½ cup flour
¼ cup whole-wheat flour
½ cup brown sugar
½ cup chopped hazelnuts
⅓ cup butter, melted

1. Preheat oven to 350°F. Spray a 9" round cake pan with nonstick cooking spray and set aside.

2. Combine blueberries in medium bowl with sugar, cinnamon, and nutmeg. Spoon into prepared pan. In same bowl, combine oatmeal, flour, whole-wheat flour, brown sugar, and hazelnuts and mix well. Add melted butter and mix until crumbly. Sprinkle over fruit in dish.

3. Bake for 35–45 minutes, or until topping is browned and crisp. Let cool for 15 minutes before serving.

PER SERVING Calories: 320 | Fat: 13g | Sodium: 10mg | Carbohydrates: 48g | Fiber: 4g | Protein: 5g

Applesauce

Applesauce is easy to make, especially when you use a slow cooker. It also freezes well.

INGREDIENTS | **YIELDS 1 QUART; SERVING SIZE: ½ CUP**

10 large apples
1 teaspoon cinnamon
⅓ cup apple juice
¼ cup sugar
⅛ teaspoon salt
3 tablespoons fresh lemon juice

Apple Choices

Because this sauce is uncooked, you can use any apple that is good for eating. Choose a tart or sweet variety depending on how you like your applesauce. Good snacking varieties include Red Delicious, Honeycrisp, Ambrosia, Braeburn, Empire, Gala, and Fuji.

1. Core and thinly slice apples.

2. Combine all ingredients except lemon juice in a 4-quart slow cooker.

3. Cover and cook on low for 8–10 hours, or until apples are very soft.

4. Using an immersion blender or potato masher, blend or mash the apples until desired consistency.

5. Stir in lemon juice. Cool and store, covered, in the refrigerator up to 5 days.

PER SERVING Calories: 130 | Fat: 0g | Sodium: 35mg | Carbohydrates: 36g | Fiber: 6g | Protein: 0g

Maple Date Carrot Cake

Free of refined sugar and with applesauce for moisture and just a touch of oil, this is a cake you can feel good about eating anytime. Leave out the dates if you want even less natural sugar.

INGREDIENTS | **SERVES 8**

1½ cups raisins
1⅓ cups pineapple juice
6 dates, diced
Water for soaking
2¼ cups grated carrot
½ cup maple syrup
¼ cup applesauce
2 tablespoons canola oil
3 cups flour
1½ teaspoons baking soda
½ teaspoon salt
1 teaspoon cinnamon
½ teaspoon allspice or nutmeg
2 eggs, beaten

1. Preheat oven to 375°F. Grease and flour a cake pan.

2. Combine the raisins with pineapple juice and allow to sit for 5–10 minutes to soften.

3. In a separate small bowl, cover the dates with water until soft, about 10 minutes. Drain water from dates.

4. In a large mixing bowl, combine the raisins and pineapple juice, carrot, maple syrup, applesauce, oil, and dates.

5. In a separate large bowl, combine the flour, baking soda, salt, cinnamon, and allspice or nutmeg.

6. Combine the dry ingredients with the wet ingredients, and add prepared eggs. Mix well.

7. Pour batter into prepared cake pan, and bake for 30 minutes, or until a toothpick inserted in the center comes out clean.

PER SERVING Calories: 450 | Fat: 6g | Sodium: 430mg | Carbohydrates: 97g | Fiber: 5g | Protein: 8g

Quick Apple Crisp

There is nothing like the taste of maple syrup, apples, and cinnamon heated together and baked—an American classic the whole family will enjoy. Serve warm with a scoop of vanilla ice cream or by itself. Delicious!

INGREDIENTS | SERVES 8

5 large red apples
½ cup raisins
½ cup apple juice
Juice of 1 lemon
¼ cup maple syrup
1 teaspoon cinnamon powder
2 cups raw oats (not instant)
½ cup walnuts
¼ teaspoon salt
1 teaspoon vanilla extract
⅓ cup canola oil
⅔ cup maple syrup

Maple Syrup

Maple syrup is made from the sap of the sugar black or red maple tree. The tree is first tapped (pierced), which allows the sap to run out freely. The clear, tasteless sap is then boiled down to evaporate the water, giving it the characteristic maple flavor and amber color, with a sugar content of 60 percent.

1. Preheat oven to 350°F.

2. Peel, core, and slice the apples. Layer in a 9" × 12" baking pan with the raisins.

3. In a small bowl, whisk together the apple juice, lemon juice, ¼ cup maple syrup, and cinnamon; pour over the apples.

4. To make the topping, process the oats in a food processor until almost flour consistency.

5. Add the walnuts and salt to the oats; pulse to lightly chop. Pour the mixture into a large bowl.

6. In a medium-size bowl, whisk together the vanilla extract, oil, and ⅔ cup maple syrup.

7. Pour the liquid mixture over the oats; use a wooden spoon to combine. You may need to use your hands to mix well enough to coat the oats and walnuts.

8. When done, spoon the mixture over the top of the apples. Bake 30 minutes, or until apples are tender and topping is a golden brown. Allow to cool slightly before serving.

PER SERVING Calories: 450 | Fat: 16g | Sodium: 80mg | Carbohydrates: 74g | Fiber: 7g | Protein: 5g

Apple Pear Cranberry Strudel

This recipe makes creative use of phyllo dough in a delicate luscious dessert. For variety, make an apple tart by layering oiled phyllo sheets in a sunburst pattern, adding apple filling in the center, and folding up edges to cover filling.

INGREDIENTS | **SERVES 8**

¼ cup sugar, optional

1 tablespoon fresh lemon juice

1 tablespoon lemon zest

1 tablespoon apple juice

½ teaspoon ground cardamom, optional

⅛ teaspoon ground nutmeg, optional

¼ teaspoon salt

1½ teaspoons ground cinnamon, optional

2 medium apples

2 medium pears, Bosc or Bartlett

½ cup dried cranberries, fruit sweetened

2 teaspoons arrowroot

¾ cup canola oil

10 sheets phyllo dough, thawed overnight in refrigerator

1. Preheat oven to 350°F.

2. Whisk together 1 tablespoon sugar, lemon juice, zest, apple juice, cardamom, nutmeg, salt, and ½ teaspoon cinnamon. Peel, core, and cut apples and pears into ½" pieces.

3. Add cranberries, apples, pears, and arrowroot to liquid mixture. Mix to combine.

4. In a separate bowl, mix together remaining 3 tablespoons maple sugar and 1 teaspoon cinnamon.

5. Place a sheet of parchment paper on flat surface. Place 1 layer of phyllo dough on parchment paper. Brush oil on phyllo dough and sprinkle cinnamon sugar mixture over sheet.

6. Lay another sheet of phyllo dough on top of first. Brush with oil and sprinkle cinnamon sugar mixture over sheet. Repeat with remaining 3 layers of phyllo dough, until all 5 sheets are stacked, one on top of the other.

7. Place a 3" wide scoop of apple pear mixture on one end of sheets, 2" from edge and sides. Lift up parchment paper and let phyllo dough roll around filling until dough is rolled into a log.

8. Brush top of strudel with oil and sprinkle with cinnamon sugar. Using parchment paper, transfer log to baking sheet. Repeat procedure for second strudel.

9. Bake for 35 minutes, or until deep golden brown. Cool for 10 minutes. Cut strudel into 4 portions, and serve.

PER SERVING Calories: 330 | Fat: 23g | Sodium: 190mg | Carbohydrate: 32g | Fiber: 4g | Protein: 2g

Almond Arrowroot Fruit Pudding

An old-fashioned cornstarch pudding, this smooth and creamy mixture replaces cornstarch with arrowroot and forms a soothing backdrop to the assertive fruit flavors. A cook's tip: Before adding arrowroot to a liquid, always mix first with a little liquid to make a paste.

INGREDIENTS | SERVES 4

3 tablespoons arrowroot

2 cups almond-flavored soymilk or almond milk

2 egg yolks

½ cup sugar

2 teaspoons almond extract

1 teaspoon vanilla extract

Pinch salt

2 tablespoons butter

1 cup blueberries

1 cup sliced strawberries

1. Combine the arrowroot with 3 tablespoons soymilk, then combine this mixture with egg yolks and sugar in a mixing bowl. Stir in ½ cup soymilk to make a paste.

2. Heat the remaining soymilk in a large saucepan over medium-low to medium heat and, stirring gently, slowly pour in the cornstarch mixture.

3. Increase the heat to medium-high and bring the mixture to a boil. Immediately reduce the heat to medium-low and, stirring gently, add the almond and vanilla extracts and the salt and butter.

4. Meanwhile, put the fruit into a 2-quart serving bowl. When the pudding mixture is thickened slightly, pour it over the fruit. Let the pudding cool slightly before serving, or chill and serve cold.

PER SERVING Calories: 310 | Fat: 10g | Sodium: 75mg | Carbohydrates: 50g | Fiber: 2g | Protein: 5g

Carrot Fruit Cup

This combination of ingredients may sound odd at first, but give it a try.
You'll be surprised by the flavor (and nutrients) packed into it!

INGREDIENTS | **SERVES 4; SERVING SIZE: ¾ CUP**

1 tablespoon raisins
2 carrots, grated
1 apple, grated
1 tablespoon frozen apple juice concentrate
1 teaspoon cinnamon
Pinch of ground ginger
1 frozen banana, sliced

1. Soak raisins overnight in little more than enough water to cover.

2. When ready to prepare dessert, drain water from raisins and pour into bowl. Add carrots and apple.

3. Stir in frozen apple juice concentrate and spices until blended.

4. Add banana slices; stir again. Chill until ready to serve.

PER SERVING Calories: 69 | Fat: 1g | Sodium: 13mg | Carbohydrates: 18g | Fiber: 4g | Protein: 1g

Fall Fruit with Yogurt Sauce

Take a trip to your local orchard to pick apples, then put together this fresh delicious treat!

INGREDIENTS | **SERVES 8; SERVING SIZE: ½ CUP**

2 cups apples, cubed
1½ cups red seedless grapes, halved
1½ cup pears, cubed
2 teaspoons fresh lemon juice
8 ounces vanilla yogurt
1 teaspoon lemon juice
1 tablespoon honey
¼ cup walnuts, chopped

1. Combine apples, grapes, and pears in medium bowl.

2. Drizzle 1 teaspoon lemon juice over fruit to prevent turning brown.

3. In small bowl, combine yogurt, 1 teaspoon lemon juice, and honey.

4. Portion ½ cup fruit per serving. Spoon yogurt dressing over fruit and top with chopped walnuts.

PER SERVING Calories: 126 | Fat: 3g | Sodium: 48mg | Carbohydrates: 26g | Fiber: 3g | Protein: 3g

Summer Fruit Cobbler

Any combination of fresh fruit will work well with this recipe. You will need a total of 4 cups of fruit. Fruit suggestions include blueberries, blackberries, peaches, mangoes, or plums. Keep in mind that nutritional analysis will vary somewhat with different fruit combinations.

INGREDIENTS | **SERVES 8; SERVING SIZE: ½ CUP**

1½ cups raspberries
1½ cups peaches, peeled and sliced
1 cup strawberries, sliced
¼ cup sugar
2 tablespoons whole-wheat pastry flour
1 teaspoon cinnamon
¾ cup whole-wheat pastry flour
1 tablespoon sugar
1½ teaspoons baking powder
½ teaspoon salt
2½ tablespoons canola oil
2 tablespoons milk
2 tablespoons egg whites

1. Preheat oven to 350°F. Spray 9" × 9" square baking pan with nonstick cooking spray.

2. Put fruit in bottom of baking dish.

3. In small bowl, mix sugar, 2 tablespoons flour, and cinnamon; sprinkle evenly over fruit.

4. In small bowl, sift together ¾ cup flour, 1 tablespoon sugar, baking powder, and salt.

5. Add oil, milk, and egg whites; stir quickly until just mixed.

6. Drop dough by spoonfuls over fruit. If desired, loosely spread dough over fruit.

7. Bake for 25–30 minutes, until dough is golden brown.

PER SERVING Calories: 140 | Fat: 5g | Sodium: 250mg | Carbohydrates: 23g | Fiber: 4g | Protein: 3g

Bubbly Berry Blast

Make your own healthy Jell-O-like dessert!

INGREDIENTS | SERVES 6; SERVING SIZE ½ CUP

2 envelopes unflavored gelatin

½ cup frozen unsweetened apple juice concentrate

3 cups (24 ounces) unsweetened sparkling water

1 cup sliced strawberries

1 cup blueberries

1. Mix gelatin and apple juice in small saucepan; stir and let stand for 1 minute.

2. Place mixture over low heat; stir until completely dissolved, about 3 minutes. Cool slightly. (Alternatively, blend gelatin and apple juice in small microwave-safe bowl; let stand 1 minute then microwave on high for 45 seconds; stir until gelatin is completely dissolved.)

3. Stir in sparkling water. Refrigerate until mixture begins to gel. Fold fruit into partially thickened gelatin mixture.

4. Pour into 6-cup mold. Refrigerate for 4 hours, until firm.

PER SERVING Calories: 61 | Fat: 0g | Sodium: 11mg | Carbohydrates: 13g | Fiber: 1g | Protein: 2g

Bananas Foster

Keep bananas in the freezer to make them last longer.

INGREDIENTS | SERVES 4

4 bananas, sliced

¼ cup apple juice concentrate

Grated zest of 1 orange

¼ cup fresh orange juice

1 tablespoon ground cinnamon

12 ounces frozen vanilla yogurt

1. Combine all ingredients except yogurt in nonstick skillet.

2. Bring to a boil; cook until bananas are tender.

3. Put 3 ounces frozen yogurt in each dessert bowl or stemmed glass; spoon heated banana sauce over top.

PER SERVING Calories: 270 | Fat: 0g | Sodium: 45mg | Carbohydrates: 64g | Fiber: 5g | Protein: 7g

Apple Bread Pudding

Bread pudding is such a comforting dessert! For this recipe, the bread should be at least 1 day old so it's fairly firm.

INGREDIENTS | SERVES 8

4 cups crumbled Cinnamon-Swirl Raisin Bread (Chapter 13), at least 1 day old

2 apples, peeled and grated

½ cup raisins

½ cup chopped pecans

1½ cups milk

3 eggs

2 teaspoons vanilla

¾ cup brown sugar

3 tablespoons honey

1 teaspoon cinnamon

½ teaspoon nutmeg

2 tablespoons fresh lemon juice

Bread Pudding Toppings

Bread pudding can be topped with everything from nonfat whipped topping to a fruit sauce or hard sauce. To make hard sauce, combine 2 tablespoons butter with ½ cup powdered sugar, ½ teaspoon vanilla, and 2–3 tablespoons skim milk, enough to make a stiff sauce. The sauce melts over the hot dessert. Yum!

1. Preheat oven to 350°F. Spray a 9" square baking pan with nonstick baking spray containing flour.

2. Combine bread crumbs, apples, raisins, and pecans in the prepared pan and spread in even layer.

3. Combine remaining ingredients in a medium bowl and mix until well blended. Be sure the bread is saturated; push it down into the liquid mixture if necessary. Let stand for 10 minutes.

4. Bake the pudding until top is golden brown, about 35–45 minutes. Serve warm with warmed honey or maple syrup.

PER SERVING Calories: 420 | Fat: 11g | Sodium: 210mg | Carbohydrates: 76g | Fiber: 6g | Protein: 9g

CHAPTER 15

Beverages, Juices, and Smoothies

Iced Ginger Orange Green Tea

If you use orange juice with pulp in it you increase your fiber content without even thinking about it, so don't pick up the pulp-free variety anymore. The same goes for grapefruit juice. For added color and fiber, eat a handful of fresh raspberries along with your juice.

INGREDIENTS | SERVES 4

2 cups water

1 tablespoon coarsely chopped crystallized ginger

2 (1") pieces orange peel

4 green tea bags

2 cups orange juice, chilled

1. In medium saucepan, bring water to boil.

2. In ceramic container, pour boiling water over ginger and orange peel. Add tea bags; cover and steep for 5 minutes.

3. Remove tea bags, ginger, and orange peel; add orange juice and stir.

4. Put ice cubes in 4 glasses; pour orange juice-tea blend over ice, and serve.

PER SERVING Calories: 62 | Fat: 0g | Sodium: 9mg | Carbohydrates: 14g | Fiber: 0g | Protein: 1g

Hot Spiced Tea

You can also chill this recipe and serve over ice for a refreshing iced tea.

INGREDIENTS | SERVES 4

2 tea bags

14 whole cloves

1 cinnamon stick

1 strip (about 3") fresh orange peel

2 cups boiling water

¼ cup orange juice

1½ tablespoons lemon juice

1. Put tea bags, spices, and orange peel in ceramic or glass container; pour boiling water over. Cover and allow to steep for 5 minutes.

2. Strain; stir in orange and lemon juices. Reheat if necessary.

PER SERVING Calories: 8 | Fat: 0g | Sodium: 3mg | Carbohydrates: 2g | Fiber: 0g | Protein: 0g

Kiwi Lime Cooler

Kiwi is also known as Chinese gooseberry.

INGREDIENTS | SERVES 2

1 cup ice cubes
1 tablespoon fresh lime juice
1 cup light vanilla yogurt
2 ripe kiwi, peeled and sliced
1 tablespoon agave syrup, or to taste
1 tablespoon chia seeds, soaked

1. Combine all ingredients in a blender; process until mixed.

2. Serve in a chilled glass.

PER SERVING Calories: 200 | Fat: 3.5g | Sodium: 85mg | Carbohydrates: 38g | Fiber: 5g | Protein: 8g

The Chinese Gooseberry

Kiwi is a very nutrient-dense food rich in vitamin C, fiber, and potassium. This versatile little fruit can be used in beverages, salads, salsas, or as a beautiful edible garnish.

Fruit Frenzy Sparkler Concentrate

This is a refreshing beverage perfect for quenching thirst and adding some nutrients at the same time.

INGREDIENTS | SERVES 8

1 cup peeled, seeded, and chopped peach or papaya
1 cup peeled and cubed fresh pineapple
1 teaspoon peeled and grated fresh ginger
1 cup orange juice
1 cup frozen banana slices
Unsweetened club soda, seltzer water, or carbonated water

1. Place all ingredients except water in a food processor; process until smooth.

2. To serve, pour ½ cup concentrate over ice in a 12- to 16-ounce glass. Complete filling glass with carbonated water.

PER SERVING Calories: 53 | Fat: 0g | Sodium: 1mg | Carbohydrates: 13g | Fiber: 1g | Protein: 1g

Blackberry Mango Smoothie

The fiber in bananas, mangoes, blackberries, and chia seeds will help you stay full for longer than if you drink plain juice for breakfast. The yogurt will add just enough protein to burn the sugar in the juice.

INGREDIENTS | SERVES 2

½ banana
1 cup frozen mango cubes
1 cup blackberries
1 tablespoon chia seeds, soaked
½ cup vanilla frozen yogurt
¼ cup orange juice
1 teaspoon honey

1. Place all ingredients in a blender and blend until smooth.

2. Pour into 2 glasses, and serve as a quick breakfast.

PER SERVING Calories: 230 | Fat: 2g | Sodium: 25mg | Carbohydrates: 51g | Fiber: 8g | Protein: 6g

Blueberry Soy Smoothie

You can vary the fruit you use in this smoothie; frozen raspberries or strawberries would be delicious.

INGREDIENTS | SERVES 2

½ cup soy milk
1¼ cups frozen blueberries
¼ cup honey
½ cup silken tofu
2 tablespoons ground flaxseed

1. Combine all ingredients in a blender or food processor. Blend or process until mixture is smooth.

2. Serve immediately.

PER SERVING Calories: 280 | Fat: 6g | Sodium: 40mg | Carbohydrates: 54g | Fiber: 6g | Protein: 8g

Dairy-Free Tofu

Make sure to read the labels of the tofu you purchase to verify it is dairy free. Most organic brands are made without milk protein. Silken tofu is very soft, almost like a pudding. It is used to make smoothies, puddings, cheesecakes, and other desserts.

Raspberry Pineapple Smoothie

This tropical treat will make a splash at your luau or pool party. Forget the alcohol and cake altogether, and serve this smoothie as a treat.

INGREDIENTS | **SERVES 4**

2 cups frozen raspberries

1 (8-ounce) can crushed pineapples, in natural juices

1 cup freshly squeezed orange juice

1 cup milk

½ teaspoon vanilla extract

2 tablespoons ground flaxseed

Handful ice

1. Blend all ingredients in a blender until smooth.

2. Serve immediately.

PER SERVING Calories: 150 | Fat: 4g | Sodium: 30mg | Carbohydrates: 27g | Fiber: 6g | Protein: 4g

Strawberry Kiwi Smoothie

Kiwifruits offer a grand amount of vitamin C and potassium (almost as much as a banana). Chia seeds are the richest source of omega-3 oils, and just a small amount boosts the nutritional value of this delicious beverage.

INGREDIENTS | **SERVES 4**

2 cups frozen strawberries, leaves removed

1 cup frozen kiwi

1 cup freshly squeezed orange juice

1 cup milk

½ teaspoon vanilla extract

2 tablespoons chia seeds, finely ground

Handful ice

1. Blend all ingredients in a blender until smooth.

2. Serve immediately.

PER SERVING Calories: 140 | Fat: 4g | Sodium: 30mg | Carbohydrates: 25g | Fiber: 5g | Protein: 4g

Peaches and Cream Smoothie

If you don't have fat-free plain yogurt in your fridge, use another flavor instead.

INGREDIENTS | **SERVES 4**

3 cups frozen peeled and sliced peaches

1 cup orange juice

1 cup yogurt

1 cup milk

½ teaspoon vanilla extract

2 tablespoons flax oil

Handful ice

1. Blend all ingredients in a blender until smooth.

2. Serve immediately.

PER SERVING Calories: 210 | Fat: 11g | Sodium: 55mg | Carbohydrates: 24g | Fiber: 2g | Protein: 6g

Very Berry Smoothie

*You can alter the amount of each berry you use in this smoothie to create fun colors.
Make a variety and serve them in clear glasses for a beautiful effect!*

INGREDIENTS | **SERVES 4**

1 cup frozen strawberries, leaves removed

1 cup frozen blueberries

1 cup frozen cranberries

1 cup orange juice

2 tablespoons chia seeds, finely ground

1 cup milk

½ teaspoon vanilla extract

Handful ice

1. Blend all ingredients in a blender until smooth.

2. Serve immediately.

PER SERVING Calories: 130 | Fat: 4g | Sodium: 30mg | Carbohydrates: 22g | Fiber: 5g | Protein: 4g

Date Milkshake

This is a smooth and creamy milkshake with lots of fiber and natural date sugar. It makes a great breakfast smoothie with loads of fiber and protein as well as flavor.

INGREDIENTS | **SERVES 2; SERVING SIZE: 12 OUNCES**

1 cup chopped dates
1 cup milk
1 banana, peeled
1 cup plain yogurt
¼ cup orange juice
1 pint vanilla frozen yogurt

1. To soften the dates, soak them in the milk for 30 minutes.

2. Purée the dates and milk in a blender.

3. Add the banana and blend.

4. Add the yogurt, orange juice, and frozen yogurt and blend until smooth.

PER SERVING Calories: 790 | Fat: 11g | Sodium: 200mg | Carbohydrates: 157g | Fiber: 11g | Protein: 25g

Yogurt Is a Carrier for Fibers

Many great fibers are very dry. These include dried fruits, seeds, and nuts. However, when these nourishing dry ingredients are mixed with some yogurt, they are much easier to swallow.

Red Bean Ice-Cream Shake

Red bean paste is a sweetened purée found in Asian groceries. Substitute red bean ice cream for the paste, if available. Red bean paste is an excellent source of both protein and fiber.

INGREDIENTS | **SERVES 2; SERVING SIZE: 16 OUNCES**

1 pint vanilla ice cream
1½ cups red bean paste
1 cup milk

1. Place all ingredients in a blender and blend until smooth.

2. Serve immediately.

PER SERVING Calories: 500 | Fat: 19g | Sodium: 810mg | Carbohydrates: 67g | Fiber: 13g | Protein: 19g

Make Your Own Bean Paste

Soak 1 cup dried adzuki beans in water overnight. Drain and put the beans in a saucepan with 4 cups water and simmer for 1½ hours. Stir in ½ cup sugar and cook for 10 more minutes, stirring often. Squash beans with a wooden spoon and stir to thicken. Remove from heat and purée in a food processor for a smoother paste. Chill in the refrigerator before using.

Standard U.S./Metric Measurement Conversions

VOLUME CONVERSIONS

U.S. Volume Measure	Metric Equivalent
⅛ teaspoon	0.5 milliliters
¼ teaspoon	1 milliliters
½ teaspoon	2 milliliters
1 teaspoon	5 milliliters
½ tablespoon	7 milliliters
1 tablespoon (3 teaspoons)	15 milliliters
2 tablespoons (1 fluid ounce)	30 milliliters
¼ cup (4 tablespoons)	60 milliliters
⅓ cup	90 milliliters
½ cup (4 fluid ounces)	125 milliliters
⅔ cup	160 milliliters
¾ cup (6 fluid ounces)	180 milliliters
1 cup (16 tablespoons)	250 milliliters
1 pint (2 cups)	500 milliliters
1 quart (4 cups)	1 liter (about)

WEIGHT CONVERSIONS

U.S. Weight Measure	Metric Equivalent
½ ounce	15 grams
1 ounce	30 grams
2 ounces	60 grams
3 ounces	85 grams
¼ pound (4 ounces)	115 grams
½ pound (8 ounces)	225 grams
¾ pound (12 ounces)	340 grams
1 pound (16 ounces)	454 grams

OVEN TEMPERATURE CONVERSIONS

Degrees Fahrenheit	Degrees Celsius
200 degrees F	100 degrees C
250 degrees F	120 degrees C
275 degrees F	140 degrees C
300 degrees F	150 degrees C
325 degrees F	160 degrees C
350 degrees F	180 degrees C
375 degrees F	190 degrees C
400 degrees F	200 degrees C
425 degrees F	220 degrees C
450 degrees F	230 degrees C

BAKING PAN SIZES

American	Metric
8 x 1½ inch round baking pan	20 x 4 cm cake tin
9 x 1½ inch round baking pan	23 x 3.5 cm cake tin
1 x 7 x 1½ inch baking pan	28 x 18 x 4 cm baking tin
13 x 9 x 2 inch baking pan	30 x 20 x 5 cm baking tin
2 quart rectangular baking dish	30 x 20 x 3 cm baking tin
15 x 10 x 2 inch baking pan	30 x 25 x 2 cm baking tin (Swiss roll tin)
9 inch pie plate	22 x 4 or 23 x 4 cm pie plate
7 or 8 inch springform pan	18 or 20 cm springform or loose bottom cake tin
9 x 5 x 3 inch loaf pan	23 x 13 x 7 cm or 2 lb narrow loaf or pate tin
1½ quart casserole	1.5 litre casserole
2 quart casserole	2 litre casserole

Index

Note: Page numbers in **bold** indicate recipe category lists.

Includes material adapted and abridged from: *The Everything® Food Allergy Cookbook* by Linda Larsen, copyright © 2008 by F+W Media, Inc., ISBN 10: 1-59869-560-6, ISBN 13: 978-1-59869-560-1; *The Everything® Flat Belly Cookbook* by Fitz Koehler, MSESS with Mabelissa Acevedo, LDN, copyright © 2009 by F+W Media, Inc., ISBN 10: 1-60550-676-1, ISBN 13: 978-1-60550-676-0; *The Everything® Bread Cookbook* by Leslie Bilderback, CMB, copyright © 2010 by F+W Media, Inc., ISBN 10: 1-44050-031-2, ISBN 13: 978-1-44050-031-2; *The Everything® Diabetes Cookbook, 2nd Edition* by Gretchen Scalpi, RD, CDN, CDE, copyright © 2010 by F+W Media, Inc., ISBN 10: 1-44050-154-8, ISBN 13: 978- 1-44050-154-8; *The Everything® Guide to Being Vegetarian* by Alexandra Greeley, copyright © 2009 by F+W Media, Inc., ISBN 10: 1-60550-051-8, ISBN 13: 978-1-60550-051-5; *The Everything® Juicing Book* by Carole Jacobs and Chef Patrice Johnson with Nicole Cormier, RD, copyright © 2010 by F+W Media, Inc., ISBN 10: 1-44050-326-5, ISBN 13: 978- 1-44050-326-5; *The Everything® Guide to Macrobiotics* by Julie S. Ong with Lorena Novak Bull, RD, copyright © 2010 by F+W Media, Inc., ISBN 10: 1-44050-371-0, ISBN 13: 978-1-44050-371-9; *The Everything® Vegan Cookbook* by Jolinda Hackett with Lorena Novak Bull, RD, copyright © 2010 by F+W Media, Inc., ISBN 10: 1-44050-216-1, ISBN 13: 978-1-44050-216-3; *The Everything® Low Cholesterol Cookbook* by Linda Larsen, copyright © 2008 by F+W Media, Inc., ISBN 10: 1-59869-401-4, ISBN 13: 978-1-59869-401 7; *The Everything® Low-Fat High-Flavor Cookbook* by Lisa Shaw, copyright © 1998 by F+W Media, Inc., ISBN 10: 1-55850-802-3, ISBN 13: 978-1-55850-802-6; *The Everything® Superfoods Cookbook* by Delia Quigley, CNC with Brierley Wright, RD, copyright © 2008 by F+W Media, Inc., ISBN 10: 1-59869-682-3, ISBN 13: 978-1-59869-682-0; *The Everything® Whole-Grain High-Fiber Cookbook* by Lynette Rhorer Shirk, copyright © 2008 by F+W Media, Inc., ISBN 10: 1-59869-507-X, ISBN 13: 978-1-59869-507-6; *The Everything® Sugar-Free Cookbook* by Nancy T. Maar, copyright © 2008 by F+W Media, Inc., ISBN 10: 1-59869-408-1, ISBN 13: 978-1-59869-408-6; *The Everything® Classic Recipes Book* by Lynette Rohrer Shirk, copyright © 2006 by F+W Media, Inc., ISBN 10: 1-59337-690-1, ISBN 13: 978-1-59337-690-1.

We Have

EVERYTHING®

on Anything!

With more than 19 million copies sold, the Everything® series has become one of America's favorite resources for solving problems, learning new skills, and organizing lives. Our brand is not only recognizable—it's also welcomed.

The series is a hand-in-hand partner for people who are ready to tackle new subjects—like you!

For more information on the Everything® series, please visit *www.adamsmedia.com*

The Everything® list spans a wide range of subjects, with more than 500 titles covering 25 different categories:

Business	History	Reference
Careers	Home Improvement	Religion
Children's Storybooks	Everything Kids	Self-Help
Computers	Languages	Sports & Fitness
Cooking	Music	Travel
Crafts and Hobbies	New Age	Wedding
Education/Schools	Parenting	Writing
Games and Puzzles	Personal Finance	
Health	Pets	